To Bill &
our Fabulous host who
have shown us the best
of Greensboro each and
every time we come

Thank you
Love Ray & Connie

28763

GREENSBORO

To Terry, Allison, and Graham, the major participants in my personal history;

To my parents, Grace and Jasper Hicks, who taught me to respect the past and plan for the future; and,

To those who taught me to understand the developments of history and the tools of interpretation.

Photographic Assistants: Karen Cobb Carroll, Stephen Catlett and Christine Dumoulin

Chronology Assistant: Kathy Devereux

Produced in cooperation with the City of Greensboro, the Greensboro

Historical Museum, Inc. and the Greensboro Public Library

American Historical Press
Sun Valley, California

GREENSBORO

A Chosen Center

An Illustrated History

Gayle Hicks Fripp

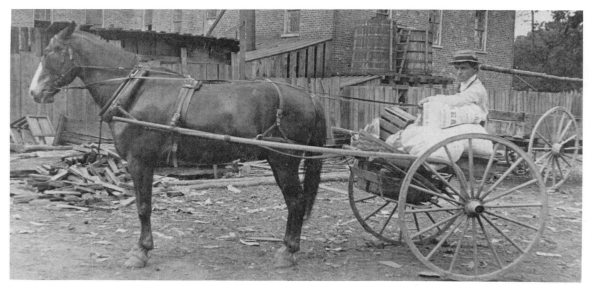

Carey B. Guthrie was employed by Tucker & Erwin Grocers at 515 South Elm. He was photographed around 1910 on a Greensboro back street, delivering groceries in a two wheeled cart drawn by Logan. (GHM)

Editor's Note: pgs. 87 & 129 True name is Ceasar Cone

Published 2001
Printed in the United States of America

Library of Congress Catalogue Card Number: 2001094642

ISBN: 1-892724-20-0

Bibliography: p. 232

CONTENTS

New Jersey Quaker John Collins visited Greensboro and the New Garden area in 1869 and 1887. He kept a journal, illustrating it with watercolor sketches. This Collins sketch of the Quaker Meeting House at New Garden includes typical vehicles and people. Courtesy, Friends Historical Collection, Guilford College

INTRODUCTION

Greensboro: A Chosen Center is an illustrated, chronological history of the city's development from prehistoric times to the year 2000. The title reflects the theme, and the book outlines some of the cultural, economic, political and social events that shaped the city.

Even before its creation as a county seat in 1808, nomadic Indians and settlers who appreciated its adequate water supplies, available land and abundant resources had chosen the site. Others selected the site for military reasons: Nathanael Greene in 1781 as a place to fight the British; Joseph E. Johnston in 1865 as a camp site along two rail lines; and the U.S. Army in 1943 as a basic training camp location. The Quakers and Methodists established schools in the 1830s that still operate as colleges today, beginning Greensboro's role as an education center. In 1873 local blacks supported by private benefactors established another school, and in the 1890s the state chartered two new educational institutions that became NC A & T State University and UNCG. The presence of these institutions greatly expanded educational and cultural opportunities.

Industrial giants located in Greensboro beginning in the 1820s with Henry Humphreys who built a large textile factory. This group included Moses and Ceasar Cone, the Sternbergers, J. Spencer Love and C.C. Hudson. One of the city's attractions was an excellent transportation system that began with the completion of the NC Railroad in 1856. Good roads, rail lines, interstate highways, and finally an airport were important economic factors.

Known as the Gate City since 1891 because of its railroad connections, Greensboro has been called the Hartford of the South because of its insurance industry and the "birthplace of the sit-ins" because of the sustained civil rights protest that began here on February 1, 1960. Leaders in many fields and countless unnamed men and women have shared in Greensboro's development. Through them the city has become a hub of education, industry, transportation, finance, health care, recreation and the arts. Today, as in the past, Greensboro is indeed a chosen center.

Gayle Hicks Fripp

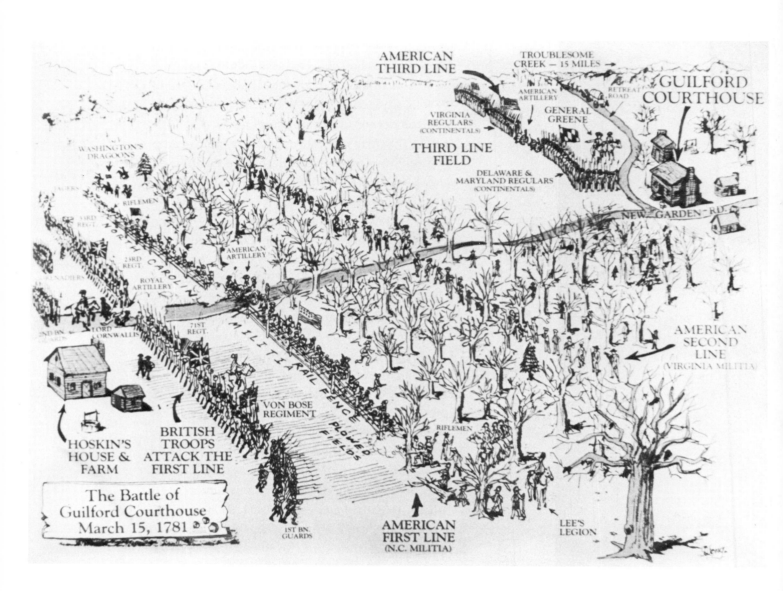

American General Nathanael Greene chose the village of Guilford Courthouse as a suitable battlefield; he liked the terrain and the road placement. This contemporary sketch shows the three lines placed by Greene, who stationed his most experienced men in the rear. Guilford militiamen were on the front line. Courtesy, Don Long, Guilford Courthouse National Military Park

Chapter One

SEEDS FOR A CITY:
TO 1800

Seven men on horseback moved slowly through a wooded area. Their leader checked his compass and signaled directions. The group had an important mission: to locate the geographic center of Guilford County and purchase a tract of land surrounding that point. The site would be used to construct a new county courthouse.

The terrain inspected that day was irregular, marked by hills and valleys, streams and marshland, cleared fields and dense timber. The explorers doubtless spotted many animals—squirrels, rabbits, deer, bear, wolves, foxes, and beaver. They probably flushed out quail, doves, turkeys, pigeons, and geese. The forest provided protection for game, an important source of food to the people of that time. Oak, poplar, pine, and chestnut trees supplied materials for houses, tools, and furniture. Other resources were invisible—fish in the waters, minerals in the earth, and the soil itself. The year was 1808, and the center of Guilford County was still largely wilderness.

* * *

In prehistoric times, 10,000 to 20,000 years ago, more than 20 nomadic groups roamed throughout Piedmont North Carolina. They hunted and fished, camped and traded. By A.D. 1200 farming was combined with hunting, and small family groups built temporary villages that were used until the soil around them was exhausted. Most of the agricultural chores, including clearing the land, were performed by women. Corn was the primary crop, but beans, pumpkins, squash, and tobacco were also planted. Long after these early farmers had abandoned the area, their cleared fields, overgrown with wild grasses, stood as reminders of their onetime presence.

Archaeological evidence of these early residents has been uncovered at approximately 150 sites in Guilford County. These spots, usually near streams or on raised ground, have yielded stone tools, mortars, and weapons. One type of projectile point has been designated the "Guilford," because it represents an Indian culture present within the central Piedmont around 4000 B.C.

One of the first European visitors to the area was John Lawson, an English surveyor and explorer who in 1701 traveled 550 miles through South and North Carolina. Lawson's *A New Voyage to Carolina*, published in 1709, contains a description of a Keyauwee Indian town situated between High Point and Asheboro.

According to this witness, a fence of pointed stakes surrounded the cabins of the town; large cornfields, grassland, and high cliffs surrounded the stockade. The town's approximately 200 inhabitants differed from others Lawson visited in that "Most of these Indians Wear Mustachoes or Whiskers." Another interesting characteristic was the "use of Lead-Ore, to paint their Faces withal, which they get in the neighboring Mountains." The exploring party was treated to a feast that included chestnuts, venison, turkey, bear, and rabbit.

By 1710 the Keyauwees had abandoned this site, moving first to the east and then into South Carolina. It is thought that they eventually merged with the Catawbas, but some descendants of this Siouan-speaking group may be the ancestors of today's Lumbee Indians.

A second tribe lived northwest of Greensboro in the 17th century, but no descriptions of their settlements survive. Known by various names, including Saura, Sawras, and Cheraw, the tribe moved into South Carolina around 1710 and joined the Keyauwees.

Colonial Pioneers

Permanent settlement of the Greensboro area began around 1740, decades later than in the eastern portions of North Carolina. The delay was due mainly to geography.

North Carolina is divided into four regions: the Outer Banks, Coastal Plains, Piedmont, and Mountains. The Outer Banks, which block the coast, prevented the creation of a major seaport during the colonial period, and the absence of rivers flowing from west to east discouraged the movement of people and goods inland. In the 18th century, a border of "pine barrens" marked the western boundary of the Coastal Plain, and the land beyond that line was hilly and hard to clear for farms. The name Piedmont, meaning "foot of the mountain," was applied to the region.

Thus, the traditional pattern of settlement in America, expansion from the coast inland, did not occur in North Carolina. Instead, people pushed southward into the Piedmont from the Northern colonies. It was these nontraditional pioneers who worked the land and shaped the

Below: This brass surveyor's compass is marked "C. Moore/ Guilford, N.C." Cameron Moore was a local silversmith in the 1780s who belonged to the Quaker Meeting at New Garden. The compass is a precision instrument, the type that might have been used to locate the center of Guilford County. (GHM)

Left: Indian artifacts and evidence of prehistoric hunting camps were uncovered by an archeological team that examined the proposed site for the new Piedmont Triad International Airport Terminal. In this photograph the crew member on the right removes plowed dirt, which is sifted through a screen by a second person. Courtesy, Archeological Department, Wake Forest University

Below: John Collins, a Quaker from New Jersey who visited the Greensboro area in 1869 and 1887, made watercolor sketches of the people and places he saw, like this interior of a Quaker sitting room. Courtesy, Friends Historical Collection, Guilford College

future.

The first groups to arrive had left Germany because of wars and religious oppression. They sought freedom in America, entering through the seaports of Pennsylvania and Maryland. As land in the Northern colonies became scarce and expensive, they moved southward, and by 1744 a number of families had settled along the Haw River in eastern Guilford County. Friedens Church, established in 1745 near Gibsonville, is the oldest church in Guilford County. One of the earliest county deeds, granting Ludwig Clapp 640 acres on Alamance Creek, was recorded in 1752. By the following year, a community known as Wachovia had been established near Winston-Salem.

Arthur Dobbs, royal governor of North Carolina from 1754 to 1765, described the Piedmont Germans as "an industrious people. . . . They raise horses, cows, and hogs with a few sheep, they raise Indian Corn, wheat, barley, rye and oats, make good butter and tolerable cheese . . . they sow flax for their own use and cotton, and what hemp they have sown is tall and good."

Quakers of English and Welsh descent settled the western portion of Guilford County around 1750; most of them came from the Northern colonies, but some migrated from eastern North Carolina. A large group from Nantucket Island arrived in 1771, and a contemporary observer named J. Hector St. John DeCrevecoeur wrote about them in his *Letters from an American Farmer:*

They have founded a beautiful settlement known by the name of New Garden. . . . No spot on earth can be more beautiful, it is composed of gentle hills, of easy declivities, excellent lowlands, accompanied by different brooks which traverse this settlement. I never saw soil that rewards men so easily for their labours. . . . It is perhaps the most pleasing, the most bewitching country which the continent affords.

One entry in the New Garden Monthly Meeting Records reads, "Dolley, their daughter was born ye 20 of ye 5 mo. 1768." The parents referred to were John and Mary Payne, members of the New Garden meeting between 1765 and 1769, when they moved to Virginia. Dolley later became the wife of James Madison, fourth President of the United States, and is the only North Carolina native to become a President's wife.

William Hockett and other Quakers settled along Polecat Creek in southern Guilford County, acquiring tracts of 640 acres each from the Earl of Granville. Their community, halfway between New Garden and Cane Creek in Alamance County, came to be called Centre, a name that survives to this day. In the southwest, Quakers settled along Deep River and established a village named Jamestown.

Around 1750, a third group of people moved into the area between the Germans and the Quakers. Commonly called Scotch-Irish, they were descendants of Scots who had lived in Ulster, Ireland, before migrating to the Ameri-

The Buffalo Cemetery, the oldest one in Greensboro, dates from the 18th century. Soldiers of the wars of Regulation and Revolution are buried here, as are David and Rachel Caldwell, Henry Humphreys, and other individuals from Greensboro's history. (GHM)

can colonies. Some settled in Pennsylvania, Maryland, and Virginia, but others moved southward where land was available and neighbors were scarce.

A large number of Ulster Scots, organized by the Nottingham Presbyterian Church in Lancaster County, Pennsylvania, arrived to claim more than 20,000 acres of land that had been selected by Nottingham Company agents. Their deeds to land on North Buffalo and Reedy Fork creeks are all dated 1753. In 1756 these settlers built a church on land obtained from Adam Mitchell and named it for North Buffalo Creek which ran close by. Representing "Old Side" Presbyterian thought, this congregation rejected the emotional, evangelical religion that had become so popular during America's Great Awakening.

Ralph Gorrell, an important figure in Greensboro history, left northern Ireland and arrived at Boston in 1750. Immigrating to Piedmont North Carolina, Gorrell settled near Alamance Creek and acquired a tract of land at the center of what would become Guilford County. A neighbor to the east, William Cusach, owned 640 acres that had been deeded to him by the Earl of Granville in 1759. In 1762, Cusach gave land for a church, neighbors built a log structure, and Alamance Pres-

byterian Church began its long history. While the distance from Buffalo Church may have made a second church necessary, the difference in religious thinking was even more important. The Alamance congregation accepted both the evangelical thrust and the emotionalism of the Great Awakening.

Both Presbyterian churches were without a pastor until 1765, when they invited a missionary named David Caldwell to serve them. Four words, inscribed on a granite marker at Guilford Courthouse National Military Park, summarize his life: "Teacher, Preacher, Physician, Statesman."

Born in Pennsylvania in 1725, Caldwell was trained as a house carpenter and then attended Tennett's Log College and the College of New Jersey (later Princeton). After a series of examinations and trial assignments, he was licensed to preach by the Presbyterian church. In 1765 he was ordained and appointed to serve as a missionary in North Carolina. The following year he married Rachel Craighead, daughter of a noted Presbyterian minister in Mecklenburg County. The Caldwells lived on a farm of 550 acres purchased from the Nottingham Company, and a portion of the plantation exists today as a memorial park. His income from farming and operating a gristmill was necessary to supplement his church salary of $200 a year.

In 1767 Caldwell started a classical school in his home and later built a log building as an academy to prepare young men to enter a university. He enrolled approximately 50 students each year, many of whom became statesmen, lawyers, judges, physicians, and ministers. Rachel assisted her husband as a teacher.

Caldwell was officially installed as minister at Buffalo and Alamance Presbyterian churches in 1768 and served until 1820. Busy as a plantation owner, teacher, and preacher, Caldwell nonetheless found time to care for the sick within a 20-mile radius of his home. Self-educated as a physician, he learned from medical books ordered from Pennsylvania and by observing a trained physician. His presence in Guilford made the frontier less primitive.

Land deeds and church records tell much about early Germans, Quakers, and Presbyterians, but there were families and individuals of other backgrounds. Indentured servants, white and black, who had fulfilled their work contracts would have moved toward freedom and opportunity. Emigrants from Scotland, France, Sweden, Ireland, and Holland may well have been present in 1765. Slaves, more numerous in America after 1700, would have accompanied their owners to the Piedmont, and it is estimated that some 500 blacks were present by 1754.

The People's War

As a colony of Great Britain, North Carolina was ruled by a governor appointed by the king and a bicameral assembly based on county and town representation. In 1771 there were 22 counties in the east and only 7 in the west; as a result, fewer than one-fourth of the representatives to the House of Commons came from the west, where almost half the colony's population lived. Local officials throughout the colony were appointed by the royal governor, who lived in the east.

Tension between east and west was augmented by additional problems. The distance between the new western settlements and the courthouses at Hillsborough for Orange County and Salisbury for Rowan County required men to spend days traveling to record deeds, pay taxes, and deal with officials they considered dishonest. The national origins and religious beliefs of residents living in the east and west were dissimilar. Finally, the small farmers of the west had little in common economically with the large landholders of the east.

The result of these increasing tensions was the War of Regulation, a five-year struggle by settlers living in the Piedmont against government officials stationed throughout the colony.

Left: In 1764 William Tryon was appointed (British) lieutenant governor of North Carolina, and the following year he became governor. Oppressive rule and high taxes (especially those used to build the elaborate "Tryon's Palace" governor's mansion) fueled the Regulators' revolt in 1771. Courtesy, Division of Archives and History, Raleigh

Right: Tryon, center, is depicted confronting a group of Regulators in this illustration, circa 1771. Courtesy, Division of Archives and History, Raleigh

Beginning in 1766 with a peaceful meeting of Orange County farmers, it ended in 1771 at the Battle of Alamance. Major causes of the conflict were the domination of government by eastern residents, usually men of wealth; an increase in taxes to pay for the construction of a palace at New Bern to house the colonial assembly and Royal Governor William Tryon; a scarcity of money necessary to pay increased taxes, rents, and fees; and the abuse of power by local officials.

The Regulator movement was formally organized in 1768. Members vowed not to pay illegal taxes and fees, stating: "An officer is a servant of the Publick, and we are determined to have the officers of this county under a better and honester regulation than any have been for some time past."

Governor Tryon replied to a 1768 Regulator petition by demanding that they give up their name and cease their activities. Since peaceful protests were of no avail, the Regulators staged riots when court sessions were held and assaulted royal officials.

In January 1771 the assembly authorized the governor to use military force against these western agitators, and Tryon called out the North Carolina militia. Approximately 1,000 men marched to Hillsborough, where court was in session, and then to Great Alamance Creek (30 miles east of Greensboro). There, about 2,000 Regulators had gathered, many of them members of the Presbyterian churches of Buffalo and Alamance. Reverend David Caldwell was present to serve as a mediator but was unsuccessful.

On May 16, 1771, after Tryon refused to accept a petition and the Regulators refused to disperse, a two-hour battle took place. The untrained and often unarmed Regulators were defeated. Nine men on each side were killed, and the militia took 15 prisoners; seven were hanged, and eight were later released. According to Governor Tryon, "a signal and glorious victory was obtained over the obstinate and infatuated rebels." As governor he offered clemency to all who would submit to his authority, and during the next six weeks more than 6,000 western residents accepted his offer.

The same assembly that authorized the governor to use military force in suppressing the Regulators four months earlier had authorized the establishment of four new Piedmont counties: Guilford, Wake, Chatham, and Surry. Together, Tryon's success at Alamance and the creation of additional counties ended the east-west struggle for political control.

Establishment of Guilford County

On January 26, 1771, the colonial assembly meeting at New Bern passed "An Act for erecting a new County between the Towns of Salisbury and Hillsborough by taking Part of the Counties of Orange and Rowan." The creation of Guilford County satisfied local Regulators because it meant political representation and a nearby courthouse; it also pleased royal officials because it weakened the Regulator movement. According to the legislation, a line, beginning 25 miles west of Hillsborough, would be drawn to serve as the boundary of a new unit to be made up of land two-fifths formerly in Orange County and three-fifths in Rowan. The act named the county Guilford after Francis North, the first Earl of Guilford,

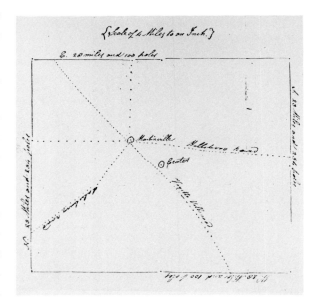

This surveyor's map, from the North Carolina State Archives, marked the center of Guilford County southeast of the 1807 county seat Martinville. A year later this "center" became the new county seat, Greensborough. From Legislative Papers, 1807, L.P. 223, N.C. Courtesy, Division of Archives and History, Raleigh

whose son Frederick was prime minister of Great Britain from 1770 to 1782. It also included provisions for a Church of England parish and a Court of Pleas and Quarter Sessions.

This court, made up of justices of the peace, was to meet on the second Tuesday of each February, May, August, and November, beginning on May 14, 1771. Robert Lindsay's house on Deep River was the original meeting place, and its great hall is considered Guilford's first courtroom. Seven commissioners were appointed to run the county's boundary line, to select a site for necessary public buildings including a courthouse and jail, and to levy a poll tax to provide revenue for construction.

The boundary line was completed on June 19, 1771, but almost three years passed before a site was agreed upon. The seven commissioners recommended a location in northwest Guilford County, and Governor Josiah Martin approved the act that confirmed their choice on March 19, 1774. The one-acre tract was purchased from Commissioner John Campbell. A log courthouse, begun in 1774 and used until 1809, became the center for the county seat known simply as Guilford Courthouse.

Guilford During the American Revolution

News of a skirmish between British troops and colonial minutemen at Lexington, Massachusetts, reached Guilford County through private letters and newspapers. From April 1775 until October 1781, the threat of war, the economic struggle for life, and the creation of a state government were major concerns.

In September 1775 the Provincial Congress of North Carolina prepared for war and authorized Guilford County to raise one company of minutemen. A number of county citizens remained loyal to the British government, however, and they responded to Royal Governor Josiah Martin's appeal for troops to conquer North Carolina. In February 1776 the two groups skirmished at Bruce's Crossroads (renamed Summerfield in 1812). The

Loyalists, or Tories, then marched to eastern North Carolina to rendezvous with other Loyalists at Moore's Creek Bridge. A battle between Revolutionary and Tory forces took place there on February 27, 1776, and the Loyalists were soundly defeated. For the next five years, military events occurred outside North Carolina.

During 1776 the Fourth Provincial Congress authorized Charles Bruce, a large landowner in northwest Guilford County, and Daniel Gillespie, a resident of the Buffalo Creek area, to procure arms for Guilford's troops placed under the command of Colonel James Martin. The same congress appointed a Committee of Safety to govern North Carolina. In December, Guilford County sent five delegates to the Fifth Provincial Congress meeting at Halifax. Three of them were major figures of the 18th century: Charles Bruce, Ralph Gorrell, and David Caldwell. On December 18, 1776, the congress adopted a constitution for the state of North Carolina. It also appointed Richard Caswell as the state's first governor.

During 1779 two acts of the general assembly affected county landowners. One called for the confiscation of property owned by residents loyal to Great Britain, and 3 of the 68 men named lived in Guilford. Proper disposal of the seized tracts was a continuing concern. A second act established a new county and stated that the southern third of Guilford would become part of Randolph.

By the summer of 1780, a military invasion of North Carolina seemed probable. Georgia had been restored to British rule during 1779, and South Carolina had fallen to the British army following the surrender of Charleston on May 12, 1780. British forces in the South, under the command of Lord Charles Cornwallis, moved to the Charlotte, North Carolina, area in September but withdrew into South Carolina. In December, General Nathanael Greene, new commander of the American army in the South, arrived at Charlotte.

In an unusual move General Greene divided

his army, sending a force under General Daniel Morgan to South Carolina while Greene moved northward. Morgan's army won a battle at Cowpens, South Carolina, in January 1781, and then began its march to Virginia. The British army followed Morgan and Greene and attempted to engage the Americans in battle. The Americans led the British across North Carolina and then used boats to cross the flooded Dan River. The British were left behind, far from their supply bases in South Carolina.

General Greene stayed in Virginia long enough to resupply his troops and to enlist additional men; then he reentered North Carolina. The American commander had studied the terrain covered during his earlier retreat and had decided that the area around Guilford Courthouse was suitable for a major battle with the British. On March 14, 1781, the American army moved to Guilford Courthouse, the village for a farming community of 300 people. Greene prepared his battle plan, stationing more than 4,000 men in three fixed lines. The North Carolina militia, including the Guilford unit under Colonel James Martin with one company led by Captain Arthur Forbis, was in the first line which stretched across New Garden Road.

Learning that Greene was inviting an attack, General Cornwallis moved his army northward from Deep River and arrived early in the afternoon of March 15, 1781. The attacking British force of 2,200 soldiers quickly routed the first line, fought through the second line of Virginia militia, and reached the third line of Continental soldiers. The savage fighting that occurred at this position was finally broken up when General Cornwallis directed the British artillery to fire into the battle's center.

Nathanael Greene, calculating that he had severely weakened his enemy, withdrew his army and retreated to Troublesome Creek in northeast Guilford County. In surrendering the field, he gave the technical victory to Cornwallis. In April Greene's army marched into South Carolina and freed that state of British control. The last major Southern battle for General Greene was at Eutaw Springs on September 8, 1781.

The British army, having lost one-fourth of its men, remained at Guilford Courthouse until March 18, 1781. The wounded were moved to New Garden Meetinghouse where Quakers cared for them, and General Cornwallis led the remainder into Randolph County and then to Wilmington. In late April 1781, the British army moved into Virginia. There, at Yorktown, trapped between an American land force and a French naval force, Cornwallis was forced to surrender on October 19, 1781.

The Treaty of Paris, signed on September 3, 1783, formally ended the American Revolution; however, the Battle of Guilford Courthouse marked its close in Piedmont North Carolina. After Cornwallis retreated to

During the Revolutionary War Nathanael Greene led the strategically successful retreat into North Carolina, which forced Lord Cornwallis to follow. Although Greene's troops "lost" the Battle of Guilford Courthouse, they weakened the British who then had to withdraw for supplies. This momument to General Greene was dedicated in 1915. Courtesy, Guilford Courthouse National Military Park

Left: Having served as county commissioner in 1771, Alexander Martin was elected governor of North Carolina in 1782. Martinville, named for the governor in 1785, served as Guilford's county seat until 1808. Courtesy, Division of Archives and History, Raleigh

Right: Daniel Gillespie (1743-1829) was an early settler on Buffalo Creek. His first land grant was made in 1765 and another for 300 acres was made in 1783. When lots in the new town of Greensboro were auctioned in 1808, he paid $136 for the southeast lot on Courthouse Square. A leader in the War of the Regulation, he was a militia colonel during the Revolution and fought at Guilford Courthouse. As an elected representative, he voted to adopt the North Carolina and United States constitutions. (GHM)

the coast, the remaining problem was the sale of confiscated Tory land. One buyer was Alexander Martin, who had served as a county commissioner in 1771. When confiscated land around the courthouse was sold, Martin and Thomas Henderson purchased 350 acres.

Elected governor of North Carolina in 1782, Alexander Martin served two one-year terms and then retired to Guilford County. On December 29, 1785, an act passed by the general assembly provided that a town with a town common be laid off around Guilford Courthouse. The established settlement, to be called Martinville in the governor's honor, covered 100 acres owned by him and Henderson. Thus, the county seat acquired a new name.

A second act, passed on the same day, provided another major change for the county. The section north of an east-west line "beginning at Haw River bridge, near James Martins" was designated a new county named Rockingham. Portions of the original Guilford, created in 1771, had now become neighboring counties to the south (Randolph, 1779) and the north (Rockingham, 1785).

In July 1788 a state convention of county delegates met at Hillsborough to consider North Carolina's adoption of the Constitution of the United States. Guilford's five representa-

tives included David Caldwell and Daniel Gillespie. The county delegation voted with a majority of representatives against ratification of the Constitution without a Bill of Rights. This action left North Carolina outside the new United States. In November 1789, at a second convention held at Fayetteville, the majority voted in favor of ratification, and North Carolina became the 12th state in the Union.

Martinville served as Guilford's county seat from 1785 until 1808, but it remained a village with one major street named for General Greene. The commissioners in 1785 were William Dent, who surveyed the settlement; Ralph Gorrell; Robert Lindsay, Jr., who ran a general store and coppersmith shop; John Hamilton; William Dick, who owned a wagon factory and blacksmith shop; Bazilla Gardner; and Alexander Martin. Crowds gathered only on the days that court was in session at the log courthouse or when stagecoaches and wagons loaded with people and trade items arrived from east or west.

In 1790 the first United States census was taken, and Guilford County's population totaled 7,291 residents. There were 3,406 white males, 3,242 white females, 27 free persons, and 616 slaves. Most of these people lived and worked on small farms, but some were large landowners: Charles Bruce, Robert Donnell, Daniel Gillespie, Ralph Gorrell, and Alexander Martin.

In June 1791, all area citizens were thrilled by a visit from the President of the United States. On his tour of the South, George Washington was eager to see the battlefield at Guilford Courthouse where Greene had so weakened Cornwallis, and he spent the morning there. After lunch, probably at Ballinger's Tavern, and dinner with Charles Bruce, Washington spent the night with Alexander Martin. He then proceeded to Troublesome Ironworks, following Greene's retreat march. Washington's tour of North Carolina did much to ease political friction created by the establishment of a strong national government.

This portrait of John Motley Morehead, governor of North Carolina from 1841-1845, was painted by William Garl Brown around 1860. Later Morehead was to use his political influence to have the North Carolina Railroad curve northward and pass through Greensboro. (GHM)

Chapter Two

A TIME OF GENTLE GROWTH: 1801 - 1860

*M*artinville's success as county seat was unlikely from the start. Its location in the northwest meant that some citizens had to travel greater distances than others to conduct official business. This type of injustice had been an issue during the War of the Regulation.

Residents of southeast and southwest Guilford began to talk about relocating the county seat, and a movement to choose a central site gained strength. Those who supported the idea were known as the Centre party. They opposed the Martinville party led by Charles Bruce and Alexander Martin. In February 1807 county officials appointed five commissioners to arrange for a new brick courthouse and jail to be built at Martinville, hoping that the construction of new public buildings would divert those who favored relocation. But their plan merely increased the strength of the opposition, and when an election was held in August to determine the permanent location of the county seat, the Centre group won. On December 16, 1807, the general assembly passed an act appointing seven commissioners "to fix on a suitable and centrical place . . . for erecting the Court House and Other public buildings." Those named were William Armfield, David Caldwell, Jr., Charles Bruce, Hugh Forbis, Jacob Clapp, George Swaine, and Nathan Mendenhall.

The Founding of Greensborough

Early in 1808, the commissioners began their task. Nathan Men-

denhall, one of the group, was trained as a surveyor and owned the necessary tools, a compass and chain. When the county's center was located, it turned out to be under water; ducks swam over it in the marshy area now known as Fisher Park. After a time of deliberation, the commissioners moved to the crest of a hill slightly to the southwest and staked a site. The new county seat, still without a name, was positioned between North and South Buffalo creeks.

The wooded area belonged to Ralph Gorrell, who consented to sell a tract of 42 acres, setting his price at $98. The deed awarding the land to the commissioners was dated March 25, 1808.

A second responsibility of the seven was to sell lots to secure the necessary funds for construction of the county's public facilities—a courthouse, jail, stocks, and whipping post. Surveyor Mendenhall drew up a village, one-fourth mile wide and one-fourth mile long, with four major streets: North, South, East, and West. The enclosed property was divided into squares which were sold at public auction.

A total of 44 lots were purchased by 33 men, at prices that ranged from $4.80 to $151. The intersection of the four streets was designated as the site of the courthouse, and neighboring land was the most expensive. For the north corners of Courthouse Square, William Ryan and Levi Tucker paid $151 and $150; for the south corners, Thomas Bevell and Colonel Daniel Gillespie paid $139 and $136; Nathan Mendenhall, Levi Huston, and Leven Kirkman

purchased three lots each; David Caldwell, Jr., Jesse Cook, Joseph Lovet, and Levi Tucker each purchased two. The total amount raised by the property auction was $1,689.39. The entire village, still unnamed, extended only two blocks from Courthouse Square. Its population was zero, and no buildings existed.

On December 15, 1808, the general assembly passed an act naming Guilford's county seat Greensborough. According to tradition, David Caldwell, Jr., a commissioner and son of Guilford's leading citizen, suggested that the town be named for Nathanael Greene in appreciation of his service during the Revolutionary War. A borough was simply an organized town; therefore, the name meant "the town of Greene." As the years passed, a shorter spelling came into use, and by 1895 Greensborough had become Greensboro.

Not until May 15, 1809, did the new village officially serve as the county's seat of government. The delay was due to construction of a courthouse and jail, which were completed for the May term of the Court of Pleas and Quarter Sessions. According to Albright's history of Greensboro, court days were also holidays:

> Both white and black, by hundreds gathered on what is now Gaston Street from Ashe to Davie, to have a good time. Watermelons, cider, ginger-cakes, pies, etc., formed the dainty menu; while the fiddle and banjo supplied the music. There was but one town constable, and he seldom had an arrest to make.

Some of Greensboro's earliest residents moved in from the county: Robert Lindsay, Jr., from Martinville; Henry Humphreys from Jamestown; John McClintock Dick from a farm in eastern Guilford; and the Caldwell twins from the west. Thomas Caldwell became clerk of the Guilford Superior Court in 1807. Serving first at Martinville, he moved to the new county seat about 1815 and built a brick house within the town's western limit. His

The Genesis Monument stands at the "approximate center of Guilford County as determined for the establishment of Greensborough as the county seat of Guilford County, 1808." In Fisher Park between North and South Park drives, it was a gift to the city in 1971, the county's bicentennial year. The donor was county historian James G.W. MacLamroc. (GHM)

brother David lived next door on a lot purchased at the 1808 auction.

Development of Town and County

In 1810 the North Carolina General Assembly adopted Greensboro's first charter. Thirteen sections outlined a system of administration to be carried out by six commissioners of police appointed by the state legislature. The only services offered to residents were unpaved streets, public water pumps, and a public well which was later enclosed at county expense. A second act, passed in 1824, allowed the "free men" of Greensboro to elect five commissioners of police, who were to serve one-year terms. A town constable was elected as the leading official. An amendment in 1828 authorized a system of fire protection. Little else is known about this period, and the earliest local records begin in 1829.

In April of that year, the commissioners of police (William Adams, John M. Dick, Jacob Hubbard, Christopher Moring, and Robert Moderwell) adopted nine town rules:

1. Every person who shall exhibit a Stud horse in any of the Streets of this town nearer to the Courthouse than the first Cross Street Shall be Subject to a fine of Five Dollars. . . .

2. Any Person Known to Keep Wood, Stone or Lumber in the Two Main Streets Crossing at the Courthouse . . . unless for the purpose of Building . . . for Twenty-Four hours shall be fined Two Dollars. . . .

3. Every Person living within the Incorporation Shall be Subject to a fine of Five Dollars For Every Ten Days his Chimney or Chimneys Shall Remain Less than Two Feet and a half Above the Comb of his house. . . .

4. Any Person Known to drive or stop a Wagon Cart Or Carriage of any description in any Street within the Corporation at any publick time For the purpose of Selling any Article Or Commodity What Ever, Shall be fined One Dollar. . . .

5. Any Waggoner or Other Person who May feed his team of horses Within the Two Main Street Crossings at the Courthouse Shall be fined one dollar for such offence. . . .

The David Caldwell, Jr., house stood on West Market Street, east of the Thomas Caldwell house which faced Ashe Street. The sites are now occupied by the 1918 Guilford County Courthouse. David Caldwell, Jr., was one of Greensboro's early residents and a pioneer physician. (GHM)

6. Any Person known to fire a gun or Pistol (the Cannon Excepted) any Where Within the Corporation . . . shall be fined one dollar. . . .

7. Any Person throwing Shavings, Straw, Leather, Ashes, or any other kind of litter in the Streets shall be fined one dollar for every Such Offence.

8. Any person Watering a horse at Either of the Publick pumps shall be fined one dollar. . . .

9. The officer of Police Shall at all times attend to the Removeale of any Nuisance when Required by any of the Commissioners under a penalty of One Dollar for each Neglect.

A tax schedule was established based on a poll tax of 50 cents and a property tax of 10 cents per $100. Licenses were required for merchants ($7), liquor retailers ($2.50), and owners of stud horses ($2).

The commissioners appointed a secretary, T. Early Strange, and a tax collector/police officer, John M. Logan. Logan, who arrived in Greensboro by stagecoach in 1821, was a leading merchant and captain of a state militia company. He was well suited for keeping both the treasury and the public peace.

On June 10, 1829, the commissioners ordered Strange and Logan to take a census and to assess real estate within the town limits. Official records indicate that Greensboro had 484 white residents (369 within its one-fourth mile borders and 115 nearby), 26 free blacks, and 96 slaves. A total of 33 families owned slaves, but the largest holder, Robert Carson, owned 15, and another family owned 6.

All the real estate in Greensboro was valued at $53,495. The wealthiest man was Henry Humphreys ($12,000), followed by Marcelles Jordan ($8,000), Jacob Hubbard ($4,200), and Jed H. Lindsay ($3,500). The town income for 1829 was:

124 taxable voters at .50 . . . . . . $ 62.00

$53,495 property (.10 per $100) . . . 53.50
5 stores ($7) 35.00
3 liquor shops ($2.50) 7.50
1 stud horse ($2) 2.00
                     Total $160.00

Some of this money was spent on maintenance of the streets ($57.50) and water pumps ($20). Logan received $15 for his work as police officer.

In 1830 the commissioners adopted a tenth ordinance, establishing a fine of one dollar for feeding a hog in any of the town streets. They also agreed on a system of night patrols. All white male citizens, except ministers, between the ages of 21 and 45 were expected to serve. Their duties included enforcing a 10 p.m. curfew for blacks, slave and free, supervising the morals of whites, and watching for fires. In 1833 the newly elected commissioners of police began a system of fire protection, requiring each household to clear its yard of rubbish and to have two ladders, one of which would reach the roof's peak.

The only public buildings in early Greensboro belonged to Guilford County. The courthouse, completed in 1809, was used for at least a decade. Little is known about it, but during the War of 1812 the Guilford militia met there to enlist volunteers to aid in the defense of Norfolk, Virginia. When no men

Militia units were both social and patriotic organizations. The Greensborough Guards had blue uniforms trimmed in buff, and leather hats the size and shape of firebuckets. Merchant Robert G. Lindsay, a West Point graduate, was the first captain of this 30-man organization. In 1847 a militia group organized by John Logan left to fight in Mexico. Courtesy, Greensboro Public Library

stepped forward, David Caldwell, then 88 years old, climbed on the courthouse bench and preached to the crowd. As a result, 167 men enlisted in two companies.

In May 1818 a new courthouse was constructed, but its poor condition was a political issue by 1826. It must have been replaced by 1828, because a tax was levied to make the third payment for the courthouse. A bell and town clock were installed after 1831.

Other county facilities were a jail, whipping post, stocks, pillory, and "place of execution." In 1845 a new county jail and an office for the county clerk were built.

In 1837 an act of the General Assembly served as a new charter; the town was incorporated, a tax schedule was adopted with $5 as the maximum real-estate tax, and the official limits were extended so that Greensboro covered one square mile. New wells were dug as a town service, and a system of drafting citizens for street work was adopted.

In 1839 the town commissioners replaced the citizen night patrols with two hired watchmen and began a beautification program by providing that elm trees be planted on the major streets leading from Courthouse Square. Gill, a "man of colour," was paid $34 to set out the trees during the spring of 1840. The same commissioners also set a fine of $50 to be paid by anyone caught playing cards within the town boundaries!

In 1843 public health became an issue when a fever epidemic swept over the town. An appointed health committee decided that the marsh area east of Elm Street should be drained. Ditches were dug where ducks and boys formerly swam.

A volunteer fire department was organized by William Caldwell and Lyndon Swaim in 1849. A hand-pumped fire engine was purchased in Baltimore for $600 and a brick fire house, 18 feet by 28 feet, was constructed near the Courthouse.

During the 1850s two pieces of legislation modified local government. The first, in 1855, provided for the election of an intendant of police (replacing the town constable) and four commissioners. The second required the county seat to name its major streets.

From the town's beginning, East and West streets had led from Courthouse Square into the country, while North and South streets ended several blocks from the square. Since some of the early shops were located on East and West, and since those streets were used to reach the stores on the square, the official name became Market Street. For North and South streets, officials chose Elm in honor of the trees planted by Gill in 1840. Other names were memorials to important men, such as (Nathanael) Greene, (William R.) Davie, and

Charles Green Yates, mayor of Greensboro from 1857-1860, built this handsome house which stood on Church Street beside the Jacob Henry Smith house. Later when the house was moved to North Elm Street, Mr. A. Wayland Cooke, an attorney and Greensboro's postmaster from 1916-1920, lived in it. The house was razed in the 1950s. (GHM)

GREENSBORO

Since 1895, the official spelling of Greensboro has not varied, but before that date two forms were commonly used.

In North Carolina legislation:
  1808-1855 Greensborough
  1855-present Greensboro
As postal cancellations:
  1810-1850 Greensboro
  1850-1895 Greensborough
  1895-present Greensboro
In the *Patriot,* leading newspaper:
  Before 1865 Greensborough
  After 1865 Greensboro

(William) Gaston. Local features, such as sycamore trees or a church, also lent their names to the principal streets.

The Revised Code of North Carolina was adopted in 1859. In the chapter regulating towns, the office of intendant of police was changed to mayor, and a provision required that the mayor and six commissioners be elected. A.P. Eckel was chosen as Greensboro's first mayor in 1859.

By 1858 a new courthouse stood on the northwest corner of Courthouse Square. This lot, the most expensive one sold at the 1808 auction, was purchased for $4,000 from Samuel Hopkins, who operated a tavern there. County officials accepted a construction bid of $17,383 by the firm of McKnight, Houston & Collier. The building was completed within a year and was, according to the *Greensborough Patriot,* "an elegant and inspiring edifice." County government was properly housed at last.

Economic Developments

By 1820 Greensboro was a center for roads that reached into Virginia and to Raleigh, Fayetteville, Asheville, Salisbury, and Salem. Some of these had been paths used by migrating animals and Indians. Now they were stage roads used to transport mail, newspapers, people, and merchandise. Men with new ideas visited the community and stayed in local inns run by leading citizens, George Albright, Peter Adams, James Bland, and Christopher Moring. The business of accommodating travelers became an important enterprise, and five inns were operating by 1850.

On July 11, 1851, people gathered to celebrate the first day of work on the North Carolina Railroad. The first shovels of dirt were moved by Calvin Graves, who as president of the North Carolina Senate voted to break a tie vote in favor of the state-owned line.

Farmers from the surrounding area came to Greensboro to obtain manufactured goods and sell surplus produce. Greensboro was their county seat, and they made frequent trips to the courthouse; it was also the place to see a militia or circus parade or consult a physician.

In 1829, when the first census was taken, five stores were licensed to operate, and by 1833 there were 27. Robert Moderwell, a successful merchant, had his house and store on Elm Street where Sycamore intersects. His stock included nails, iron, lead, sugar, glass, and books. Other shops sold jewelry, furniture, and leather goods.

During the 1850s, W.C. Porter opened a drugstore, Andrew Weatherly operated a dry goods shop, E.W. Ogburn sold books, R.G. Lindsay specialized in hardware, and T.M. Woodburn was known for confections. General stores were run by John L. Hendrix, W.S. Gilmer, John M. Logan, and the firms of Rankin & McLean and McAdoo & Scott. James M. Hughes was a tailor, and A.P. Eckel was a jeweler.

Early factories were frame or brick buildings located beside houses, stores, and churches. At the corner of West Market and Greene, P. Adams & Sons made fur and high silk hats, and on South Elm Street, Rose & Overman produced carriages. Other successful businesses were a tannery with a harness and saddle shop operated by W.R.D. Lindsay and John Hoskins, Samuel Shelton's furniture plant, and James Brannock's shoe factory.

In 1828 Henry Humphreys built the town's

By 1840 there were stores on three corners of Courthouse Square: T. Caldwell & Sons' Cheap Store, Humphrey's, and Lindsay's. McConnel's Cheap Store stood on West Market, the primary business street before 1850. From the *Greensboro Patriot*

first textile mill, Mount Hecla. It was the first steam-operated cotton mill in North Carolina, operating 3,000 spindles and 75 looms by 1833. Its products, including woven cotton material and cotton yarn, were shipped to neighboring counties and states. Humphreys, Greensboro's leading businessman and wealthiest citizen, also served as chairman of the town commissioners in 1832 and 1834. His three-story house on the southwest corner of Courthouse Square was called Humphrey's Folly; it served as home, office, and general store.

During the 1840s a second major industry began. A factory operated by Reuben Dick was located near the Presbyterian Church; it manufactured cigars, snuff, and plug tobacco. Greensboro's location at the center of the Piedmont meant that tobacco was grown nearby and farmers needed a convenient market. The Civil War briefly interrupted the development of this industry which continues today.

The manufacture and sale of tin goods, tobacco products, furniture, and hats continued during the 1850s, but Mount Hecla Mill was moved to the Catawba River to take advantage of steam power. An important new firm was Pioneer Foundry, which produced metal plows and tools. During the Civil War this factory was converted to the manufacture of guns.

A number of influential men settled in Greensboro between 1820 and 1850. James Turner and John Motley Morehead, students of David Caldwell and graduates of the University of North Carolina, were lawyers. Active in state politics, the Moreheads also owned mills and plantations north of town. In 1841, John Motley Morehead was elected governor of North Carolina and served two two-year terms. He returned to Greensboro in 1845, and Blandwood, his remodelled house, became a center for social activities.

The Morehead brothers married sisters, daughters of Robert Lindsay, Jr. His sons, Jesse, J. Harper, and Robert Lindsay, were involved in town and county affairs. Their store on Courthouse Square was a gathering place for the community.

In 1850 the first insurance company in

Mount Hecla Steam Cotton Mill occupied a 150x50-foot building near the Greene/Bellemeade intersection. The company issued its own scrip, pictured here. (GHM)

town, Greensborough Mutual Fire Insurance, was established, and in 1853 the *Greensborough Patriot* reported that the business had moved from "under Squire Peter Adams hat" to "one of the best business rooms in town."

In 1851 the Bank of Cape Fear in Wilmington established a local branch. Jesse H. Lindsay was cashier, and five local businessmen served as directors. A second banking and insurance company, Greensborough Mutual Life Insurance and Trust, was chartered in 1851 and opened in 1852. Ralph Gorrell, grandson of the landowner who sold Greensboro its site, was the president, and Lyndon Swaim, editor and architect, was vice-president. Finally, in 1859, the Farmers Bank of North Carolina opened a Greensboro branch which later became bank headquarters. None of these institutions survived the chaos of the Civil War.

Business establishments opened in response to local growth. In 1851 Joshua Lindley moved his nursery business from Chatham County to the New Garden settlement, possibly so that his son John could attend the boarding school. Dating back to 1842, Lindley Nurseries has changed names and locations several times.

Schools, Churches, and Social Institutions

A concern for education was demonstrated early in Greensboro's history, and in 1816 charters were drawn up for male and female academies. The Male, or Greensborough Academy, soon opened in a Sycamore Street building with Nathaniel Harris as principal. In 1819 the Reverend William Paisley became director, and on January 1, 1820, the Female Academy opened in a building behind the Paisley house. It was directed by Paisley's eldest daughter, Polly, and a board of trustees.

Reverend Paisley was also a Presbyterian minister, and in 1824 he organized the first congregation to meet within the town limits. Using the Male Academy for services, First Presbyterian Church began with 12 members, eight whites and four slaves. In 1830 the Greensborough Female Benevolent Society organized to raise funds for a building, and in 1832 a small brick church was constructed on land donated by Jesse H. Lindsay. By this time church membership had grown to 38. The building was only 30 feet wide and 40 feet long, but it had two doors, one used by the women and one by the men. The cemetery that adjoined the building is still a doorway to Greensboro's past.

The Presbyterian church was not the town's first, however. Followers of the Methodist movement had migrated to the area as early as 1770. Missionary preachers, known as circuit riders, were assigned to the colony, and in 1783 the Guilford Circuit was established as one of 12 in the state. Peter Doub, a Methodist minister assigned to the Guilford Circuit in 1830, succeeded in building Greensboro's first church in 1831. Its initial membership was 68. Located at 318 South Elm Street, it was a two-story brick building with an upstairs gallery used by black worshipers.

Before 1850, to attend church within the town limits one had to worship as a Methodist or Presbyterian. The Quakers, Lutherans, and German Reformed, long present in the county, were not yet organized in Greensboro. The Baptists were represented in this early period by one man, Major Jones Johnson, the only "professing Christian" discovered by Paisley

Sawmills, tin and blacksmith shops, and shoemaking and tailoring establishments were early local enterprises in Greensboro. Albright's *Greensboro* states that "tinware and the repairing of copper stills were profitable industries before 1857 when the railroad reached the town." This tin assortment is from the Greensboro Historical Museum collection. (GHM)

In 1859 Jacob Henry Smith became pastor at First Presbyterian Church, serving until his death in 1897. A year earlier the Smith family gathered for a photograph. From left to right, the seated grandchildren are Mary Norris, Lunsford and Laurinda Richardson, and Egbert and Margaret Virginia Smith; in the second row are Lynn Richardson, Mrs. Lunsford Richardson, the Reverend and Mrs. Smith, Hay Watson Smith, and Mrs. Egbert Smith; and in the third row are H. Smith Richardson, Lunsford Richardson, Henry Louis Smith and wife, Samuel Smith, Mrs. R.G. Vaughn and husband holding Mary Watson Vaughn, and Egbert and Alphonso Smith. (GHM)

Frances Webb (1819-1898), was teaching school when Reverend Sidney Bumpass proposed by sending her a New Testament with marked passages. Married in 1842, they moved to Greensboro in 1846 and lived on South Mendenhall Street. The neighborhood, known as "Piety Hill," included many Methodist residents, a college, and a church. Between 1852 and 1872 "Auntie" Bumpass printed *The Weekly Message*, a religious newspaper founded by her husband shortly before his death. (GHM)

on his arrival in 1819. David Caldwell continued to serve the Presbyterian congregations at Buffalo and Alamance, but an assistant minister named Eli Caruthers was called to help. By 1820 Caruthers was in charge of both churches.

In 1851 the Methodists moved from South Elm to a new building on West Market Street which had central heating and gas lights. Many Methodist ministers and laymen built houses near their church, and the neighborhood was often called "Piety Hill" (now College Hill). One resident was Frances Webb Bumpass, widow of a Methodist minister who had founded a religious newspaper *The Weekly Message* in 1850. Continuing her husband's work, Mrs. Bumpass edited the paper and printed it in her home for the next 20 years.

The empty Methodist church on South Elm Street was purchased by Elias Dodson, a missionary for the Baptist Home Mission Board, and used for services after 1851. The Greensboro Baptist Church was officially organized on March 13, 1859, and its membership of 20 included blacks and whites. Elder John Mitchell was the first minister.

Soon after the Methodist church was completed, members financed a female school which opened nearby on South Elm Street in 1833. Five years later it was chartered as Greensborough Female Seminary by the General Assembly, and in 1843 construction began on a building on West Market Street. Greensboro Female College opened in 1846. The Presbyterians were also interested in a church-related school. Dr. Joseph Caldwell, president of the University of North Carolina, headed a committee chosen to select a site; the group decided eventually on a South Elm Street location. Caldwell Institute, which opened in 1835, attracted young men from several states until 1843 when it moved to Hillsborough, North Carolina, following a fever epidemic. (Neither the Institute nor Joseph Caldwell had any relation to David Caldwell and his "log college.")

West of town New Garden Boarding School admitted 25 boys and 25 girls when it opened on August 1, 1837. It was the first coeducational institution in North Carolina. The Quakers of New Garden had begun planning for the school in 1830 and in 1834 a charter had been obtained. The school's primary purpose was to teach advanced students to teach others.

In 1840 John Motley Morehead founded a

school for girls, naming it Edgeworth after an Irish writer. With five daughters to educate, a local seminary seemed a good idea, and the building was constructed on a site that bordered the grounds of Morehead's home. Music, art, literature, foreign languages, math, and science were taught to the young ladies who came from many towns in the state.

In addition to the private institutions, free schools were established for local children. The General Assembly adopted a common or public school plan in 1839, and Guilford County voted in favor of setting up a local committee to manage state funds and supervise school operations. An advertisement in the *Patriot* of July 10, 1841, urged attendance at one such school held at the home of Thomas Beattie. Children of both sexes, ages 5 to 21, could attend the three-month session.

During the 1850s a number of new schools were opened, including the Greensboro Classical School for boys on Edgeworth Street, the Greensborough Male High School in the old Caldwell Institute Building, and Hoyle School for girls.

A Greensboro citizen was elected state superintendent of education when that office was created by the General Assembly in 1852. Calvin H. Wiley, lawyer and author, worked to develop North Carolina's system of public schools, which included 118,852 children in 1860. He also organized a State Teachers Association and established the *North Carolina Journal of Education.* Perhaps his greatest accomplishment was keeping the public schools of North Carolina open throughout the Civil War.

Greensboro's adult population learned by reading. The Librarian Society, located first at the Courthouse and then at the Male Academy, provided resources for some people, but a local newspaper, the *Patriot,* was much more important. Established before 1826, the paper was purchased by William Swaim in 1829. In his first issue the editor announced that the publication was:

> Devoted to . . . public education, the encouragement of manufactures in Southern States, a general improvement in the condition of our coloured population; a change in the policy of our banking institutions, and a total overthrow of the system of electioneering which has disgraced the character of our country.

This progressive thrust continued until William Swaim's death in 1835; its influence, though difficult to measure, was significant.

In 1839 Jesse Lindsay contacted Lyndon Swaim, a printer in Randolph County who had worked with his cousin William on the *Patriot,* and urged him to buy the *Patriot.* Swaim agreed, and he ran the newspaper with Michael Sherwood for the next 15 years. His purpose was given in his first editorial: "We shall advance all well-judged plans for the improvement of the internal commerce of the state and that system of school education which may reach every child in the land."

Social life in the town was centered in the

Left: Edgeworth Female Seminary was established in 1840 by John Motley Morehead, the father of five daughters. The building, pictured on this piece of early sheet music, was designed by New York architect Alexander Jackson Davis. It was located on Morehead's property, northwest of his residence. (GHM)

Above: This house was built around 1850 for Michael Swaim Sherwood, editor of *The Greensborough Patriot*. His partner Lyndon Swaim boarded at the Sherwood House briefly with his wife and stepdaughter Mary Jane Virginia, who became the mother of the writer O. Henry. The house was listed on the National Register of Historic Places in 1978. (GHM)

Right: The Richard Mendenhall plantation house in Jamestown is thought to have been a depot for the Underground Railroad. Built around 1811, the house is listed on the National Register of Historic Places. Surviving outbuildings were used by Mendenhall, a farmer and tanner. (GHM)

homes, but it included church and school activities. Adult males could belong to "Old 76," the Lodge of Mason organized in 1821.

Social issues were also important, and many people, particularly the Quakers, felt that slavery was wrong. By 1816 they had established local branches of the Manumission Society of North Carolina. Editor William Swaim was a later spokesman for this movement.

In 1817 an interesting trial opened at the Guilford County Courthouse; it involved a freed slave, Benjamin Benson, who had been kidnapped in Delaware and brought to Greensboro to live. His "owner" John Thompson refused to release Benson, and he was placed on trial. The case which continued for two years ended with Benson freed. More significant than his victory, however, was the stimulus given to the proslavery and antislavery forces.

State laws were passed making it illegal to educate slaves (1831) and difficult to free them. In 1835 all blacks, slave and free, were forbidden to vote. The continued existence of slavery and increasingly harsh laws were more than many people could bear, and many Guilford County Quakers moved westward. The manumission societies ceased to exist, and escape to a free territory seemed the only answer.

During the slavery era, many black men, women and children used a system of trustworthy people and routes known as the Underground Railroad to escape to freedom. The railroad had depots where fleeing slaves could hide or rest, and it depended on conductors to direct the passengers. There were depots in Guilford County, and it is believed that John Dimrey was the first slave to travel the route from Guilford to Indiana in 1819. Vestal Coffin of New Garden is considered the creator of the railroad, and his cousin Levi was later called "president." Vestal's widow Alethea, the Mendenhalls, the Worths, the Beards, and a slave named Sol were among those who risked much to aid fleeing slaves.

Railroad development of a different kind brought excitement to the community on January 29, 1856, when many local citizens witnessed an event that was to be a symbol of the town's future. The two ends of the North Carolina Railroad were joined near Jamestown, and two engines pulled cars of cheering workers east to Greensboro for a celebration. State Representative D. Frank Caldwell drove the last spike, but the real hero of the day was John Motley Morehead. He had worked for two decades to create a railroad system for the state, and his skill as a politician resulted in an east-west line of tracks that curved miles to the north to pass through his town. Greensboro's period of "gentle growth" was drawing to a close.

A Confederate officer signs his parole while others wait, in this *Harper's Weekly* illustration. Although 39,000 paroles were printed in Greensboro, only officers were released in the town; enlisted men were discharged by their officers as they reached their homes. The Albright brothers reopened their printing shop to prepare the parole forms. From *Harper's Weekly*, 1865

Chapter Three

A TIME OF CRISIS
AND CALM:
1861 - 1876

On February 28, 1861, voters in Greensboro joined others across North Carolina to defeat a referendum which authorized a convention to consider the state's secession from the United States. Although the proposal failed by a mere 651 votes (46,672 to 47,323), it was favored by only 113 in Guilford County and opposed by 2,771. Just six weeks before the outbreak of the Civil War, there was little local sentiment for separation from the national government.

The Civil War Years: 1861-1865

Seven southern states which had seceded met during February 1861 and formed the Confederate States of America. Federal property within those states was seized but Fort Sumter in the harbor at Charleston, South Carolina, was one of two still controlled by the U.S. Army. Attempts to supply the men stationed there were unsuccessful, and on April 12, 1861, Confederate troops at Charleston opened fire on the fort and forced its surrender.

President Abraham Lincoln called for 75,000 volunteers to put down this Southern insurrection and proclaimed a blockade of Confederate ports. North Carolina governor John Ellis, forced to choose between the Union and the Confederacy, ordered the seizure of all U.S. forts within the state, the federal arsenal at Fayetteville, and the federal mint at Charlotte. He called for volunteers to fight for the Confederacy, and on May 20, 1861, North Carolina seceded from the U. S. and joined the C.S.A.

On April 18, 1861, the *Greensborough Patriot* ran the following editorial:

> *It is with deep regret and most painful anticipation of the future, that we announce to our readers that the war has commenced. . . . But yesterday, all was quiet, peace and happiness; today, terror, excitement, and confusion rule the hour. The Stars and Stripes, the Flag which we have been taught to reverence, and which we all so much love . . . has been dishonored, and that, too, by the hands of those, who of all others, should have been the first to defend it.*

On that same day the Guilford Grays met at the courthouse, and 45 of the men, supplied with three days' rations, boarded a train and left Greensboro. The company musicians were from the "colored troops": Jake Mebane as fifer, Bob Hargrove as kettle-drummer, and Caesar Lindsay as base-drummer. The first of six local units, the Grays became Company B, 27th North Carolina Troops. They fought at New Bern and in Virginia and Maryland; 12 of them surrendered at Appomattox with Robert E. Lee and were paroled to return home.

A second volunteer outfit, the Guilford Dixie Boys, left in June. This group became Company M, 21st North Carolina Troops. Their organizing officer was a lawyer and former teacher at Edgeworth, William Lafayette Scott.

During the four years of civil conflict, Greensboro citizens concentrated on the needs of the Confederacy. In 1862, the congregation of First Presbyterian Church voted to give its church buildings to the Confederacy to use as a war-service unit and donated the church bell to be melted down for ammunition. Its pastor, Reverend Jacob Henry Smith, served as a Confederate chaplain spending part of his time with General Scales' Brigade and part at

Wilmington. He visited the Guilford Grays at their winter quarters near Orange County Courthouse, Virginia, and preached in a log tabernacle at Christmas. His wife, Mary Watson Smith, helped organize a canteen at the railroad station, and its other hostesses met the passing trains and shared food with the troops. Other mothers, sisters, wives, and daughters spent hours preparing bandages and comfort kits to be sent to local men wherever they were stationed.

Although a fire forced Greensboro Female College to close in 1863 and Edgeworth Seminary closed in 1864, New Garden Boarding School remained open throughout the war. Two seminary teachers, Richard Sterling and James D. Campbell, joined with James W. Albright to begin a publishing company. Working out of the offices of the *Greensborough Patriot,* the trio began producing a series of school books called Our Own, because they reflected the ideals and ideas of the Confederacy. Paper made of cotton was run through a press operated by a horse-powered

Thomas Johnson Sloan, one of the Guilford Grays, posed for this picture in 1861. The militia company ordered uniforms from Philadelphia (note the "GG" on the hat) and received them in May 1860. (GHM)

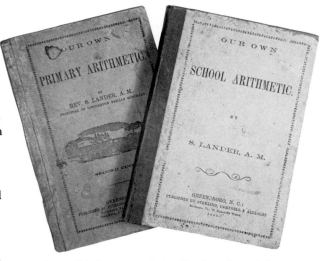

Nineteen books were prepared under the "Our Own" label. Paper made from cotton was run through a press operated by a horse-powered engine, which had originally been developed by A.P. Boren to grind cane. Thousands of books were sold before April 1865, when U.S. General Schofield ordered that publication cease. (GHM)

engine which was originally developed by A.P. Boren of Pomona to grind cane. Thousands of books were printed before 1865 when Federal troops occupied the town.

Another firm founded in 1861, J.&F. Garrett & Company, manufactured guns and sewing machines. On February 14, 1863, Jere H. Tarpley, who had become a partner, registered a patent for a breech-loading carbine, and after that date the firm of Tarpley, Garrett & Company concentrated on manufacturing the Tarpley carbines.

By 1864 Greensboro residents suffered from food shortages created by the blockade of Southern ports. Sugar and coffee were prewar luxuries; cornbread, sorghum molasses, sweet potatoes, rabbit, and fatback meat were staples for people of all classes. At the wedding

celebration of John Alexander Gilmer, son of the former congressman, and Jesse Lindsay's daughter, Sallie, tallow-dip candles lit the rooms and a fruitcake prepared with dried huckleberries and molasses, not raisins and citron, was served.

During 1864 a railroad line linking Greensboro with Danville, Virginia, was completed. The 40-mile line, suggested by Governor Morehead as early as 1857, was built by the Confederate government so that men and supplies could move in a north-south direction.

Greensboro became both storehouse and railroad center, and its citizens, especially the women, were kept busy caring for the troops. As Mary Watson Smith later recalled:

> *Weary, footsore, and needy soldiers were daily passing through the town, who needed to be clothed, fed, and comforted; and whenever the Danville train came in with Graycoats on board it was a signal to broil bacon, bake cornbread, and set out all the milk, buttermilk, and sorghum one could lay hands on, the only delicacies that one could then afford.*

Greensboro became a center for military activity early in 1865. In February Robert E. Lee was named general-in-chief of the Con-

Many Confederate soldiers left or arrived in Greensboro at the Richmond & Danville Railroad depot. President Jefferson Davis stopped at the depot on September 21, 1864, to make a brief speech. Located near the intersection of South Elm and East McGee streets, the building looked out of place in the 20th century. It was razed and its site became a park for "Hamburger Square." (GHM)

federate army, and he placed General Joseph E. Johnston in command of the Confederate army in the Carolinas. Johnston's assignment was to stop the northward advance of a Union army under Major-General William T. Sherman. As Sherman entered North Carolina in early March, he ordered his soldiers to "deal as fairly and moderately as possible" with the citizens and property of the last state to leave the Union; therefore, destruction was less severe than in other areas. On March 19, 1865, the invading army was surprised by a Confederate attack near Bentonville. The battle continued for three days before Johnston withdrew his outnumbered and battered troops. More than 900 of the wounded Confederate soldiers were transported to Greensboro by train, so that they would not be captured. The Presbyterian and Methodist churches, the courthouse, and Edgeworth Female Seminary all became temporary hospitals. Refugees from the eastern portion of the state also were sheltered in the town, which became headquarters for the 20,000-man army under General P.G.T. Beauregard, Johnston's second in command.

On April 2 President Jefferson Davis and his cabinet moved from Richmond to Danville, Virginia, and the next day Federal troops occupied the former Confederate capital. On April 9, at Appomattox Courthouse, Robert E. Lee surrendered the Army of Northern Virginia to General Ulysses S. Grant, and Jefferson Davis, hearing that report, left Danville for Greensboro.

Traveling on the same train was a great deal of money which belonged to the Virginia banks and the Confederate treasury. According to contemporary accounts, approximately $39,000 of this fund was buried at Rose Villa, residence of Mayor A.P. Eckel. General Judson Kilpatrick, who lived at Rose Villa during the period of Federal occupation and had the grounds searched for valuables, failed to uncover the cache. After Kilpatrick's departure, the money was recovered by Confederate

agents and shipped southward.

On April 11, 1865, Jefferson Davis arrived in Greensboro, and for a few days the town was the seat of the Confederate government. Meeting with Generals Johnston and Beauregard, Davis learned that both opposed further military action, and he reluctantly agreed to a conference between Johnston and Sherman. President Davis then left on horseback for Charlotte.

Johnston and Sherman met near Durham's station at a log house owned by James Bennett on April 17, and at a second meeting on April 18 they agreed on a surrender plan and a 48-hour truce. When this news reached Greensboro, riots broke out as soldiers and civilians tried to capture the supplies of food and clothing stored by the Confederate army. Only the presence of armed troops prevented total chaos. Many soldiers deserted, and Johnston saw his army of 50,000 men "melting away like snow before the sun."

Both generals forwarded copies of the preliminary treaty to their superiors, and Davis approved for the Confederate States of America. General Grant and Secretary of War Stanton, officials of the U.S., did not. While

Rose Villa, the home of Mayor A.P. Eckel, was built during the 1840s. In 1865 Confederate officials visited the house and buried bags of silver under a yellow jasmine vine in the backyard. When U.S. General Judson Kilpatrick occupied the house in May 1865, he searched the grounds for hidden valuables, but he did not discover the cache. Rose Villa, which stood on the southeast corner of Washington and Davie, was surrounded by beautiful grounds, which earned Greensboro the nickname, "the city of flowers." It burned in 1881. (GHM)

Johnston prepared for a possible battle by moving his army from east of Greensboro to the west, Grant traveled to Raleigh to advise Sherman of acceptable terms. Sherman and Johnston met again at the Bennett place, and there, on April 26, 1865, Johnston surrendered all the troops under his command.

Governor Zebulon B. Vance had left Raleigh shortly before Federal troops occupied the capital, and he established a temporary headquarters at Greensboro in the law office of Levi and William Scott. When the governor received the news of Johnston's surrender, he prepared his proclamation of April 28, the last official act of the Confederate State of North Carolina. Then he went home to Statesville.

Letitia Morehead Walker recalled the appearance of new leaders. "One fine morning amid the sound of bugles and trumpets and bands of music, the Federals entered Greensboro, fully thirty thousand strong, to occupy the town for some time." Four United States Army generals—Jacob D. Cox, Ambrose E. Burnside, John M. Schofield, and H. Judson

Kilpatrick—called at Blandwood to see her father, Governor Morehead. During the first days of Federal occupation, before the Confederate soldiers departed with their paroles, approximately 80,000 soldiers were in Greensboro, a town of 2,000 residents.

Edmund J. Cleveland, a New Jersey soldier in Greensboro on May 8, 1865, recorded in his diary, "Greensboro is a nice county seat but thinly settled. Two of the churches are now being used as Confederate hospitals. There are several other hospitals in town—all filled with sick & wounded." On June 4 he attended a Presbyterian service held at the former Methodist church building on South Elm Street, then being used by Baptists. His diary states: "The Church was well filled with soldiers and civilians. There were many charming young ladies present. The choir accompanied by a fine organ was a good one."

Another eyewitness was William Sidney Porter, a young boy who lived on West Market Street near Edgeworth Seminary. Union soldiers were camped nearby, and many of the men used the Porter well, dug for cressy greens and onions on the property, and talked to the neighborhood children. Years later, Will Porter used material from the occupation period in short stories published under the pseudonym O. Henry.

The Carpetbag Era: 1865-1876

In June 1865 William L. Scott, a former Confederate officer, was appointed mayor of Greensboro, by W.W. Holden, who had been named the provisional governor of North Carolina by President Andrew Johnson. Holden also appointed the town commissioners: Lyndon Swaim, Jacob Hiatt, A.C. Caldwell, A.P. Eckel, W.C. Porter, and Dr. D.W.C. Benbow.

New residents greatly influenced the town's postwar years. One who left his imprint on Greensboro and North Carolina was Albion Winegar Tourgee. Arriving in the fall of 1865 with his wife and $80,000, the Ohio native purchased a house on South Asheboro Street and invested in a nursery four miles west of town. Considered a "carpetbagger" and often threatened for his belief in civil rights for blacks and whites, Tourgee organized the Union League in several Piedmont counties and established two newspapers that supported the Union League and the Republican Party.

Attending a convention in Philadelphia in 1866, Tourgee spoke out about the terrible conditions for Negroes and Unionist whites in North Carolina and Guilford County. His accusations, unsupported by any evidence, were printed in North Carolina newspapers; they strengthened the Ku Klux Klan in Guilford which boasted 800 members.

On the positive side, Tourgee was elected a county delegate to North Carolina's constitutional convention of 1868, and he drafted much of the document that is still in use. Educated as a lawyer, he was an effective United States judge for the Seventh Judicial District from 1868 to 1874. A member of the Methodist Episcopal Church, he helped to establish a school for blacks which became Bennett College.

Tourgee was also a talented writer. He published a novel entitled *Toinette* while living in Greensboro, but a later novel, *A Fool's Errand* (1879), is a significant book in American liter-

This turn-of-the-century painting depicts "a shaking of hands" on Memorial Day. The holiday was first observed in Greensboro in May 1866, when women decorated the graves of the Confederate dead. It became an annual event, with concerts and speeches. The artist Clarence F. Underwood was also an illustrator for popular magazines like *The Saturday Evening Post* and *Harper's*. (GHM)

ary history. Autobiographical in nature, it concludes that the main character was a fool for believing that an ex-Union soldier could help heal the wounds left by the Civil War.

Another influential newcomer was Yardley Warner, a Quaker and a member of the Philadelphia Association, an organization formed to help freed blacks. Warner purchased a 35-acre plot south of Greensboro's one-mile limit for the sum of $2,260; he deeded it to the Philadelphia Association and divided it into acre lots which were sold to blacks. He also began a school for black children in his home and, in 1867, built a community school where adults and young people could learn gardening and other trades, as well as the basic skills of reading and writing.

Harmon Unthank, an ex-slave who purchased a lot, became a leader in his community and is credited with naming it Warnersville. A carpenter by trade, he served on the county school board and as a bank director. Albion Tourgee, who knew Unthank, modeled one of his fictional characters around him. Alice Unthank Reynolds, a daughter, left this description of growing-up in Warnersville:

My father went to work at 6 a.m. and worked until 6 p.m. He arose at 4 a.m. and worked his garden which supplied his family, the neighbours who had none, and all that the children could sell to make their own money. That's the way we dressed ourselves. We had every fruit and berry that grew. I got up every morning and set out plants until time to go to school. He had considerable land and used great tracts for a garden.

Warner moved to Tennessee in 1881, returned to the Archdale area in 1883, and died of typhoid fever in 1885. His community grew and prospered, according to this 1889 description by English Quaker Henry Newman:

I have today been to Warnersville, visited the coloured people in their own houses, examined their garden plots, seen their schoolhouse and their church, and can bear testimony to the thriving character of the population. They number between 500 and 600 people, all coloured. Warnersville has extended far beyond the original purchase of Yardley Warner when he commenced the project about 1869. They have about 200 coloured children attending their school. They have a good house as a residence for the school teacher, who has two well-qualified assistants. I find that in the adjoining city of Greensborough, there is a very friendly spirit between the white people and the coloured. Coloured men are occupying several public offices, and a number of them are successful men of business managing their own stores.

Tourgee, Warner, and other "carpetbaggers" had been welcomed to Greensboro by Lyndon Swaim, editor of the *Greensboro Patriot*, in an editorial of 1869: "they bring money; they bring skill; they bring habits of economy and industry; they bring character; they bring willing hands and big hearts, to join our own people in a long pull and a strong pull for the prosperity of our war-wasted land."

Thomas Settle, a leader in the Republican Party and a justice of the state supreme court from 1868 to 1871, was even more outspoken:

We want their capital to build factories and workshops and railroads and to develop our magnificent water powers. We want their intelligence, their energy, and enterprise to operate the factories and to teach us how to operate them. Let hate and prejudice have no place here. Elevate yourselves, but pull nobody down. Go for the education and progress of mankind without regard to race or color and invite all to come forward and assist in the development of our common country.

This attitude of openness and welcome, shared by Cyrus P. Mendenhall, R.P. Dick, and other leading citizens, helped Greensboro move forward instead of looking back.

As "carpetbaggers" continued to arrive, many became community leaders. Thomas B.

Albion Tourgee, with "carpetbag" in hand, is caricatured leaving Greensboro in 1876. Will Porter drew the cartoon when he was 14, and throughout his life the future O. Henry sketched people and places. Although he had considered becoming a cartoonist, he turned from pictures to words and became a writer. (GHM, copy)

Keogh, a Wisconsin native, established a building and loan association, began a real-estate development, and encouraged others to immigrate to North Carolina. In 1873 he was elected a city commissioner, and he was a director of the Guilford Battle Ground Company.

Local Republicans assumed leadership roles. Cyrus P. Mendenhall, a business associate of Albion Tourgee, was elected mayor in 1874. Robert Martin Douglas, who moved to Greensboro in 1873 as United States marshall for North Carolina, was a Rockingham County native who had served four years as secretary to President Ulysses S. Grant. Douglas, later a lawyer and state supreme court justice, was a builder of the Republican Party in North Carolina, despite the fact that his father Stephen A. Douglas had been the presidential candidate of the Democratic Party in 1860.

Another important leader in Republican politics was Greensboro native, Robert Paine Dick. A noted lawyer and a state supreme court justice from 1868 to 1872, Dick then became a United States district judge. The 1874 marriage of his daughter Jessie to Judge R.M. Douglas was one of the happiest events of the Reconstruction period.

In 1870, a Democrat, Robert M. Sloan, was elected mayor of Greensboro. James W. Albright, Julius A. Gray, John Alexander Gilmer, and A.J. Brockmann were elected town commissioners. This council decided to draw up a new charter for Greensboro which would designate it as a city divided into two wards. It set the city limits as the borders of a school unit and provided that the schools, to be maintained by state and local funds, would operate eight months of the year.

On March 28, 1870, the General Assembly passed the necessary legislation, and on May 25 the new charter was adopted by the voters of Greensboro. Thus the town of 2,000 residents, still only one mile square, officially became a city.

In May, 1871, a group of 60 Northern news-

Robert Moderwell Sloan, shown here with his six daughters, was elected mayor of Greensboro in 1869. A leading merchant, he was the first local agent for the Southern Express Company. His son John was a Confederate officer, and his daughters married prominent businessmen. Pictured standing from left to right are Mrs. Clark Porter, Mrs. John Barringer, and Mrs. Jefferson Scales, and seated from left to right are Mrs. Neil Ellington, Mrs. John Logan, and Mrs. Nick Mebane. (GHM)

paper editors arrived in Greensboro, a stop on a 1,500-mile railroad excursion through the South. The purpose of the trip was to establish a better relationship between the people of the two regions by educating those who shaped public opinion.

In *The Pine and the Palm*, a published account of the excursion, the stay in Greensboro is described. Arriving at the railroad depot in early afternoon, the editors were welcomed by local leaders and a crowd "of all sizes and all colors." They were led by a band through the sandy streets to the Benbow House, "a new and commodious hotel, not yet quite completed." Following a midday dinner, accompanied by toasts and speeches, the group took a walking tour. Later they were entertained at a ball on the open balcony of the Benbow House.

The beauty and fashion of the city were in attendance.... At midnight a most elegant repast was served in the dining-room, consisting of every delicacy in early fruits, dessert and viands. The dance continued till nearly five A.M., but 'tired nature' compelled us to withdraw at a much earlier hour. The music was particularly excellent, and drew a large party of listeners. . . . The neighboring fences and trees were crowded with recently legalized 'men and brethren' of African 'scent, watching with intense interest the movements of brave men and fair women in the mazes of the waltz and polka and intricate figures of the quadrille and lancers.

On the following day the editors toured other local sites and noted the beauty of certain residences and their surrounding grounds. This favorable impression remained with the writers, and one of them referred to Greensboro as "The City of Flowers," a nickname that was used throughout the 19th century.

In 1872 the city's financial statement listed receipts of $1,550.14 and disbursements of $1,480. The cost of constructing and maintaining streets, bridges, and water pumps was $937.14, almost two-thirds of the total spent. Salaries for officials accounted for $319.45, with the constable receiving $180.50 and the mayor $100. Claims against the city had been settled for $196.06.

Citizens were pleased with the frugality of Mayor Sloan and his commissioners, but some were critical of the rather primitive living conditions. An editorial in the Republican newspaper *New North State* decried "the accumulation of filth within its limits" and the fact that "hogs, the greatest of all nuisances, are permitted to run at large, gaining their living from garbage left in the streets." The editorial continued:

Such a condition is a disgrace to any place, particularly one claiming the dignity of a city. A pound ought to be built, into which every stray hog and cow should be driven and kept until redeemed by the

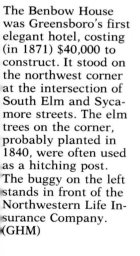

The Benbow House was Greensboro's first elegant hotel, costing (in 1871) $40,000 to construct. It stood on the northwest corner at the intersection of South Elm and Sycamore streets. The elm trees on the corner, probably planted in 1840, were often used as a hitching post. The buggy on the left stands in front of the Northwestern Life Insurance Company. (GHM)

owner. Every merchant ought to be obliged to sweep and clean to the middle of the street in front of his place of business at least once a week and the piles of dirt so collected ought to be carted away.

Greensboro's development was temporarily halted in June when a fire swept through the business district destroying the courthouse, two rows of frame law offices beside the courthouse, Southern Hotel, Farmers Bank, and Porter's drugstore.

Work was begun immediately on a new courthouse, and the same site and design were used. When the building was completed, a pump and watering trough were placed at the entrance. The statue of an angel was added as a symbol of relief from thirst for man and beast.

While Cyrus P. Mendenhall was mayor (1874-77), a number of improvements were made. In 1875 the city's charter was amended to allow an increase in local taxes and the number of commissioners. A city market house and a graded school for white children were constructed, and a municipal court that met each morning to handle city cases was initiated. The commissioners passed an ordinance requiring small pox vaccination and employed Dr. R.K. Gregory to provide this as a free service. Brick buildings replaced several landmarks that had burned in 1872. South Elm Street, cobblestoned after the war, was paved with macadam, and brick sidewalks were laid along major streets. On January 15, 1875, the business district of Greensboro was lit by kerosene fixtures, an exciting improvement for its residents.

In 1876 Greensboro was a "dry" city; citizens could neither buy nor sell alcoholic beverages within its limits. The issue quite literally divided the town in 1877, when Gilmer Township, east of Elm Street, voted in favor of keeping its "dry" status, while Morehead Township west of Elm voted "wet," approving the sale of alcohol. After that there were bars

on the west side of Elm but none on the east, until 1878 when Gilmer voters endorsed liquor sales also.

Economic development resumed after the war, beginning with the production of wooden objects needed to build and furnish houses, repair wagons, and produce textile goods. Thomas McMahan established a Spoke and Handle Factory, and W.H. Snow opened a similar plant which also produced furniture items. Related businesses were lumberyards and sawmills.

In 1869 the Sergeant and McCauley Manufacturing Company was organized from the Yarborough and Tarpley Foundry. The new company specialized in cooking and heating stoves, but it also produced farm implements and tools. In 1873 Giles T. Glascock,

The "graceful wooden tower" of the 1858 stuccoed brick courthouse caught fire in 1872. The building was lost, but it was replaced with a similar structure whose tower had clock faces on all four sides. (GHM)

who had worked for Yarborough and Tarpley
during the war, established the Glascock Foundry and Machine Shop, which also produced
stoves and implements.

The tobacco industry was revived, and
several firms manufactured products for shipping. Colonel E.P. Jones, the first businessman
to ship tobacco from Greensboro during the
prewar years, used the former Caldwell Institute as a plant, and Eugene Morehead built
Greensboro's first warehouse for tobacco and
processed items. In 1872 the Tobacco Board of
Trade was established to regulate and
encourage the industry.

Below: The Bogart
house with its picket
fence, outbuildings,
and tree-shaded yard,
was on North Church
Street across from the
Jacob Henry Smith
house. Home enter-
tainment in the late
1800s included taffy
pulls, charades, and
musical perfor-
mances. Young
people could also
swim, skate, bicycle,
and dance. (GHM)

As manufacturing increased, so did the
number of business establishments along
South Elm. In 1871 J.W. Scott opened a grocery store, and in 1872 J.A. and J.H. Odell and
W.H. Ragan opened a general store. To pay for
Northern goods shipped in by train, Mr. J.A.
Odell shipped out agricultural products—dried
apples, blackberries, and sassafras roots—
obtaining these items by bartering with area
farmers; as principal partner, he used the
profits to enlarge the store.

Three new banks, two private and one chartered by the North Carolina General Assembly,
opened between 1867 and 1871, but none survived. Only the Bank of Greensboro,
reorganized in 1869 from the Bank of Cape
Fear, managed to grow, and in 1876 it changed
its name to the National Bank of Greensboro.
Thomas Keogh's building and loan association
prospered, as did the Greensboro Building and
Loan Association established in 1870 by
N.D.H. Wilson. Warnersville, the city's first
planned suburb, was a real-estate success.

Much of Greensboro's economic activity
depended on the railroad. Goods were shipped
in to local merchants and out by local
manufacturers and dealers. The city's location
on an east-west (North Carolina Railroad) and
a north-south (Piedmont Railroad) line
encouraged trade. In 1873 an additional line
(Northwestern Railroad) was completed to
link Greensboro and Winston-Salem. A
Western Union office, which opened in 1870,
improved business communication.

Schools, Churches, and Social Institutions

The outcome of the Civil War also stimulated religious activity. The city's established
churches lost many of their black members to
newly formed congregations. Providence Baptist Church organized in 1866 and constructed
its first building on East Market Street in 1871.
This one-room church was used as a community school also. In 1876 the congregation
built the first brick church for a black congregation in North Carolina.

A Methodist church which would become St. Matthews was organized in the Warnersville community. A second congregation of black Methodists, established in 1869 by the African Methodist Episcopal Church, would become Bethel. Its first building was completed in 1874 and stood at the intersection of Regan Street and Gaston Avenue.

St. James Presbyterian, another congregation active in Greensboro today, was organized in 1867. The nucleus of its membership came from First Presbyterian Church which had been integrated from its beginning in 1824.

All of the prewar congregations continued to grow, except for the Baptists. In 1871, when its South Elm Street church was condemned, that membership numbered only a dozen. Calling Dr. J.B. Richardson as their minister, the Baptists began a campaign for a new building which was soon completed.

Greensboro Episcopalians had been meeting together since 1863 and had organized a parish in 1869. Their first church, St. Barnabas, was built in 1871. It stood on the corner of Greene and Gaston and is supposed to have been the first church in the city with stained glass windows. Roman Catholics were meeting together by 1870, and they constructed a small frame building for worship in 1877. Named St. Agnes, the church stood on Forbis Street.

During the 1870s educational activity resumed. Greensboro Female Seminary reopened on August 27, 1873, and the Reverend Turner M. Jones, president from 1854 until 1890, returned to the city. His wife, Lucy McGee Jones, who taught at the seminary, was described in *Founders and Builders of Greensboro* as "a woman of remarkable gifts, highly cultured, deeply religious, exceedingly diligent in administering the onerous duties of her high calling."

During 1873 classes sponsored by local blacks and their friends who were interested in advanced education met in the basement of Warnersville Methodist Episcopal Church (St. Matthews). In 1875, 20 acres of land were purchased for an advanced school with dormitories. A campaign for building funds began

J.W. Scott (1843-1918), Guilford County native who fought in the 53rd North Carolina Confederate Regiment, worked for two Greensboro merchants before opening a grocery store on South Elm Street in 1871. The company later became a wholesale firm selling groceries and dry goods, doing business throughout the state with its catalogue *Our Commercial Traveler*. (GHM)

By 1876 the first building had been erected on the campus of Bennett Seminary. The Methodist-supported school, which admitted both male and female students throughout the 19th century, was chartered as a college in 1889. It included a college preparatory department until 1926. This photograph was made when W.F. Steele, a clergyman from New England, was president of the college. (GHM)

successfully with a $10,000 gift from Lyman Bennett of New York, and the first building was named for him. In 1878 the coeducational seminary was dedicated in his honor, and Bennett's bronze bell was given in his memory.

Greensboro's charter of 1870 had provided for tax-supported public schools, but there is little information about any that opened before 1875. In January of that year, a school "free to all the white children within the corporate limits of the city of Greensboro" was opened in a small brick building at the corner of Lindsay and Forbis. Its six rooms accommodated 147 pupils, who were divided into eight grades. Jesse R. Wharton was the school's first principal. A separate school, "free to all colored children within the corporate limits," was organized under Henry C. Mabry. These students gathered in a room at St. James Presbyterian Church, where more than 150 were taught by four teachers. In August, Professor Alexander McIver became superintendent of both schools; his annual salary was $1,000. Teachers' salaries ranged from $30 to $40 a month.

The beginning of Greensboro's city school system was made possible by a schedule of taxes that supplemented the state allotment. The taxable list included more than 30 enterprises—among them sewing machine companies, grain distillers, bowling alleys, stage players, rope walkers, and "Ethiopian serenaders." This system was the first in the state to be permanently supported by special local taxes agreed to by the voters. In 1875 the city's contribution amounted to $3,000, and in 1876 the city's revenue was only $8,728.

Several private schools were started in the postwar period. The best-remembered of these was operated by Miss Lina Porter, a graduate of Greensboro Female Seminary, who lived with her mother, Ruth Worth Porter, on West Market Street. This female household had changed drastically in 1865 when Dr. Algernon Sidney Porter, son and brother of the women, returned home with his two young sons, Shell

and Will. Dr. Porter's wife, Mary Jane Virginia Swaim Porter, had died, and he needed help rearing his sons.

At first the young brothers were free to play and explore, but by 1867, when Shell was seven and Will five, their aunt decided to educate the boys. Using a front room of her mother's house, she taught them to spell, read, and do simple arithmetic. As the neighbors learned of the boys' progress, they began to send their children for lessons. In 1872 a separate schoolhouse was built on the Porter property. Some of Miss Lina's students later recalled that she read to them during recess, used story-telling games, and led country hikes. All of these activities influenced her nephew, Will (O. Henry), who stored up both experiences and fantasies. He remained her student for 10 years and then enrolled for at least one year at the Greensboro Graded School. By 1879 he was employed as a clerk at his uncle's drugstore, and he never returned to school.

By 1877 Greensboro was a changed city. Its new charter and buildings, educational development, and economic activity were evidence of confidence in the future. Once again leaders were local men willing to invest in schools and businesses. Reconstruction was complete.

Facing West Market Street, circa 1885, Steam Fire Company #1 was prepared for a demonstration and parade. The fire engine was drawn by two horses, and the hose reels were pulled by volunteer fire fighters. (GHM)

Chapter Four

A RECONSTRUCTED CITY:
1877 - 1890

*T*he winning candidate for mayor in 1877 was Silas Dodson, one of the dozen Guilford Grays who surrendered with Lee at Appomattox. Having run on a platform of economy, reduced taxes, and retrenchment, he and his six commissioners cut taxes in half, establishing the poll tax at $1.50 and the property tax at 37-1/2 cents per $100. City services were not increased until Dodson's tenure ended in 1881, and city revenue declined in 1881-1882 to $7,424.

David Schenck, who moved to Greensboro in 1882 as general counsel of the Richmond and Danville Railroad, described his new home:

> *It is painful to see how filthy this little city is permitted to become. The town authorities are elected from year to year without change, a set of old fogies pledged to oppose reforms and governed by a sort of commerce class who dictate their policy and keep a town which ought long since to have been a big city from its natural growth. These are a strange and eccentric set of people to me: conservative to indifference, prudent to timidity, without any enthusiasm, heroism or adventure. The old citizens obstructing all progress and trying to push everything into the ceaseless circles of antiquated customs. A few young men, outside the old families, have pushed forward in spite of these old fossils and built up a right good trade and erected some beautiful stores and houses.*

North Elm Street was not paved until a progressive mayor was elected in 1882. Small law offices and shops shaded by elm trees stood opposite the courthouse. Telephones were installed in some homes and offices during the 1880s. The bond issues passed in 1887 provided funds to extend North Elm beyond the Bellemeade intersection. (GHM)

Robert Ruffin King, a practicing attorney and partner of Judge John Henry Dillard, was mayor from 1882 until 1888 and during those six years, Greensboro grew and prospered. King had been drafted as a candidate by progressives who wanted better streets, expanded educational facilities, and active encouragement of industry and commerce.

In 1887 a system of waterworks was begun. A tower near the end of South Elm Street provided storage and the direct pressure needed to force water through pipes. Sewer mains were installed in portions of the city for the first time, and a sanitary engineer was hired to supervise the system.

Lighting in the business district was also improved. The kerosene lamps installed in 1875 were ignited and extinguished by lamplighter Mebane Apple, until they were replaced with piped-gas fixtures during the early 1880s. By 1887 downtown was lit by electric lamps, and some residential areas were using electricity by 1890.

The idea of a city-owned cemetery had been discussed in 1879, but the conservatives in power were unwilling to spend the necessary money. In 1882 Green Hill Cemetery became a reality, and by 1887 a gate keeper was employed and provided with living quarters.

In 1884 the volunteer fire department with 100 members was reorganized under Chief C.F. Thomas. Two years later a modern, steam-operated fire engine was purchased in New York and shipped by train. Housing for the "General Greene," its horse power, and maintenance then became city expenses. Cisterns were installed at major intersections for water storage.

All of these projects required public funding, and Greensboro's first bond issue was proposed and passed in 1887. A significant step for the city, the bond issue provided $100,000

The Dick & Dillard Law School was located on Courthouse Square between 1878 and 1893. The published course of study was supplemented by a review course and "frequent extra examinations and lectures during the month that precedes each session of the Supreme Court." (GHM)

to be used for opening streets, paving, water-works, sewers, electric lights, schools, and the cemetery. The election of 1887, according to an early biographical sketch of David Schenck, "was to really determine whether the town should continue to stand still or go forward." Schenck, a city commissioner, became chairman of the committees on schools, on extending North Elm Street, and on improving and expanding the cemetery.

In May 1888 Colonel John Alston Barringer, an attorney and a progressive, became mayor and he continued implementation of the King program. Another attorney, James Wiley Forbis, followed Barringer as mayor and served from 1889 until 1891 and by then the mayor's salary was $800 a year. The city engineer received $60 a month.

The state legislature revised Greensboro's charter in 1887, dividing the city into four wards; three commissioners, elected at large, represented each ward and served with the mayor as a council. A revision in 1889 substituted the term alderman for commissioner.

The expansion of city government was closely tied to economic development, and both were influenced by the creation of the Chamber of Commerce. Established in 1877, it was North Carolina's first such group located inland. Julius A. Gray, dissatisfied with the existing Board of Tobacco Trade (1872), called a meeting at his home, Blandwood, to discuss the need for business development and a balanced community that offered civic and cultural opportunities. Robert M. Douglas helped to organize the council and served as an original officer. In 1888 the Chamber of Commerce was incorporated.

The founding of new banks also influenced economic growth, and three opened in Greensboro: the Piedmont Bank of Greensboro (1885); the People's Five Cent Savings Bank (1886); and the Savings & Deposit Bank of North Carolina (1887). A fourth financial institution, the National Bank of Greensboro,

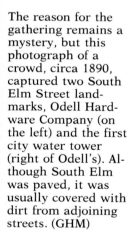

The reason for the gathering remains a mystery, but this photograph of a crowd, circa 1890, captured two South Elm Street landmarks, Odell Hardware Company (on the left) and the first city water tower (right of Odell's). Although South Elm was paved, it was usually covered with dirt from adjoining streets. (GHM)

traced its origin back to the Bank of Cape Fear (1851). The most unusual bank for the period was the People's Five Cent Savings Bank, which quickly dropped the "Five Cent" from its name. Organized by the president of Bennett College, a white Methodist minister named W.F. Steele, the bank had as a trustee Harmon A. Unthank, the black leader from Warnersville. It is believed that Unthank was the first black bank director in the state, and that the bank itself was North Carolina's first mutual savings institution.

Traditional types of manufacturing continued into the 1880s; small foundries, textile mills, woodworking establishments, and tobacco plants produced goods for local use and shipping. A developing business was the export of processed materials: thousands of pounds of sumac used in tanning hides; sassafras oil and bark used in medicines and beverages; and carloads of dried fruit, notably blackberries. The largest blackberry shippers were Odell & Company and J.W. Scott. Pomona Nursery, founded decades earlier by Joshua Lindley and now owned by his son, J. Van Lindley, sent cut flowers, trees, and plants to points within a 500-mile radius. Other well-known nurserymen were James R. Ragsdale, James M. Ward, S.W. Westbrook, C.P. Mendenhall, and John A. Young.

Greensboro's significance as a tobacco town was increased in 1881, when John King and C.D. Benbow opened a twist-and-plug factory. Next came the construction of several large warehouses: W.C. Bevill's Farmers' Warehouse in 1882; James W. Albright and David Scott's Star Warehouse in the old *Patriot* newspaper office in 1883; the Houston Brothers' Davie Street building; and, in 1885, the Banner Warehouse on West Market Street.

New plants were established to produce a variety of products. The Eagle Foundry on Lewis Street made manhole covers and iron guttering. M.G. Newell manufactured buggies and later dairy equipment. The Greensboro Knitting Company, promoted by J.W. Scott, manufactured knitted underwear. Greensboro Sash & Blind Company (1881), Guilford Lumber Company (1884), and Thomas Woodroffe Company (1886), turned out special wood items.

On August 12, 1886, a group of men met in

Farmers from Virginia, Tennessee, and the Carolinas sent their prepared tobacco to the Greensboro market. This interior view of Banner Warehouse at 210 West Market Street shows wagons at the left and men moving the tobacco flats. Note the skylights in the roof. The Banner became a popular spot for political conventions and local entertainment. (GHM)

A multipurpose building and a dormitory were constructed on a site east of the business district, and A&M opened in the fall of 1893 with 37 students. Dr. John O. Crosby, elected the first president of A&M in 1892, served until 1896; Charles H. Moore became vice-president and later head of the English department. In his later years Moore worked to set up black preparatory schools across the state.

When President Crosby resigned in 1896, the board of trustees elected James B. Dudley, who served until 1925. Dudley expanded the curriculum and the physical campus (125 acres), secured funding for additional buildings, and established a summer session for teachers. Under his leadership A&M became an outstanding institution for the education of blacks, and its presence on East Market Street provided a focal point for the black citizens of Greensboro.

Greensboro's public school system also grew during the 1890s. Extension of the city limits in 1891 meant additional children to educate, and two new schools were constructed: Warnersville for blacks in 1892, and Asheboro Street for whites the following year. When enrollment went over 1,500 in 1896, temporary classrooms were established at the city market and the Eagle Hose Firehouse.

George A. Grimsley was elected superintendent of Greensboro schools in 1890, at a salary of $1,200 a year; teachers were paid $30 a month. While working to build up Greensboro's school libraries, Grimsley also worked for the creation of public-supported community libraries throughout the state. Enlisting the support of the Century Club, together with P.P. Claxton and Annie Petty, he drew up a bill providing that towns of more than 1,000 residents could establish a public library, maintain it with tax money, and operate it as part of the school system. The bill was introduced in the North Carolina legislature by Senator A.M. Scales, and under its provisions Greensboro would obtain its first permanent library in 1902.

Patriotic and military organizations were popular with the men, and a total of 15 such societies, 4 for blacks and 11 for whites, were listed in the city directory published in 1892. At the YMCA on East Market Street, white men could use "a cosy library room . . . parlors furnished with games of Crokinole, Checkers and Chess. Also a fine Piano. The Gymnasium . . . very well equipped with nearly all kinds of apparatus for physical development. The Bath Rooms . . . Two Shower and Two Tub Baths, with plenty of hot and cold water." A membership at the Y cost three dollars a year, and meetings were held every Sunday afternoon. The YMCA for blacks met at St. James Presbyterian Church. Special-interest clubs for men included local branches of the United American Mechanics (1893), the Knights of Pythias (1895), and Woodmen of the World (1898).

The Merchants and Manufacturers Club (men only) was chartered in 1897.

A number of women's groups were organized during the 1890s. A county chapter of the United Daughters of the Confederacy began in 1899. In 1894 the Coney Club adopted a constitution and a new name, Euterpe, meaning "one who delights." The Reviewers Club, a literary organization for women, was chartered in January 1895. Its 12 charter members, all residents of the fashionable Asheboro Street neighborhood, met in each other's homes at night so that husbands, who were considered associate members, could attend. A second literary organization, the Century Club, had male and female members, including Annie Petty, one of the first trained librarians in the state; George Grimsley, school superintendent; and state

Some traveling groups performed outside rather than in a hall. On March 28, 1895, the United States Marine Band, composed of 54 musicians, played in Greensboro. The identity of the woman is not known. Military bands often visited Guilford Battleground. (GHM)

The master of the short story, O. Henry, was born William Sidney Porter in southern Guilford County in 1862. Perhaps his best-known story is *The Gift of the Magi*. From Cirker, *Dictionary of American Portraits*, Dover, 1967

Below: The Brockmann School of Music orchestra posed during the 1890s. Seated from left to right are Upton Staples, Walter Sergeant, Dottie Garland, Appleton Staples, Ernest Vernon and Claude Elam; and standing from left to right are Gaither Scott, Ed Wills, Laura and Charles Brockmann, Elsie Weatherly and Tom McAdoo. (GHM)

senator A.M. Scales.

In 1895 the Greensboro Athletic Association was organized to support local baseball activity. The club used an enclosed baseball park on Ceasar Cone's property, and stockholders had season tickets in the grandstand. Bicycle races, extremely popular during the Gay Nineties, were held at a track built east of the business district near the A&M campus and at Guilford Battleground. The Greensboro Bicycle Club was organized in 1896.

Benbow Hall, 218 South Elm, served as a theater, opera house, and dance hall, playing host to traveling troupes. In 1893 Calvin McAdoo purchased the old Methodist church on West Market and converted it into a 900-seat theater called the Academy of Music. In addition to visiting performers, the Greensboro Dramatic Club used it for programs, and on October 3, 1896, the Greensboro Minstrel

The C.M. Vanstory family was photographed around 1898. A fifth child, C.M. Vanstory, Jr. was born in 1901, and he served as mayor in 1945-1947. A third son Bill was born in 1905. (GHM)

Show was held there. Dances were held at the Odd Fellows Hall, Bogart's Hall, and Neese's Hall, which also offered roller skating and wrestling. Black citizens used Day's Hall on South Elm Street.

Fourth of July celebrations were held at Guilford Battleground during the 1890s and the annual fair was held at the new West Lee Street Fairgrounds after 1899.

An exciting event for the entire city was the outbreak of America's war with Spain in April, 1898. Captain Percy Gray recruited a new company of Guilford Grays, and 120 volunteers left for Raleigh in May. The unit became Co. D, 2nd North Carolina Volunteers. A black company of 40 men, led by Captain David Gilmer, was named the Maine Memorial Light Infantry. Although 234 men left the city prepared to fight, not a single one ever reached the battlefield.

Greensboro was a "wet" city throughout the Gay Nineties, but in July 1899 a coalition of people opposed to liquor sales in private estab-

This young lady, daughter of W.F. Alderman, was a student at Greensboro Female College. The photograph was taken in 1882 by her brother, Sidney L. Alderman, who had recently opened a studio on South Elm Street. Miss Alderman married Charles Ireland, a prominent businessman and churchman. (GHM)

lishments forced another vote on the prohibition issue. The result was Greensboro's adoption of a federally operated dispensary system, and the closing of all private saloons.

On June 9, 1899, the new Southern Railroad Station on South Elm Street was officially opened, and Greensboro at last boasted a point of entry befitting the Gate City. In the decade since that term was first coined, the city had experienced a fourfold increase in population; a tenfold increase in business; development of the best railroad system in the South, excluding Atlanta and Richmond; establishment of the Cone enterprises, which were national in scope; and the founding of a college for women that now had a waiting list.

Greensboro, claimed the editor of the *Patriot*, "is today such an intermixture of educational, commercial and industrial enterprise as no town of like size in this broad nation can excel, and few equal."

On July 18, 1899, Greensboro voters ratified a $300,000 bond issue, of which $100,000 was to be used to purchase and improve the waterworks system; $75,000 to improve streets; $65,000 to extend the sewerage system; $35,000 to build a firehouse, city hall, and market; and $25,000 to purchase and expand the electric power and light plant and the gas plant. With big plans, and the money to realize them, Greensboro was prepared to enter the 20th century.

John S. Barnes built this handsome house at 704 Asheboro Street in 1899, next to the grocery store he operated. The Barnes family was photographed around 1905. Courtesy, Mrs. Louise Reynolds

An unusual float to entertain the crowd and encourage business rolls north on Elm during the Fireman's Parade of 1899. Many organizations and businesses prepared floats for the parade. (GHM)

Volunteer fire companies were social organizations as well as service groups. Their conventions included team competitions and "the team that made the best time in throwing water" was highly praised. Horses and wagons were carried to conventions and parades like these in box and flat railroad cars. (GHM)

The Greensboro Public Schools proudly announced that the city had "the first public school in North Carolina supported by a special tax" on their Fireman's Parade float. (GHM)

Proud of its new name, the State Normal and Industrial College entered a float in the Fireman's Parade of 1899. The tracks visible on South Elm Street were for horse-drawn trolley cars. (GHM)

Nine Greensboro women of the 19th century were brought back to life by their descendants during the 1924 centennial celebration of First Presbyterian Church. From left to right, Mrs. Max Payne portrayed Frances Paisley; Mrs. Thomas Crabtree, Parthenia Dick; Mrs. C.A. Mebane, Julia Paisley; Miss Lizzie Lindsay, Letita Lindsay Humphreys; Mrs. Kate Faulconer, Lydia Hogg; Miss Anne Wright' her great-grandmother; Miss Anne Mebane, Anne Mebane; Miss Mattie Caldwell, Elizabeth Caldwell; and Miss Frances Cartland, Anne Houston. (GHM)

Chapter Six

A PROPER CELEBRATION: 1901 - 1920

*I*n October 1908 Greensboro celebrated its 100th birthday, and the party lasted for six days; many of the events were held at the Hippodrome, Greensboro's newest entertainment facility. The business area was draped in bunting, accented by pillars and arches, and illuminated with thousands of electric lights. The U.S. War Department even provided a search beacon. Centennial Week, a tremendous success, was a proper celebration for a city proud of its past, pleased with its present, and optimistic about its future.

City Government

In 1901 the term of office for Greensboro's mayor and 12 aldermen was extended to two years. In 1903 the number of aldermen was reduced to six, one for each ward, but all were still elected at large. Only the mayor and the city treasurer (one of the aldermen) were paid salaries, and all positions were considered part-time.

In 1910 the Chamber of Commerce endorsed a new form of city organization based on commissions and full-time leaders. The proposed plan called for the election of three commissioners—one (the mayor) responsible for public accounts and finance, another for public works, and the third for public safety. The commissioners would serve two-year terms and be paid $2,400 a

In 1908 Greensboro's
auditorium, the Hip-
podrome, was a cor-
rugated iron building
at Sycamore and For-
bis streets containing
a cinder racetrack
and seating for
20,000. The Greens-
boro Auditorium
Company purchased
the structure from the
Jamestown Exposi-
tion of 1907. It was
sold to the State Fair
Association of South
Carolina in 1911 for
$6,000. (GHM)

Education Day of
Centennial Week fea-
tured a parade of
10,000 pupils, teach-
ers, and administra-
tors, led by a Marine
band. This group is
shown marching in
the 200 block of
South Elm Street.
Other activities in-
cluded a re-enact-
ment of the Battle of
Guilford Courthouse
on Military Day, a
city history parade on
Fraternal Organiza-
tion Day, and a
parade honoring vet-
erans, especially
Confederates, on Vet-
erans Day. The Good
Roads Conference, the
North Carolina Peace
Congress, and the
Central Carolina Fair
all met during the
week. (GHM)

Charles M. Stedman,
a major in the
Confederate army,
was a prominent at-
torney. Shown here
on North Elm Street
(which at the time
was decorated for
Centennial Week),
Stedman was elected
to the U.S. House of
Representatives and
was the last Confeder-
ate veteran to serve
in Congress. Courtesy,
Greensboro Public Li-
brary

Top: Turn-of-the-century birthday parties involved children of all ages, mothers, and nurses. (GHM)

Above: A. Wayland Cooke and Charles Stedman are shown in their law office in the Mendenhall building. The site is now occupied by the N.C.N.B. building. (GHM)

appreciated improvement. Baths may now be indulged in as a luxury, while formerly such a performance was resorted to only as a physical necessity."

In 1902 the city sold its gas and electric plants to the Greensboro Electric Company, which inaugurated a system of electric cars in June. A decade later 12 miles of track reached from East Market Street to Lindley Park on the west and from South Greensboro to White Oak Mill on the north. In 1909 the North Carolina Public Service Company took over management of the electric railway, along with the provision of light, electric power, and gas. The company expanded to serve other communities, and by 1917 it had 9,000 customers.

A city board of health was established in 1905, and Dr. Edmund Harrison, the first full-time city physician, proposed restrictions on meat and milk sold within the city limits. In 1914 the Greensboro Women's Club pushed for more sanitary conditions in local grocery stores, and a new ordinance prohibited street displays of produce and crates of live poultry. In 1916 the regular inspection of restaurants began, and in 1919 scheduled trash removal replaced the former Easter "clean-up days." Among the major concerns of health officials were typhoid, malaria, and diphtheria, which killed many children every year. Even smallpox, preventable by vaccination, remained a threat, and Greensboro experienced epidemics in 1915 and 1916.

Spanish influenza, a new enemy, swept across North Carolina in 1918, striking 20 percent of the population and killing 3,000. Despite a city quarantine and the closing of all schools and churches, Greensboro reported 1,200 cases. During the 1920 epidemic 6,118 cases were reported in Guilford County. Old-fashioned remedies such as asafetida bags were used, and products like Vick's VapoRub had to be rationed.

In 1909 Dr. W.P. Beall reported that one of every seven deaths in the county was caused by tuberculosis (TB), and the Guilford County

year. On February 8, 1911, Greensboro citizens adopted the plan by a vote of 693 to 353.

City services improved after 1900. A street committee was established in 1907, and by 1919 there were 29 miles of paved roads. Having purchased the waterworks in 1901, the city doubled the system's capacity within six years. A 1904 description of Greensboro noted, "The recent installation of a filter plant, rendering the present supply clear and potable, is a much

GOOSE GREASE LINIMENT and Mother's Joy

Manufactured by the
GOOSE GREASE CO.
GREENSBORO, N. C.

Left: The seventh Guilford County Courthouse, shown circa 1945, was ready for occupancy in 1918. Construction of the building, which was designed by Harry Barton, required removal of many early Greensboro homes, including those of Thomas and David Caldwell, Jr. (GHM)

Above: This advertisement for Goose Grease Liniment often was brought to life for parades and holiday celebrations. Two live geese marched with a drummer who chanted the benefits of the "cure-all." (GHM)

Right: By 1917 Dick's Laundry, established in 1890, had a fleet of delivery vehicles: six wagons and three automobiles. The firm was located at 111 West Market Street. (GHM)

Anti-Tuberculosis Society was formed. In 1920 the Greensboro District Nurse and Relief Committee opened a small six-room sanatorium at Glenwood, with district nurse Clara Peck as matron. In 1920, when the cottage opened, there were 125 deaths from TB in Guilford County.

In 1911 members of the Civic League urged the newly elected commissioners to provide a "beautifully planned city for the future." A professional planner, Charles M. Robinson, was hired, but his design for Greensboro was incomplete when he died in 1917. Two years later the general assembly gave cities the power to establish planning commissions, and Greensboro established the first one in the state in 1920.

In 1900 W.C. Bain was awarded the contract for a city hall and market to be located at Elm and Gaston. A decision to include an auditorium led to the addition of a dome with windows, an architectural feature that made the building a landmark. Called the Grand Opera

House, the theater had a seating capacity of 950.

A public library opened in three rooms on the third floor of the new city hall on February 4, 1902, with Bettie Caldwell as librarian. Public response was enthusiastic, and in 1903 the city accepted $30,000 from Andrew Carnegie to construct a separate library building. The community donated funds for a lot, and the aldermen pledged $3,000 a year for an operating budget. The Carnegie Library, which opened on April 16, 1906, was described as "one of the handsomest and best appointed library buildings in the country." By 1920 it was the third largest library in the state.

In 1911 a grand jury evaluated the county courthouse, and the verdict was negative: maintenance was difficult, ventilation was poor, and the open windows let in so much traffic noise that juries could barely hear witnesses and lawyers. In 1913 the general assembly granted Guilford County the right to sell its courthouse and build a larger one. After con-

Above: In 1897 Blandwood became the Keeley Institute, a hospital for the "cure of the Liquor and Opium Habits, Nervous Diseases and Tobacco Habit." Courtesy, Gravure Illustration Company

Above right: The Greensboro *Daily Record* began in 1890 in the Benbow building basement. This Greene Street building was its third location in 1903.

siderable controversy, the building was finally sold to Jefferson Standard Life Insurance Company for $171,000 and a new site was chosen. Architect Harry Barton designed a Renaissance Revival structure to be built of Mt. Airy granite with terra cotta trim. The estimated cost when work began in 1917 was $350,000, but by 1920, when the courthouse was dedicated, its worth was believed to be $750,000.

Economic Developments

Progressive Greensboro, a promotional pamphlet published by the Young Men's Business Association in 1903, estimated a total of 50 manufacturing firms in the city producing 30 kinds of goods. Most important was the textile industry, including three cotton mills, one carpet mill, a finishing mill, and a factory that produced pants and overalls, followed by the city's three furniture factories and seven lumber companies. Other firms made and sold a wide range of products, including candy, chewing gum, drugs and medical supplies, flour, canned goods, shirts, hats, boots and shoes, wagons and carriages, mattresses, sewer pipe, tile, tinware, and sheet metal. Also enumerated were five hotels, with a combined capacity of nearly 1,000 guests, five colleges, and five local publications—two daily newspapers, two religious weeklies, and one magazine.

The Cone brothers created two more textile giants in the early years of the 20th century. White Oak Mill, completed in 1904, employed 2,500 workers operating 2,500 looms and 35,000 spindles. Proximity Print Works, established in 1912, used special machinery to produce printed cloth and was the first of its kind in the South. All of the Cone mills were managed by the Proximity Manufacturing Company, a name used until 1948.

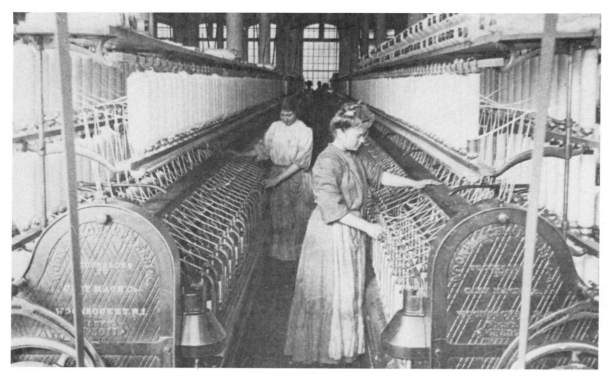

This 1907 photograph of White Oak Mills is from a stereograph entitled "Speeders." White Oak Mills was completed in 1904 and employed 2,500 workers on 2,500 looms with 35,000 spindles. (GHM)

The American Realty and Auction Company (109 East Market Street) was organized in 1902 by the five Thomas Brothers. It merged in 1906 with the American Land Company, Inc., which featured the Penny Brothers— "the world's original twin auctioneers." They used special methods and "whirlwind" speed to sell lots "anywhere on earth." Other local auction firms included the Southern Realty & Auction Company, founded in 1907, and the Acme Auction and Commission Company, which handled articles other than real estate. From *Greensboro, The Daily Record,* 1910

Blue Bell grew out of a small overall factory originally located over a South Elm Street grocery store. Charles C. Hudson reorganized the firm and moved it to Arlington Street. By 1910 the company was back on Elm at Lee, and by 1919 it was producing bib overalls with the "Blue Bell" labels.

In 1904 J.E. Latham moved from New Bern to Greensboro and established a cotton brokerage firm with branches in four states. Similar firms were operated by Leon J. Brandt (1900), Thomas Crabtree (1904), P.C. Rucker (1905), and Robertson & Cone (1912). Latham's future son-in-law, John A. Kellenburger, moved to Greensboro as general manager of the Sterling Furniture Company.

In 1901 the E.A. Brown Co. was established to manufacture "Plug, Twist, Navy, and Smoking Tobaccos." Two years later the American Cigar Company opened a factory employing hundreds of workers. The El-Rees-So Cigar Company began in 1913 with three cigar makers; in 1917 it opened a three-story factory employing 300 "pretty white girls." Seidenberger & Company, Inc., opened its five-story factory in 1917, employing 300 workers to produce fine cigars including the Prince George brand.

In 1905 Lunsford Richardson organized the Vick's Family Remedies Company. He also established the city's first Pepsi-Cola bottling plant, and for a while the drug firm was located in rooms behind the Pepsi plant. In 1907 H. Smith Richardson convinced his

Dan Hudson, shown standing, joined the sales force of Vick's Family Remedies in 1909; he was one of the company's first full-time salesmen. Hudson, pictured with his helpers and some samples, was photographed behind the Milton Street plant, which was built in 1910. Courtesy, Richardson-Vicks, Inc.

father to concentrate on one successful product, Vick's Salve (renamed VapoRub in 1912). By 1910 the firm had built its first factory on Milton Street, and in 1911 it became Vick Chemical Company. Sales were increased through the distribution of free samples, and five million jars were sent out to potential customers in 1917. When flu swept across the nation the next year, many people remembered the relief given by VapoRub, and by 1919 Vick's sales had increased from 11 million jars to 17 million. In 1919 the company was incorporated, and its worth was stated at $1.5 million.

By 1917 there were 75 factories in Greensboro. Carolina Steel produced fabri-

cated goods used to construct buildings and bridges across America.

Greensboro was an important retail center for the Piedmont, and merchants eagerly occupied sites along Elm Street. Leading dry-goods stores were Gilmer's (1902), Ellis, Stone & Company (1903), and Sapp's (1904). In 1905 the Meyer Brothers of Richmond opened a department store with "lunch counters and ladies parlors upstairs." C. Scott and Company, at 314 South Elm, was the largest mail-order seed house in the state. It manufactured fresh peanut butter daily, and visitors were invited to watch the process. S.H. Kress & Co. opened in 1904, as did Wills Book Store. South Side Hardware, at 525 South Elm,

Shaw Brothers & Company at 328 South Elm Street specialized in "staple and fancy" groceries. The firm was a local agent for Chase & Sanborn coffees, Heinz pickles, California canned fruits, and flours. Catering to a "first class family trade," it also ran a mail-order business by 1903. (GHM)

Zimrie E. and Marion W. Noah operated a grocery store at 122 North Elm Street. This 1915 interior view shows items neatly arranged on shelves and in boxes or barrels. Clerks gathered merchandise for the shoppers. (GHM)

helped pioneer the growing business district south of the tracks. In 1908 the Greensboro Merchants Association was organized, and it soon had 97 members.

Twentieth-century buildings were indications of Greensboro's development as a city. More than granite, steel, and bricks, they were points of community pride. New hotels included the Guilford (1900), the Huffine (1901), the Benbow (1902), the Benbow Arcade (1904), and the O. Henry (1919). The

O. Henry, the most famous landmark of this period, was named for Greensboro's most famous literary figure, who died in 1910. New office buildings were named for leading citizens (the McAdoo in 1908 and the Banner in 1912) or for large business firms. A five-story skyscraper built in 1904 became the Dixie Building, and a nine-story structure built for the American Exchange National Bank in 1918 became the Southeastern Building around 1930.

In 1904 the Southern Railway moved its

The Greensboro Drug Company was located on the street floor of Humphrey's Folly, the southwest corner of Courthouse Square. Its soda fountain was a popular gathering spot, and the tables with swing-out seats generally were filled. Pictured from left to right are clerks Pete McDaniels, Clifford Woodard, Hugh Johnson, and Burke Frailey. (GHM)

Clerk and assistant manager Cliff Woodard is shown behind the cigar counter of Greensboro Drug Store. Popular magazines of 1917 are displayed, along with cigars aplenty, including one named for O. Henry. (GHM)

division freight office to the Gate City from Raleigh, and in 1914 the United States government opened a parcel post depot in the annex of the Hotel Huffine on Buchanan. Increased rail activity made it necessary to lay a parallel track through the Piedmont so that traffic could move constantly in both directions. The Pomona train yard was enlarged to include a 13-stall roundhouse and a storage shed that could hold 21 locomotives. By 1920 there were 1,100 Southern employees in the Greensboro area, and 85 trains passed through the city daily.

The superior railroad system assured good mail service, but local leaders supported a growing telephone system as a supplement to mail ordering. In 1900 there were only 300 telephones in Greensboro, a city of more than 10,000 people. By 1910 the number of subscribers had increased to 1,750. Southern Bell Telephone & Telegraph, which bought the McAdoo family exchange in 1903, built an of-

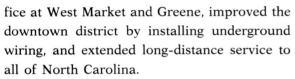

fice at West Market and Greene, improved the downtown district by installing underground wiring, and extended long-distance service to all of North Carolina.

Greensboro entered the 20th century with three banks, and in 1907 three more were organized: the American Exchange Bank, Greensboro Commercial & Savings Bank, and Home Savings Bank. In 1911 the American Exchange Bank absorbed Greensboro Commercial Bank and became the American Exchange National Bank. The Textile Bank opened that same year in White Oak Village and operated until 1920, when it was absorbed by a new bank, the Atlantic Bank & Trust Company.

Three building and loan firms were organized between 1902 and 1914. James Dudley, a leader in the black community, promoted Pioneer Building & Loan (1902-1932), a first for black businessmen. Gate City Building & Loan opened in 1903, and Home Building & Loan in 1914. The Southern Loan & Trust Company created the Southern Real Estate Company in 1905; one of its first projects was Irving Park.

The Southern Loan & Trust Company also managed four fire-insurance companies, known as the "original four": Southern Stock-Mutual (1895), Underwriters of Greensboro

(1898), Home Insurance (1902), and Southern Underwriters (1903).

In 1905 the North State Fire Insurance Company was organized and in 1906 Dixie Fire Insurance began. Within 10 years Dixie was the largest fire insurance company in North Carolina, and among the largest in the South. Licensed in six states, the firm employed 30 clerks and occupied the entire fourth floor of the Dixie Building, which was named for the company.

Above: The Guilford Hotel was similar to the Benbow House that it replaced. One of the finest hotels in the country, it could accommodate 200 guests, and its conveniences included telephones, private baths, and electric lights. In 1903 room rates ranged from one to four dollars. (GHM)

Right: The northeast corner of Courthouse Square was the site for the Lindsay Building (pictured) as it was being razed to construct the Fisher Building in 1900. The Fisher Building was later replaced by the Southeastern Building. (GHM)

Left: The O. Henry Hotel, completed in 1919, was designed by a New York firm, and Charles Hartmann returned to Greensboro to serve as supervising architect. The O. Henry was razed in 1979. (GHM)

Far left: A Greensboro landmark, the Banner building was headquarters for Home Industrial Bank, which opened in 1930. Completed in 1912, the building was named for Dr. C.W. Banner, an eye, ear, nose, and throat specialist who came to Greensboro around 1900. Its six floors housed 82 offices and was considered Greensboro's finest office building. (GHM)

Right: Southside Hose Company #4 was organized in 1891 by community leader D.W.C. Benbow. The company posed circa 1910 with a prize belt and their two mascots—a child and a rooster. (GHM)

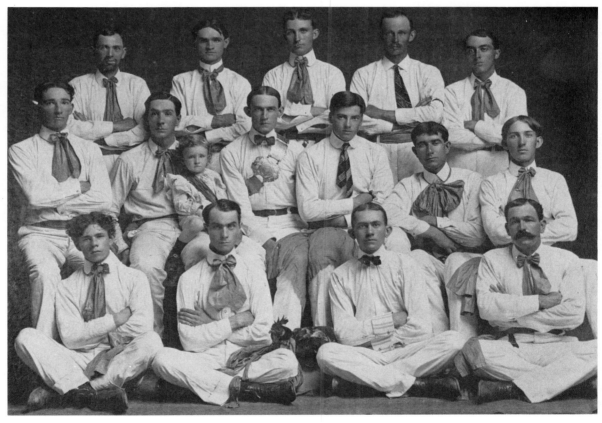

The first local life insurance company in the South, Security Life & Annuity Company, was established in 1901, with J. Van Lindley as president. In 1903 Southern Loan & Trust began an insurance department, and in 1905 the company's name was changed to Southern Life & Trust. In 1924 the insurance department was reorganized as Pilot Life. The Greensboro Life Insurance Company opened in 1905, and the Gate City Life Insurance

West Market Street M. E. Church
Greensboro, N. C.

Company in 1908.

In 1912 Security Life and Annuity and Greensboro Life Insurance merged with a Raleigh firm, Jefferson Standard Life Insurance (1907); the new company relocated in Greensboro. By 1917 the firm employed 75 clerks, and under the leadership of Julian Price, president from 1919 until 1946, it experienced vigorous growth.

Schools, Churches, and Social Institutions

The city directory of 1904 listed a total of 29 churches in the city, and at least 15 more churches and one synagogue were established before 1920. The First Christian Church of Greensboro (Congregational United Church of Christ), First Reformed Church (Peace United Church of Christ), and First Lutheran Church were all founded in the early years of the 20th century. Some members of St. Barnabas and St. Andrews' Episcopal congregations merged to form Holy Trinity, while black Episcopalians founded the Church of the Redeemer. Presbyterians, Methodists, Baptists, and Friends all added new congregations or built new houses of worship.

In 1908 the Reformed Hebrew Congregation

Above left: Washington Street Baptist Church changed its name to First Baptist Church in 1902 and built the sanctuary, shown with a hearse parked in front, in 1906. (GHM)

Above right: The oldest congregation of Methodists within the Greensboro city limits built a third and final church in 1893, West Market Street United Methodist Church. (GHM)

Top: Greensboro's police and fire departments posed at city hall, which stood on the northwest corner of Elm and Friendly. The angel statue mounted on the watering trough fountain was originally at the 1872 Courthouse and is now lost. The motorized fire engine, the first in Greensboro, was part of an expansion of fire services brought on by a rash of conflagrations in 1904. (GHM)

Right: Nina Troy, granddaughter of Frances Webb Bumpass, left Greensboro in 1912 to serve as a missionary in China. Her farewell party at the Troy-Bumpass house (now listed on the National Register) was given by the Woman's Society of Christian Service of West Market Street Church, her sponsor for the mission field. Miss Troy taught in Soochow until she was placed in a concentration camp in 1943. Following World War II she returned to Greensboro and lived with her sisters in the family home on South Mendenhall Street. (GHM)

was chartered; its founders included David Stern, Max Block, Emanuel and Herman Sternberger, and Simon Schiffman. It was a unique Jewish congregation in that both Orthodox and Reform views were represented. The former Friends Meetinghouse on Lee Street was purchased as the community's first synagogue, and Rabbi Mendelsohn was chosen as leader. Orthodox and Reform Jews continued to share a building until 1949.

Greensboro's public school system at the turn of the century was inadequate for the growing number of school-age children, and the existing school buildings (Lindsay and Asheboro Streets for whites and Percy Street and Warnersville for blacks) were operating on two shifts of three hours. School bond issues passed in 1910 and 1915, though still insufficient, allowed construction of three new schools for whites (Cypress, Simpson, and Lee Street) and two for blacks (Ashe and Washington Street). A white high school was built on Spring Street in 1910, and classes were enrolled there in 1911. Black students could continue their education at the preparatory departments of Bennett and A & M or at two new preparatory schools, Palmer and Immanuel Lutheran.

In 1917 Frederick Archer became school superintendent and a school board was appointed. For the first time women were allowed to serve and Mrs. J.P. Turner and Mrs. Julius W. Cone were appointed.

Palmer Memorial Institute, located east of Greensboro, was founded by Charlotte Hawkins in 1902; it closed in 1971 when integration and adequate high schools made a separate black preparatory school less attractive. Immanuel Lutheran College moved to Greensboro from Concord, North Carolina, in 1905. Located on East Market at Luther Street, the school drew boarding students from North Carolina and other states.

Greensboro Female College faced a major crisis in 1903 when the stockholding company decided to close the school and sell its property. President Lucy Owen Robertson, the first female college president in North Carolina's history, worked with loyal alumnae to raise $25,000, and in 1904 the school was again adopted by the Methodist Episcopal Church, South. In 1912 its name was changed to Greensboro College for Women, and in 1920 it became Greensboro College. Silas A. Peeler, a student at Bennett from 1883 to 1889, became president of that Methodist-related college in 1905, serving until 1914.

Charles D. McIver, who had played such a major role in establishing and developing the State Normal & Industrial College, died suddenly in 1906. He was succeeded as president

of the college by Julius I. Foust, who served until 1934. In 1919 the school became the North Carolina College for Women and began offering graduate-level courses. Dean Walter C. Jackson did much to encourage the development of courses other than those required for teacher training.

The Agricultural & Mechanical College changed significantly after 1900. Females were not admitted after 1901, and in 1915 the school became the Negro Agricultural & Technical College of North Carolina, the largest of

Top left: This second-grade class at Lindsay Street School was taught by Miss Rosa Abbott. (GHM)

Top right: The school in East White Oak Village was built by the Proximity Manufacturing Company. From *World Leadership in Denims*, Proximity Manufacturing Company, 1925

The crowd that had gathered on South Elm Street to welcome presidential candidate William Jennings Bryan in September 1906 was shocked to learn that Charles Duncan McIver, had died on the train ride between Raleigh and Greensboro. (GHM)

Left: Prominent Greensboro residents served on the Guilford County Board of Education in 1915. Thomas R. Foust (second from the left) became county school superintendent in 1902, when the school term lasted about 85 days. (GHM)

its kind in the nation. During 1917-1918 many soldiers were trained at A & T, while a unique summer-school program made further education possible for male and female teachers.

The commercial development of Elm Street, North and South, meant that downtown was no longer a place to build homes, and a number of new residential areas were developed. Caesar Cone built his house within walking distance of Proximity Mill. Summit Avenue was extended by the city to serve as an access road, and other families, including the Sternbergers, built their homes nearby.

Special workers' neighborhoods or "mill villages" grew up around the major manufacturing plants. Most notable was White Oak Village for employees of the Proximity mills, which featured single-family houses with free electricity and water, nine-month schools, churches, and YMCAs, all subsidized by the company. Company-operated stores sold beef and pork raised on Proximity's Reedy Fork Ranch and dairy products from herds raised on a 75-acre farm near White Oak Mill, while

Proximity lakes and processing plant provided a safe water supply. East White Oak, the community for blacks employed at the three plants, had streets with the same names, churches, a school, and a Y. Although paternalistic by today's standards, the Proximity villages were considered utopias in their day and were recommended as models for other communities.

One of the first neighborhoods to be promoted through the newspaper was Glenwood, which opened in 1909 with houses ranging in price from $1,000 to $30,000. The new subdivision was described as "one of the greatest developments ever attempted in North Carolina."

Real-estate developer Basil J. Fisher donated parkland along North Elm Street to the city in 1901 and laid out residential streets as borders. Elegant houses soon stood on Fisher Park Circle and on North and South Park Drive. The Fisher house, Eagle's Roost, was built on South Park in 1902, and the James E. Latham House on Fisher Park Circle in 1915. Guilford Realty Company built 15 houses in the area in 1915, and A.K. Moore, who managed the sales, noted one drawback: the houses in Fisher Park were too far from town! The blocks of North Elm that ran through the park were soon lined with mansions and acquired a special nickname, the Gold Coast.

Irving Park was a project of the Southern Real Estate Company. President A.W. McAlister, who introduced golf to Greensboro, had the idea of building a neighborhood around a golf course and clubhouse. The Greensboro Country Club opened in 1912, and during the next decade many prominent families moved into Irving Park. Other planned neighborhoods were Westerwood, developed by Guilford Insurance and Realty, which featured Greensboro's first demonstration home, and Cumberland, a development that grew up around the Agricultural and Mechanical College.

The issues of the day—prohibition, child labor, women's suffrage—might divide Greensboro residents, as they did other Americans, but patriotism always brought them together. In 1903 a North Carolina Reunion was held in the city and famous people from 30 states gathered to celebrate. The Fourth of July celebration at Guilford Battleground was an annual social event with prominent speakers and bands featured. The 1904 celebration was highlighted by the unveiling of a monument to David Schenck, founder of the Guilford Battleground Company, who had died in 1902. In 1915 an elaborate ceremony, including military companies from the 13 original states, marked the dedication of a monument to Nathanael Greene. On July 4, 1919, the Battleground festivities were held in honor of the soldiers returning from Europe.

While live performances and minstrel shows remained popular, the newest form of entertainment was the moving picture. In 1907 Walter Griffith opened a theater where patrons paid 10 cents to watch three reels lasting 45

minutes. Other early movie houses were the Crystal, the Lyric, the Ottoway, the Airdome, and the 250-seat Amuzu. In 1915 Elm Street had three theaters: the Piedmont, which became the Victory, then the Imperial, and finally the Center; the Bijou; and the Elm. By 1917 the Grand Opera House had become the Grand Theater, and in November of that year Greensboro's largest movie house, the Isis, opened with a seating capacity of 1,000.

For outdoor recreation, baseball was still the most popular sport, and local industries as well as schools had teams that competed against each other. Each year the University of

Robert Dick Crabtree, son of Thomas and Lizzie Dick Crabtree, is shown in a sailor suit with a land machine, an early 20th-century tricycle. He was the great grandson of Judge R.P. Dick. (GHM)

Cotton broker Thomas Crabtree's house on Isabel Street was representative of many homes in Fisher Park. It was built of stone and shingles and had a gambrel roof. (GHM)

This kitchen interior from the Hagan house on South Park Drive reveals "modern" appliances and furnishings. Constructed for the Marley family in 1922, the house had electric lights and wall sockets. (GHM)

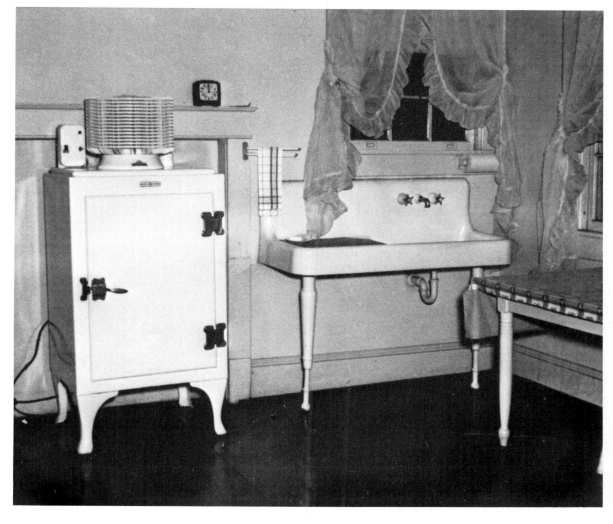

North Carolina and the University of Virginia played one game at Cone Park, and 6,000 people attended in 1903. A professional baseball team, organized in 1902, won the league pennant in 1908 and 1909, and after a wartime hiatus the Greensboro Patriots were organized in 1919.

Battleground, Fisher, and Cone parks were popular spots for courting, picnics, and games. On July 4, 1902, the Greensboro Electric Company opened Lindley Park at the southwestern end of its electric-car line. There, on 26 acres donated to the city by J. Van Lindley, were a casino for concerts, a pavilion for dances, refreshment booths, an artificial lake, "bowling alleys, shooting alleys, and every kind of rational and innocent amusement." Some Greensboro residents can still recall excursions to this wonderland, which began (and ended) with a one-and-a-half-hour ride in an open streetcar.

A number of organizations for men were established in the new century. Fraternal societies included the Benevolent and Protective Order of Elks (1900), the Knights of Columbus (1904), and the Moose (1918).

This early 20th century parade included Confederate veterans on horseback! South Elm Street buildings shown include J.W. Jones & Company Grocers, the McAdoo Hotel, and M.G. Newell's. A sign for C.C. Townsend Company is visible; Mr. Townsend's son James served as city manager from 1947 to 1961. Although South Elm was paved, dirt usually covered the stone surface. (GHM)

The first Elk's Club was on the southeast corner of Greene and Sycamore streets. The R.G. Lindsay house had occupied this site for decades and was moved south to face Greene Street. (GHM)

The Albright house and outbuildings were located on Battleground Road, which was not paved until 1923. The site near the Cornwallis Drive intersection was later purchased and used by the Elks organization for their second clubhouse. (GHM)

Nationally affiliated civic organizations were the Rotary Club (1917), Kiwanis (1919), Civitans (1921), and Lions (1922). An American Legion post was established in 1919. The Ministerial Association, formed in 1901, campaigned successfully for prohibition, which returned to the city in 1905.

Greensboro women organized a chapter of the Daughters of the American Revolution in 1902 and the American Red Cross in 1917. The Greensboro Woman's Club was formed in 1909, and in 1921 the club purchased the David Weir house on Edgeworth Street as its headquarters. The Business and Professional Women's Club (1919) replaced an earlier organization, the Business Girls' Club (1915), reflecting a growing awareness by women of their changing image and role in the community. The Greensboro section of the National Council of Jewish Women was organized in 1919 also.

Three organizations for young people were the Boy Scouts, whose first troop was formed in 1910; Girl Scouts (1916); and Children of the Confederacy (1919).

Associated Charities, organized in 1907 to coordinate private assistance to those in need, became the Interchurch Association in 1912, the Social Welfare League in 1914, and the Greensboro Welfare League in 1919. Also formed in 1907 was an ambulance society, which raised funds to purchase "a beautiful coach, rubber tired, painted in maroon with gold trim." A second campaign in 1915 replaced this horse-drawn vehicle with a more modern ambulance.

Special-interest groups included the Greensboro Gun Club, the Spinster Girls, the Audubon Society, and the Guilford County Literary and Historical Association. T. Gilbert

Miss Florence Hunt's music class posed for a recital photograph in June 1922, on the steps of the Smith Memorial Building. Miss Hunt came to Greensboro in 1908 and taught music for the next 60 years. Another outstanding musician, Hermene Eichhorn, began her Greensboro career in 1926. (GHM)

This postcard view of the Y.M.C.A. building on the northwest corner of Greene and Sycamore streets was taken around 1915. A decade later the building became Clinic (later Piedmont) Hospital. The modern 60-bed facility installed Greensboro's first blood bank in 1935. Today the site is part of the City-County Governmental Center. (GHM)

Pearson, a biology teacher at the State Normal & Industrial College, began the North Carolina Audubon Society in 1902 and helped form the National Audubon Society in 1905. The Literary and Historical Society, founded in 1906, was active during the centennial celebration of 1908, reflecting a renewed pride in Greensboro's historic past as the city embarked upon its second century.

On April 6, 1917, almost three years after World War I began in Europe, the United States Congress declared war on Germany. In June two National Guard units, the Guilford Grays and the Engineers, and an ambulance company organized by Dr. J. Wesley Long left the city for France. Approximately 1,400 Greensboro men volunteered or were drafted during the war, and 85 were casualties. Four-

teen area women, including Suzanne Hoskins and Dolley Conyers, served as nurses, and one, Annie Reveley, died in France. Two local men made unusual contributions to the war effort: Lieutenant Edwin C. Klingman became an ace for the Canadian Royal Air Force, and Dr. Henry Louis Smith devised a plan to drop information in Germany by using gas-filled balloons.

Civilians conserved resources, recycled materials, and sacrificed luxuries. Students at the Normal & Industrial College raised vegetables, canning 8,000 gallons of produce during 1917. A.W. McAlister headed a statewide fuel conservation agency, and other business leaders produced goods and services that supported the war effort.

On November 11, 1918, at 4 a.m., the telegraph editor of the *Daily News* received word of the armistice in Europe. Sirens

Harold Trigg, son of the president of Bennett College, fought in World War I. He is pictured on his return to Greensboro in 1918. Trigg earned his doctorate and later taught at Bennett. Courtesy, Mrs. Anita M. Rivers

Right: Red Cross representatives were kept busy by the large number of troop trains that stopped at the Greensboro station, circa 1917. The women shared refreshments with the soldiers and gave comfort kits to local boys who enlisted. (GHM)

Right: The people of Greensboro gathered at Courthouse Square to celebrate Armistice Day in 1918, and Fire Chief Ed Bain had all four fire trucks circle the city with sirens blasting. The buildings pictured on the right are the Federal Courthouse, Post Office, and Southern Life and Trust, the first building in Greensboro to have an elevator. (GHM)

clanged, whistles blew, and church bells rang
out to announce that the war was over!

Sketches of Greensboro, published in 1917,
summarized a vision of the city shared by
many:

> *Greensboro has always been a Southern
> town, both of the old and of the new
> South; the old South of high culture in art
> and literature, of the best ideals in morals,
> of a high bred social spirit and a courtly
> hospitality, which have created an
> atmosphere which renders habitation here
> a charm and pleasure; the new South of
> energetic, progressive, commercial and
> industrial ideas which have borne fruit in
> the city's progress and in the growth of her
> many large and varied business interests.
> The spirit of the old South has fostered its
> churches, its schools and its club life; the
> spirit of the new South has given existence
> to its commercial, industrial, and
> transportation facilities.*

The coming decades would bring significant
changes, but Greensboro's respect for tradition
and receptivity to new ideas would meet the
challenges that lay ahead.

Greensboro High
School was located
on Spring Street from
1911 until 1929, when
it moved to Westover
Terrace. This photo-
graph of the soph-
omore class at the
Spring Street school
was taken in 1921.

Opened in 1926, Greensboro's Central Fire Station at 318 North Greene Street included a training facility complete with tower. The structure, now on the National Register of Historic Places, was designed by Charles Hartmann and constructed by C.W. Angle. As the new structure was occupied, the former volunteer fire department was converted to a paid staff of fire fighters. The training center was later moved to Church Street to allow more space for men and equipment. (GHM)

Chapter Seven

GREATER GREENSBORO INDEED: 1921 - 1950

*D*uring the 1920s Greensboro grew from a large town into a small city, expanding in size and population and diversifying its commercial, industrial, and financial institutions. The effects of the Great Depression were less severe than in some parts of the country, and recovery began in 1934. The war years brought a halt to many of the city's normal activities, as thousands of Greensboro residents saw combat and thousands more were involved in wartime support activities. With the war's end, the city experienced an influx of residents, old and new, and commercial expansion and building activity resumed.

Development of City Government

By 1920 Greensboro had a population of 19,861, and in 1921 the commission form of government was replaced by a city council-manager plan. A council of seven members, elected at large, chose one of their number as mayor and appointed a city manager. In 1923 the general assembly approved a revised city charter, dramatically expanding the city's limits. As a result Greensboro's area more than quadrupled, from 4 to 17.84 square miles, and the city's population jumped to 43,525. "Greater Greensboro" was now the state's third largest city.

New public buildings included a city hall (1924), designed by Harry Barton,

The city council held its first meeting in the newly-constructed city hall in September 1925. E.B. Jeffress (shown on the left) served as mayor from 1925 to 1929 and was the target of a recall election in 1927. Opponents of city growth and development through the expenditure of public funds were defeated, and Jeffress served a second term. (GHM)

The Municipal Building or city hall, on the northeast corner of Greene and Friendly (Gaston), was constructed in 1924 and used until the 1970s. Designed by Harry Barton and built by C.W. Angle, the building housed city offices and a jail. (GHM)

This view of Greensboro was probably photographed from the Jefferson Standard building around 1930. West Market Street Methodist Church's education building and the Carnegie Public Library are on the left. Gaston Street, now Friendly, is near the center; it narrows at the Eugene Street intersection. Many residences were still downtown. (GHM)

In November 1923 the city ran out of filtered water, and a $1.5-million bond issue was passed in 1925 to improve the water system. Although sewer lines were extended during the twenties, many areas still had outhouses, which were violations of a 1917 ordinance. Elm Street was surfaced with asphalt in 1922, and Greene and other major streets were widened and extended, while Gaston remained a narrow residential street until the 1930s.

Gas, electric, and electric-car lines were installed to reach many neighborhoods. Southern Public Utilities, which owned the franchise after 1927, added 10 gasoline buses and some trackless trolleys to the electric-car system in 1934. The following year the company merged with Duke Power.

In 1923 the city council approved a reorganization of the city's health services, and in 1924 Dr. C.C. Hudson became health officer, serving until 1942. Problems addressed included restaurant sanitation, venereal diseases, tuberculosis, and infant mortality. The health department hired 11 nurses to provide services to the local schools. In 1925 the city built and operated a modern abattoir where animals were slaughtered and meat was inspected and packed.

The general assembly in 1923 granted cities the power to provide public recreation facilities, and the Greensboro Park and Playground Association was formed. A committee was appointed to plan a comprehensive recreation program, including a country park, a circle of parks around the city, swimming pools, and rest rooms. By 1926 the city was operating 16 playgrounds, 19 tennis courts, and a variety of activities including soccer football.

In 1933 the city council established the Greensboro Recreation Commission, and planning for two community parks began. The one in the east became Nocho Park; the one in the west was the "country park" proposed earlier. Mayor Paul Lindley (1931-1933) used unemployed men on the city's relief roll to build a recreation center at Country Park, located on 79 acres borrowed from Forest Lawn Cemetery. A federal program, the Public Works Administration, provided funds to complete the park in 1934. Facilities and activities included a zoo, picnic sheds, a bandstand, a clubhouse, and three lakes for swimming, boating, and fishing.

Greensboro officials faced a number of problems during the Depression years 1932-1933. With many citizens unable to pay their taxes and assessments, the salaries of city and county workers were reduced. When the city was unable to pay its bonded debts, Mayor Roger Harrison (1933-1939), City Manager Andrew Joyner, and Councilmen Julius Cone and A.S. Keister traveled to New York and refinanced Greensboro's loans. Their efforts made it much easier for the city to recover from the Depression.

Money was scarce, and the city welfare board paid those on its relief roll with grocery orders. In April 1933 officials had to handle a strike by 300 men who were paid 80 cents a day to work on projects; the strike settlement increased the daily wage to $1.05. There were no funds to maintain streets, water mains, and sewage facilities, and citizens who lived near the North Buffalo sewage plant complained of odors.

State government suffered from a loss of income also. In an attempt to keep all schools open, North Carolina levied a temporary 3-percent sales tax to be used for education and assumed control of local systems. The state established the school year at eight months, which reduced Greensboro's nine-month year; state cutbacks also made it necessary to eliminate some school programs and a number of teacher positions.

The federal government intervened in May 1933 by establishing the Federal Emergency Relief Administration which was authorized to provide direct and work relief to those in need. It was a positive step at a time when the unemployment rate was estimated at 25 per-

In 1927 Paul Lindley sold 112 acres, including a landing field and hanger, to the Tri-City Airport Commission for a modest $21,250. A modern airport terminal was added in 1937. Another building contained a U.S. Weather Bureau station which began keeping official records in 1929. (GHM)

On December 10, 1930, a group of brave passengers and airline personnel posed before take-off of the initial passenger flight from Lindley Field on Eastern Air Transport. Eastern Air Transport formed from Pitcairn Aviation, and later became Eastern Airlines. (GHM)

America's flying hero Charles A. Lindbergh spoke at a banquet held in his honor on October 14, 1927. He is shown with (left to right) Governor A.W. McLean, County Commissioner and Manager J.A. Rankin, and Greensboro Mayor Jeffress. (GHM)

Approaching from the southwest, the tornado that swept through Greensboro on April 2, 1936, moved east and northeast along West Lee, McAdoo, and Gorrell streets. The building pictured above, at the corner of South Elm and Bain streets, was a block from the main path of the tornado. The storm caused about $2.5 million worth of damage, leaving 500 people homeless and 13 dead. (GHM)

cent. Federal programs provided funding and employment for a number of local projects, the most interesting of which was a cannery located on Commerce Place. The plant, which operated 24 hours a day and employed 170 workers, produced canned beef for the poor. A second project involved the airport, which had been closed by the Federal Aviation Administration in January 1935 because of its grass runways. Men began working in August to pre-

pare the land for paved runways, and the airport reopened in May 1937.

Economic Development

During the 1920s real estate was the key to economic growth, and at least 17 residential areas were promoted. Sedgefield, the second major project of the Southern Real Estate Company, was designed to include a golf course, a resort hotel (Sedgefield Inn, 1927),

Above: Mules and men provided the necessary labor to clear building sites at Sedgefield and Hamilton Lakes, developments of the 1920s. The Great Depression temporarily halted the real estate projects. (GHM)

Golf became a popular recreational activity in Greensboro soon after it was introduced by A.W. McAlister. By 1930 there were four courses, Greensboro Country Club, Valley Brook at Sedgefield (1924), Green Valley (1928), and Starmount. The first GGO (Greater Greensboro Open) tournament was held in 1938. (GHM)

an area for horse shows, and elegant houses. Hamilton Lakes, incorporated as a town with developer A.M. Scales as mayor, featured parks, lakes, and a golf course. Less extravagant developments also flourished, including Sunset Hills begun by A.K. Moore and Alan Turner in 1924. A neighborhood for middle-class blacks was developed in eastern Greensboro, and in 1925 it was named for J.R. Nocho, an early teacher, mail agent,

and civic leader in the black community. James Latham donated 100 acres of land along Buffalo Creek to the city in 1924, and the Latham Park neighborhood became a popular new area.

Many of these real-estate projects were built on credit, however, and as the Depression deepened a number of companies failed. The Hamilton Lakes development collapsed before the stock-market crash, and the area eventual-

Above: During the Depression the Greensboro Red Cross chapter stayed busy; one of its projects was sewing items for the needy. The sign on the left states that Brockmann Music Company had loaned a sewing machine for the effort. (GHM)

South Elm Street between Sycamore and Washington was a prime location for merchants during the 1920s. (GHM)

Greensboro's success as the central city of the Piedmont depended on transportation, and for the automobiles that brought students and businessmen to the city, service stations were essential. This typical 1930s gas station has electrical pumps and gasoline for 19¢ a gallon. (GHM)

ly came under the control of Blanche Sternberger Benjamin and her husband Edward. He developed a private country club and public golf course in the new neighborhood during 1930, choosing the English translation of Sternberger for its name, Starmount. In 1931 the Sedgefield operation was sold at auction, and by 1934 the Moore-Turner firm was bankrupt. Construction activity, constant during the twenties, declined to a minimum, and many city residents, particularly the unskilled, were without work.

Finance was a second area of heavy business activity, and 13 banks opened during the 1920s. Only two survived the Depression, and neither offered commercial banking services. Greensboro citizens were without a bank for several months following the National Bank Holiday on March 6, 1933, because none of the commercial banks ever reopened. The North Carolina Bank & Trust Company (1929) was liquidated, its depositors receiving 65.6 percent of the funds invested. The failure of this institution marked the end of earlier firms that

had merged with North Carolina Bank & Trust: The Bank of Cape Fear (1851), Southern Loan & Trust Banking Department (1900), Textile Bank (1911), and Atlantic Bank & Trust (1920). The Cone family donated approximately $300,000 to repay Textile Bank depositors the difference between their investments and the 65.6-percent liquidation settlement, an action that received national coverage in *Time* magazine.

Five life-insurance and five fire-insurance companies continued to operate throughout the Depression. In 1928 Pilot Life moved to its new location in Sedgefield, and in 1930 Jefferson Standard acquired a controlling interest in the company. During 1931 the Dixie Life Insurance Company (organized in 1927) moved to Greensboro from Raleigh, and the following year it merged with the Southern Life & Accident Insurance Company. W.L. Carter was president of the firm, which eventually became Southern Life. The Dixie Fire Insurance Company joined the American Insurance Company of New Jersey in 1929 but

On December 1, 1937, North Carolina s first supermarket was opened on West Washington Street in Greensboro. The Big Star Stores were operated by the Pender Grocery Company, which advertised low prices based on volume purchasing. "Self service" was a new concept for local consumers. (GHM)

During the 1930s, Greensboro merchants led a fight against "chain stores" that were trying to interest shoppers of the Piedmont area. (GHM)

operated as a separate company until 1948.

There were changes in the textile industry also. Mock, Judson, Voehringer Company, created in 1926, produced silk hosiery in its Howard Street factory. Despite the Depression, it expanded production between 1930 and 1932, as did Proximity Manufacturing Company and Blue Bell. In 1933 Proximity employees, working overtime to meet orders, were paid in scrip and in cash borrowed from New York. In July the firm reduced its operating hours to comply with a 40-hour limit set by Congress; this caused unrest among employees, but company officials refused to violate the government code.

In 1934 the local textile companies cut production levels to cooperate with federal recovery measures, and this led to serious disturbances. The Textile Workers Union sent groups called "flying squadrons" to Greensboro and other mill towns to generate support for a general strike, but violence was more often the result. Nonstriking employees and National Guard units prevented successful strikes in Greensboro.

In 1934 the Blue Gem Manufacturing Company was organized to produce overalls, and in 1935 a company based in Burlington, North Carolina, moved to Greensboro. Burlington Mills, founded by J. Spencer Love, continued to diversify, and by 1936 the company had 22 plants.

Greensboro's retail trade prospered during the 1920s. New firms included Younts-DeBoe (1923), Wright's (1926), E.L. Brownhill's (1926), Straughan's (1924), and Phipp's (1925). In 1927, a few months after its local mail-order business was begun, Sears opened its first retail store in North Carolina at 105 South Greene Street. Although business declined in the early 1930s, Greensboro's retail trade was not severely damaged by the Depression and recovered rapidly after 1933.

Schools, Churches, and Social Institutions

Three of Greensboro's colleges were accredited by the Southern Association of Colleges and Secondary Schools: the North

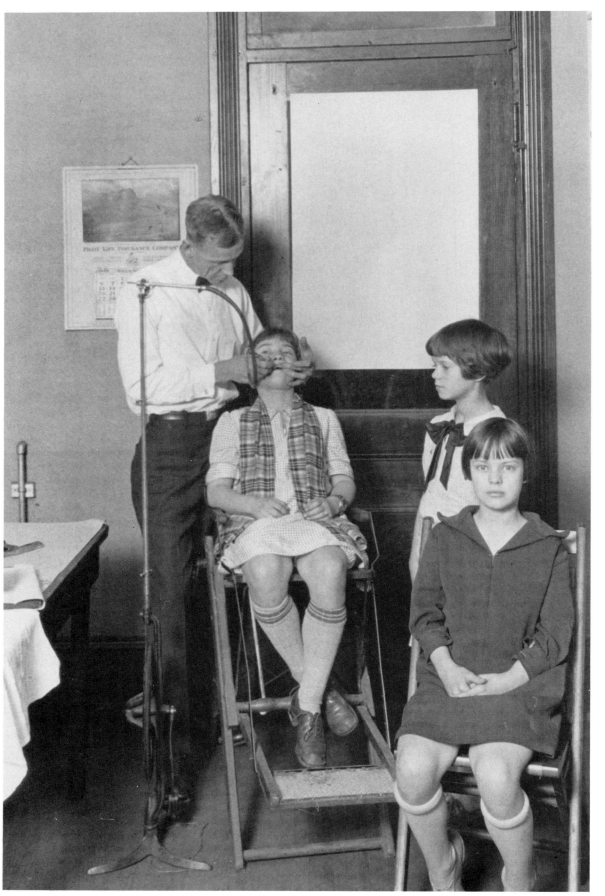

In 1925 Dr. Long, school dentist, inspected children's teeth and did minor repairs as part of the public health program. His equipment was portable. Courtesy, Greensboro Public Library

Pomona High School's baseball team won the state championship in 1923. Schools in the Pomona neighborhood were later brought into the Greensboro school system. (GHM)

Athletics have always been an important aspect of school life at North Carolina A & T. This basketball team from the 1930s, when the school was known as the Negro Agricultural and Technical College of North Carolina, is representative. (GHM)

State Champions of N.C. High Schools
Season 1923

Carolina College for Women in 1921, and Greensboro and Guilford colleges in 1926. In 1933 NCCW became Woman's College, a branch of the new Consolidated University created by the state general assembly, and by 1934 it was the third largest college for women in the United States.

Students at WC were taught by a number of outstanding female educators, including Harriet Elliott, Louise Alexander, and Elizabeth Weatherspoon. Dean Elliott taught history, but in 1935 she was granted a semester's leave to work for the Democratic National Committee; in 1936 she was one of the first women to serve as a delegate to the Democratic Platform Committee. Miss Alexander, an attorney who was to fill in for Elliott, began teaching history in 1935 and retired in 1957. Three years later she was described as "Greensboro's number one catalytic agent to sanity, good will, and progress through intellectual means." Elizabeth McIver Weatherspoon, who taught art at Curry from 1910 until 1939, joined the college art department when it was established

in 1935; she was an early promoter of a statewide school art competition which became the North Carolina State School Art Exhibition in 1934.

Bennett College went through a complete reorganization in 1926, terminating its preparatory department and emerging as a four-year college for women. Dr. David Jones, a Greensboro native who graduated with honors from Wesleyan University (Connecticut), was president during the reorganization and for the next 25 years. Under his leadership Bennett developed into an outstanding college with excellent facilities. In 1957, the year after Jones' death, it became the first women's college for blacks to be accredited by the Southern Association.

Dr. Ferdinand Bluford followed James Dudley as president of A & T, serving from 1925 to 1955. He expanded the academic program and worked for the admission of women students, which began again in 1928. Graduate programs in agriculture, education, and engineering were added in 1939.

The bookmobile of the Greensboro Public Library, which began operating in 1926, was the first one in the South. One vehicle (which covered the county) was supported by the county dog tax, and it was supplemented by a bookmobile that visited city neighborhoods. The Council of Jewish Women provided volunteers for the city service. During its first year, the bookmobile circulated 62,026 books. (GHM)

Over the years many community organizations have met at the Hayes-Taylor Y.M.C.A. at 1101 East Lee Street. Dedicated in 1939, the facility grew through the efforts of a group of chauffeurs who organized a black branch of the "Y" in 1932. Major financial support came from Ceasar Cone II, and additonal funds came from J. Spencer Love and a local fund drive. The building was named for two long-time employees of the Cone family. (GHM)

The Greensboro city school system, headed by Superintendent Frederick Archer, was greatly enlarged during the twenties. Aycock, McIver, and Caldwell schools for whites and Price School for blacks were constructed in 1922. Eleven county schools were brought into the city system when Greensboro extended its limits in 1923, and in 1925 a proposed single countywide system failed by approximately 1,000 votes. In 1926 voters approved a 30-cent special tax to operate on a nine-month school year and a $2.3-million bond issue to provide building funds. Four elementary schools were constructed before 1929, and Dudley (1928) and Greensboro (1929) senior highs opened just as the Depression ended this educational explosion. In 1935 the city schools began another building-improvement campaign which was funded by a $225,000 bond issue.

The Carnegie Library was an important educational resource for children and adults. Nellie Rowe, librarian from 1920 to 1949, began gathering information and objects related to local, county, and state history, and a basement room of the library became the city's first museum. In 1924 a society was formed to collect, preserve, and exhibit historical artifacts, and on Armistice Day 1925 the Greensboro Historical Museum opened with an exhibit of 186 items carefully arranged by volunteers.

Funds for a library to serve the black community were obtained through the Carnegie Fund, and in 1924 a library was built on East Washington Street. The city provided funds for its operation and maintenance. The library opened with only 150 volumes, but by 1928 the number had increased to 3,500, and a total of 14,846 books were circulated that year. Martha O. Sebastian, the primary organizer of the library, served as librarian until 1948.

In 1939 Greensboro acquired a civic center. The former buildings of First Presbyterian Church, vacant since 1928, were purchased for $125,000 by Mrs. Lunsford Richardson and her three daughters, Mrs. C.I. Carlson, Mrs. Karl Prickett, and Mrs. W.Y. Preyer, who donated them to the city. An additional

$100,000 was spent renovating the structures to create a single building that would house the library, museum, art center, and civic and social service organizations.

New houses of worship were constructed in Fisher Park. On June 5, 1925, the Greensboro Hebrew Congregation dedicated its temple, designed by Hobart Upjohn of Boston. In 1928 First Presbyterian moved into its new building, designed by Upjohn assisted by Harry Barton. Holy Trinity Episcopal dedicated its chapel in 1922 and used it until 1950 when a sanctuary was dedicated.

By 1920 the YWCA had constructed a meeting hut on its Davie Street lot, and in 1921 the cornerstone for a permanent building was set. The Y provided rooms for unmarried working women and supported a cottage for unwed mothers. A new YMCA built at 517 West Market Street in 1925 contained an indoor swimming pool and a gymnasium with seating for 300.

In 1921 R. Odell Holland began the city's first radio station, WQAZ; the *Greensboro Daily*

News paid for the license. Using electric power from the trolley wires to broadcast, the station operated for about 18 months before a studio fire ended its service. In 1926 station WNRC went on the air, operating on 10 watts of power from a studio on the eighth floor of the Jefferson Building, with a transmitter on the roof. Wayne Nelson, who owned the radio equipment, was paid by the Chamber of Com-

In 1925 the local American Legion post raised $100,000, during one week, to build War Memorial Stadium. The 9,100-seat facility, which opened in November 1926, was the center of sports activity for the next two decades. (GHM)

The Carolina Theater opened in 1927 with the film *Painting the Town*. Described as a movie palace, the theater was a showpiece of the area. Outstanding movies were booked at the Carolina, and Laurel and Hardy features were favorites. (GHM)

Eleanor Roosevelt visited Greensboro on several occasions. She is shown here with members of the Junior League at the Summit Avenue home of her hostess Mrs. Julius Cone. Mrs. Roosevelt returned in 1945 and 1953 to speak at Greensboro and Woman's Colleges. (GHM)

merce to operate as often as possible. In 1930 Edney Ridge became manager, and the station's call letters were changed to WBIG, "We Believe in Greensboro."

Another communications change occurred in 1930 when the *Greensboro Record* was purchased by the *Greensboro Daily News*. In 1927 out-of-state businessmen had acquired the paper, and Greensboro citizens welcomed a return to local ownership. Abram D. Jones served as editor from 1930 to 1948.

Theaters provided entertainment for all ages, and the National, which opened in 1921, was considered among the finest in the South. It replaced the Grand as the site for touring shows, and the old opera house was razed in 1926. Other new theaters included the Alamo (later the State), the Carolina, and the Criterion.

Aycock Auditorium opened at the North Carolina College for Women in 1927, providing a home for the symphony orchestra organized by college musicians in 1920, as well as for theatrical performances. Cultural pro-

grams and organizations were neglected during the Depression years, but many were revived in the late thirties. In 1936 the WPA supported an orchestra at WC and by 1939 the college was able to sponsor the Greensboro Symphony, made up of community and campus musicians. The Civic Music Association, established in 1927, brought in outstanding performers: Jascha Heifetz in 1937, Arthur Rubinstein in 1938, and Sergei Rachmaninoff in 1939.

War Memorial Stadium, located at Yanceyville and Lindsay streets on 11 acres donated by the Cone family, was dedicated on April 5, 1927, during the North Carolina State-Wake Forest baseball game. Football, track, and boxing events drew large crowds, and patriotic rallies were held there.

A number of volunteer organizations had their origin during this period. In 1922 the Chamber of Commerce established the Community Budget, later the Community Chest, and two years later the Greensboro Council of Social Agencies was created to allocate funds

to worthy community programs and projects. In 1925 Greensboro women established a local chapter of the Colonial Dames of America, which promoted local history and preservation. The Charity League formed in 1926 and became the Junior League in 1928. The Altrusa Club was formed in 1928, and the Junior Women's Club in 1930. The Little Gate Garden Club began in 1929, and by 1931 a total of 11 clubs sent representatives to the organizational meeting of the Council of Garden Clubs, which promoted citywide plantings and beautification.

The War Years

In 1940 Greensboro's population exceeded 60,000. The Cone mills were the world's largest producers of cotton denim, Blue Bell was the nation's leading overall manufacturer, and Burlington Mills was the world leader in rayon weaving. The city was the commercial hub of an area 50 miles in radius, with a regional population of more than one million.

On September 16, 1940, the expanding world war touched the city with the mobilization of the National Guard. Three hundred men left with the Second Battalion, 252nd

On March 7, 1930, the Guilford Battle Chapter of the Daughters of the American Revolution marked the site of Dolley Payne Madison's birth with a four-ton stone and bronze plaque. The brick house behind the stone is a 20th century version of an early house. The actual Payne log house, which stood north of what was then Friendly Road, no longer exists. (GHM)

On January 2, 1941, the last issues of the *Patriot* rolled off the presses, ending more than a century of publication. The newspaper was purchased by the *Daily News* and redesigned as an agricultural weekly, *The Patriot Farmer* (which was sold to *Southern Agriculturalist* in 1950). This upstairs office, at 205½ North Greene Street was near city hall. (GHM)

A group of grateful mothers gathered at Sternberger Hospital (715 Summit Avenue) which operated from 1930 to 1953. Opened by Blanche S. Benjamin as a memorial to her family, the facility provided maternity and pediatric care for many women and children. Today a small park is located on the site. (GHM)

Coast Artillery, nicknamed the Guilford Grays. The Grays trained in South Carolina and Georgia before leaving the country early in 1941; assigned to duty on the island of Trinidad, the unit lost many members through transfers and eventually ceased to exist. Seven of its original members were killed during World War II.

The commanding officer of the Grays was Mayor Ralph L. Lewis, who resigned his office when the unit was called up. He was succeeded by Huger King, who resigned for military duty in 1942. King's replacement, William H. Sullivan, served until 1945.

Although some North Carolina cities were stimulated by military spending, Greensboro experienced an economic slump in 1941-1942. A few of its largest industries converted to wartime production—Proximity Manufacturing Company made tent and camouflage material, Blue Bell produced garments for the armed forces, Vick Chemical manufactured rocket fuel, Carolina Steel won military contracts, and several companies made aircraft

parts—but other firms, especially in construction, were idle during much of 1942. The Greensboro Housing Authority, established in 1941, had drawn up plans to build 2,500 units of public housing over the next 10 years, but the project was deferred because of the war and not reactivated until 1949.

When city officials learned that the army needed a North Carolina site for a 5,000-man training camp, they were quick to promote Greensboro. A site was selected in the northeastern part of the city, and construction began in 1942. The only army camp in America situated entirely within a municipality, it was also the last one to be built from the ground up. Civilians erected more than 900 prefabricated buildings that became barracks, mess halls, libraries, and theaters, and a $5-million hospital was completed in November. A total of $15 million was spent in the creation of Basic Training Camp-10 (BTC-10), which received its first troops on March 1, 1943.

Approximately 87,000 men trained at Greensboro during the next 13 months. In

MAIN ENTRANCE

April 1944 the facility became the Overseas Replacement Depot (ORD) for the Army Air Corps in the Eastern United States, and during the next 13 months, 240,000 men and women were processed there.

The camp boosted Greensboro's economy. As many as 1,200 civilians worked at the facility, and their payroll checks totaled $300 million. Military personnel spent money in the city—an estimated total of $42 million, plus another $5 million for construction materials.

The city remained a transportation hub. In 1940 Southern Railway ran 39 passenger and 29 freight trains through the city each day, and its north-south lines through Greensboro were the only double tracks in the southeast. At Union Bus Station each weekday 61 buses were dispatched, and on Sundays 92 buses arrived or departed. There were 1,100 miles of paved highways and 160,000 car owners within the "50-mile magic circle." When gasoline rationing began in 1942, many of these vehicles were parked. In 1941 the general assembly established a Greensboro-High Point Airport

Authority, but the airport soon came under the control of the Army Air Corps, which suspended passenger and mail service.

In the communications field Ralph Lambeth received a license for a new radio station in 1941, but the attack on Pearl Harbor postponed its opening. Greensboro's second station began programming on February 16, 1942, under the call letters WGBG, "We're Going to Beat Germany." Radio listeners heard correspondent Edward R. Murrow analyze the war news, opening his famous broadcasts with the terse phrase, "This is London," and signing off with the equally familiar "Good night and good luck." Murrow, the pioneer of broadcast journalism, was born in eastern Guilford County, but his family moved away from North Carolina when he was still a child.

Civilians were involved in a number of activities. In 1942 Woman's College celebrated its 50th anniversary with a special theatrical production and the opening of Weatherspoon Art Gallery, named for Elizabeth M. Weatherspoon. At A & T College, the ROTC program

People across the country probably received postcards like this one of the main entrance to ORD (Overseas Replacement Depot). The Army camp opened in 1943 on a 652-acre site. Civilians erected over 900 prefabricated buildings, and a $5 million hospital was completed in 1942. The site closed in 1946. (GHM)

Construction of the second Southern Railway passenger train station began in 1926 and was nearly complete when this photograph was made. Many early Greensboro houses were razed to clear the building site. During World War II thousands of soldiers used the million-dollar facility as they arrived for basic training in Greensboro or left for overseas duty. In 1979 Southern Railway gave the building, "the finest that Southern ever built," to the city of Greensboro. (GHM)

was an important source of black officers for the armed forces. Greensboro's public schools remained open throughout the war, and a 12th grade was added in 1943.

In 1942 the Civilian Defense Volunteer Organization (CDVO) trained 150 men and women to staff its control center and enlist others to work. The agency sponsored an emergency rescue truck, arranged recreation and entertainment for soldiers, and coordinated the activities of the USO and the Red Cross. Individuals cultivated "victory gardens" and participated in scrap drives, saving paper, cans, and clothing.

Three people stand out in Greensboro's World War II history. Harriet Elliott, dean of students at WC, became consumer adviser on the National Defense Advisory Commission, serving from May 1940 to November 1941. In 1942 she joined the advisory commission investigating a women's auxiliary for the navy and helped organize the WAVES. She also organized the women's division of the War Bonds Program and in 1945 was one of the 14

American delegates at the conference to set up the United Nations Educational, Scientific, and Cultural Organization (UNESCO). Dean Elliott died suddenly in 1947, but her contributions to college, city, state, and nation were acknowledged when the new student-union building at WC was named for her.

Mary Webb Nicholson gained fame another way. In 1928 she had obtained a private pilot's license, the first one granted by North Carolina to a female, and in 1936 she earned a transport license from the U.S. Department of Commerce. Early in the war, Miss Nicholson and 24 other women were trained by Britain's Royal Air Force to transport Canadian planes to England. On May 22, 1943, while flying a plane to a combat area, she was killed. Greensboro citizens honored her memory by contributing funds to purchase a hospital plane.

Greensboro's greatest war hero was Major George E. Preddy, who joined the Guilford Grays in 1940; transferring to the Army Air Corps, he earned his commission in December

Far left: In 1942 First Lieutenant George Preddy returned to Greensboro for a week's leave. He is shown here with his mother at N.C. State University, where his brother Bill was a student. In August 1944 Major Preddy returned on a 30-day leave, and a large celebration was held in his honor at World War Memorial Stadium. (GHM)

Left: George Preddy was photographed in northern Australia, in his fighter plane nicknamed "The Tarheel." Preddy had his first plane ride in November 1938, and decided then to become a pilot. (GHM)

Right: A soldiers' lounge was in operation in Greensboro before the United Service Organization (USO) provided funding. Community groups provided operating funds, and the Kleins (Al and Min) donated hours of service. In 1943 the lounge became an official USO lounge, the only one in the U.S. to be directed at the local level. A USO for black soldiers opened in 1944 on East Market. Eight hundred women served as hostesses for these facilities. (GHM)

Booths to sell war bonds and stamps were located throughout the city. This unusual one at the National Theater attracted many buyers and a photographer. (GHM)

1941. Preddy's first assignment was in the Pacific flying a P-40. Wounded while training, he recuperated in Australia and joined the Eighth Air Force in England. While flying P-51s Preddy is credited with destroying five planes on the ground, and aerial victories that range from 24 to 27 plus 1.5 to 1.83 shared victories. He became America's leading air ace on August 6, 1944, when he shot down six German planes within five minutes. On Christmas Day 1944, while pursuing a plane over Belgium, Preddy was stuck by US antiaircraft fire and killed. His brother William destroyed three planes before he was shot down over Czechoslovakia in 1945.

On May 7, 1945, Germany surrendered to the Allied powers, and Greensboro's ORD became a redistribution center for military personnel. After Japan's surrender on August 14, 1945, it became a separation center, discharging 500 soldiers daily and troop trains moved continuously in and out of the city. A year later the barracks were vacated and the facility closed down.

According to records kept by the public library and the American Legion, 9,763 Greensboro people served in the armed forces during World War II; 267 of them did not return. The city honored its dead on Recognition Day, celebrated at War Memorial Stadium on November 6, 1946, and again when a memorial auditorium and coliseum were built with funds raised by the American Legion and civic groups. As in the past, however, the city was ready to put the war behind it and eager to face the future.

The Postwar Years

The site of Greensboro's wartime ORD, more than 600 acres of developed land, was offered for sale in 1946 by a Proximity Manufacturing Company subsidiary. A & T College purchased 52 acres and the ORD hospital; Bessemer Improvement Company, organized by Oscar Burnett, bought almost all of the remaining land and buildings, for $200,000. In 1947 the city council rezoned the property north of Bessemer Avenue for light

industry and residential housing, and the area developed quickly as many of the army buildings were converted to civilian use. In 1949 Summit Shopping Center opened as a focal point for the new neighborhood—the first shopping center in Greensboro, and the second in North Carolina.

Following the war, the city annexed small sections in east and south Greensboro and the northwestern residential area known as Kirkwood. Although the neighborhood had been laid out in the 1920s, only a few houses had actually been built before the Depression. After the war, Weaver Construction Company and an Asheville firm used some of the first available building materials to construct more than 100 Kirkwood houses. Priced from $9,000 to $12,000, they sold quickly, many of them to young couples just returning from military assignments. A strong community spirit developed as people used the neighborhood's only telephone, arranged car pools, and shared lawnmowers. Consumer items were still scarce in 1946-1947.

In 1947 a planning and zoning commission was established to integrate proposed projects involving city land, air and water, major streets, community buildings and playgrounds, and public utilities. Fielding Fry, who became mayor in 1947, asked Greensboro citizens to make suggestions about their city's future development. Among the major concerns expressed were the need for an adequate water supply, more businesslike financing, expansion of recreational facilities, better streets and sewers, and the construction of low-rent housing. During the 1950s a number of these citizen suggestions would become city council goals.

Between 1945 and 1950 Greensboro resumed its development as a regional center. In 1946 the United States Post Office Department selected Greensboro as a "mail hub" serving the area between Washington, D.C., and Atlanta. A new mail terminal, dedicated on March 13, 1948, served 5,331 post offices in five states. Sears, Roebuck also chose Greensboro as the site for its southeastern warehouse and mail-order plant. The new Sears building on

Manuel's Cafe at 112 West Market Street was a popular gathering spot and outstanding restaurant. When the city of Greensboro began its restaurant inspection program, Manuel's received a perfect score for its facilities. The restaurant continued the tradition of quality dining that made Greensboro a stop for "more than 1,000 traveling men." (GHM)

Lawndale Drive was completed in 1947 at a cost of $2 million.

In 1948 a third radio station, WCOG, began operating from a studio beside the Carolina Theater. WGBG, the city's first FM station, proved to be "static-free even in the worst thunderstorms," and the Greensboro News Company constructed a second FM station, WFMY, on North Davie Street beside its headquarters.

On August 18, 1949, WFMY-TV transmitted a live image and voice, a first for North Carolina. For the next 30 days, it ran a test pattern. Then, on September 22, 1949, the station signed on the air with an evening of programs: "Introducing WFMY-TV" (30 minutes); a newscast (5 minutes); a local film (10 minutes); a musical show (15 minutes); the CBS "Arthur Godfrey Show" and "College Football Thrills." There were approximately 2,000 television sets in the Piedmont area, and their owners could now receive programming six days a week, three hours a night. On Saturday there was only a test pattern.

During the polio epidemic of 1948, Greensboro became a regional medical center, caring for patients from 16 counties. Cases of this dread disease had been reported in 1935 and 1944, but the number of people stricken in late 1947 and early 1948 caused the National Foundation of Infantile Paralysis to issue a warning to the entire state of North Carolina. The number of cases reported locally was 3 in April, 8 in May, 24 in June, and 43 in July, at which point the city closed all recreational facilities, including the YMCAs. By August 1, 1948, 10 people had died and many more were permanently paralyzed. When the epidemic finally ended in September, statistics revealed that Guilford County had more polio cases than any region in the country.

Responding to the emergency, community leaders requested contributions to build a temporary hospital at an estimated cost of $60,000. Within two weeks $100,000 had been received, and campaign leaders decided to build a permanent 125-bed hospital instead. The Central Carolina Convalescent Hospital, designed by Edward Loewenstein and Charles Hartmann, Jr., was built in only 94 days. Union and nonunion, skilled and unskilled workers donated more than 5,500 hours of labor, while groups of churchwomen provided them with meals. The facility, which opened in October 1948, served the community for 10 years.

Established industries converted to peacetime production and new companies were organized in the postwar period. In the textile field, J.P. Stevens acquired Carter Fabrics (1937), and Blue Bell added Western wear under the trademark Wrangler. Burlington Industries continued to diversify by adding ribbon production and purchasing Cramerton Cotton Mills. In 1946 a new textile company was established by James M. Hornaday, who had been in the feed and hatchery business; the first Guilford Mills plant had six knitting machines and six employees.

In September 1949 a traditional enterprise, the storage and sale of tobacco, was revived. A new warehouse, built at a cost of $180,000, was dedicated, and more than 12,000 people attended the ceremony and barbecue. After 20 years Greensboro was once again a tobacco-selling center. Guilford County remained among the top five tobacco-producing counties in North Carolina, while the El Moro Cigar Company made Greensboro the state leader in cigar manufacturing.

During the 1940s Greensboro's business district, with its large department and furniture stores, specialty shops, and clothing establishments, was the retail center of the Piedmont. In 1949 Sears opened a retail store at Friendly and Eugene, having purchased the Van Noppen house (1853) which stood on the site. Citizens were so upset about the loss of this historic property that they failed to see the move as a threat to the inner city. When Greensboro's first shopping center opened, tenants hesitated to move as far away as Summit and Bessemer. Downtown seemed secure despite a 1949 traffic plan which created one-way streets in the business district.

In 1947 Randall Jarrell, an outstanding teacher and nationally acclaimed poet, arrived to teach at WC. Having served three years in the Army Air Corps, Jarrell wrote many poems dealing with the horrors of war; two of his best known are "Eighth Air Force" and "The Death of the Ball Turret Gunner." In addition to seven books of poetry, he published three collections of essays, four children's books, and one novel. *The Woman at the Washington Zoo* (1960) won the 1961 National Book Award for poetry.

Clara Booth Byrd, WC alumnae secretary for 25 years, reached beyond the campus to establish an organization that provided educational opportunities to adults across the state. The Historical Book Club of North Carolina, founded in 1947, serves to stimulate interest in current literature and to encourage creative writing.

Many veterans who settled in Greensboro

The Central Carolina Convalescent Hospital (the complex of buildings on the left) was built near the Evergreens County Home (on the right) in 1948. Known throughout the Piedmont as the "polio hospital," it operated as an integrated, special-care medical facility until 1958. In 1963 it housed civil rights protesters who were students at Bennett College. Courtesy, Evergreens, Inc.

were eager to use education funds provided by the GI Bill of Rights. Only A & T and Guilford College admitted men, however, and their classes were held during the day. The Greensboro Chamber of Commerce approached WC with a plan for evening classes. They were refused on the grounds that men on campus would be a danger to a female college! In 1948 the Greensboro Evening College opened, offering liberal arts courses but emphasizing business education, and in 1952 it became a division of Guilford College.

Many people who chose to settle in Greensboro in the postwar years commented on the city's friendliness and openness. Civic organizations accepted newcomers, colleges provided a variety of educational and cultural opportunities, and businesses encouraged their employees to participate in community projects.

Many Greensboro leaders came from traditional areas. Businessmen C.M. Vanstory, Jr., and Benjamin Cone served as mayors, while Caesar Cone was a member of the airport authority from 1942 until 1967. Alonzo C. Hall, Ferdinand D. Bluford, Walter C. Jackson, David D. Jones, and others came from the colleges to serve as members of city boards, commissions, and committees or to be active in civic and professional associations.

Leadership also emerged from other sections of the community. In 1947 Grace Donnell Lewis, president of the Greensboro branch of the National Council of Negro Women, founded the Metropolitan Day Nursery to replace wartime federal day-care centers; in 1967 this organization became a part of United Day Care, a United Way agency. Elreta M. Alexander, another black woman, began practicing law in Greensboro in 1947; 20 years later, she was elected a district judge. In 1949 Juliette Dwiggins was elected to the city council, becoming its first female member.

Blacks and whites, Gentiles and Jews, worked on projects to improve the city and aid its citizens. Although many problems existed, a spirit of cooperation was developing and would prove a valuable resource for the future.

The Sisters of Charity operated St. Leo's Hospital from 1906 to 1954. The hospital's nursing school graduated approximately 600 nurses over a 47-year period. This graduating class is a representative one. There were also nursing schools at the Wesley Long, Clinic, and L. Richardson hospitals. (GHM)

The Rogers Plan of 1963 was developed around a city like the one pictured. One change underway by 1965, when this aerial photograph was made, can be seen left of the Jefferson building. The steel framework for the Wachovia building stands behind the old city hall. The 1918 Courthouse and the two blocks behind it soon were transformed by the Governmental Center. (GHM)

Chapter Eight

CONCRETE CHANGES:
1951 - 1980

*O*n June 15, 1950, North Korean troops invaded South Korea, beginning another war which involved Greensboro citizens and industries. Edward R. Murrow reported on the conflict using radio broadcasts and television clips which made the war visible. Burlington Industries produced nylon fabric at its Elm Street Weaving Plant for many of the parachutes used over Korea, and Vick's Manufacturing Division made a number of war-related chemical products. When a truce was signed on July 27, 1953, American communities could concentrate once again on local concerns.

The Physical City

Annexation drastically changed Greensboro, which grew from 18.4 square miles in 1955 to 60.5 square miles by 1980. On July 1, 1957, Greensboro extended its four sides, adding more than 31 square miles. Although much of the "new city" was west and south of the 1923 boundaries, the Bessemer community on the east was annexed. Hamilton Lakes was also included at this time, in a merger move initiated by the community's mayor, E.R. Zane. Hamilton Lakes was guaranteed zoning protection and continued private use of its recreational facilities, and Zane became a member of the Greensboro City Council.

In 1962 the town of Guilford College was annexed, and Clyde Milner gratefully retired as mayor, a position he had held since 1935 in addition to being president of the college. A large area south of Guilford College was annexed in 1969, and the Brightwood area, the northern tip of the city, was added in 1970.

Public-housing projects also changed the city physically. In 1952 Morningside Homes (for blacks) and Smith Homes (for whites) were completed; Morningside had a waiting list from the first day. In 1959 the Greensboro Housing Authority built its first units for the elderly, including them in a new project named for Ray Warren, the agency's first director. In 1965, as part of an urban redevelopment plan, portions of the Warnersville community were razed and replaced by Hampton Homes. By 1969 Greensboro had four public-housing complexes, all of them in the southeast, and GHA approved the scattered-site concept to prevent further concentration of low-rent housing. Alonzo Hall Towers on Church Street, built in 1970, was the city's first high-rise complex for the elderly; a second, Gateway Plaza, opened five years later. In 1979 Village Green was established as a retirement facility for middle-income people, and in 1980 the first 157 scattered-site units were ready for occupancy.

During the 1950s the city expanded its parks and recreation program, adding baseball fields, a golf course, and a pool. The lake at Country Park had to be closed to swimmers in 1951 because of pollution, but the Natural Science Center opened there in 1957. During the 1960s public facilities were integrated, and Hagan-Stone Park was acquired. Bryan Park was dedicated to Mr. and Mrs. Joseph M. Bryan on May 20, 1971, and the Bryans reponded by donating funds for the Bryan Enrichment Center. Today the park occupies more than 1,500 acres that include two golf courses, a new club house, tennis courts, and a soccer complex, as well as picnic and play areas. In 1975 the Greensboro Jaycees developed a 75-acre park adjacent to

the city's Country Park; public and private funds totaling $2 million were used to build a tennis area, athletic fields, and a tram system. With the development of Oka T. Hester Park in the southwest quadrant of the city in 1977, the planned expansion of Greensboro's recreation program was complete. The city owned and operated 14 recreation centers, 40 playgrounds, and 75 tennis courts; it managed three reservoirs, 2,886 acres in parks and open space, and a complete athletic program using volunteers as coaches and organizers. In 1979 the National Sporting Goods Association awarded Greensboro its gold medal, meaning that it had the best recreation program in the nation for a city its size.

The Greensboro Coliseum, built on the site of the old fairgrounds on Lee Street, was dedicated on October 24, 1959; a crowd of 8,000 attended the ceremony which opened the "living memorial" to the casualties of World War II and Korea. In 1969-1970 a vertical addition to the coliseum gave it a seating capacity of more than 16,000, making it the second largest city-operated coliseum in America. The Exhibition Hall was part of the same $6.5-million expansion.

The first sports event in the arena was a hockey game featuring the Greensboro Generals, who played in Greensboro until 1971. A professional basketball team, the Carolina Cougars of the ABA, were headquartered at the coliseum from 1969 until 1974. The facility was selected for ten ACC tournaments played between 1967 and 1980, and in 1974 it hosted both ACC and the NCAA Final Four tournaments. The 1976 and 1979 NCAA Eastern Regionals were held there, as were many CIAA and MEAC tournament.

Greensboro's professional baseball team, the Patriots, was acquired by the Chicago Cubs in 1951, then sold to the Yankees in 1958 and to the Houston Astros in 1968, after which the club was terminated. A decade passed without professional baseball, but in 1979 the Greensboro

In 1966 the Wendover Avenue extension was the most expensive thoroughfare in North Carolina's history. The 10.3 mile, six-lane road cuts from old U.S. 70 on the east to Interstate 40 on the west. Construction of its road bed and 16 bridges with ramps took a decade and cost $12.5 million. In 1980 an estimated 125,000 vehicles traveled Wendover daily. This photograph of East Wendover shows early construction in the Raleigh Street-Huffine Mill Road area. (GHM)

Hornets of the South Atlantic League began playing at War Memorial Stadium.

In 1954 consultant Frank Babcock designed a thoroughfare plan to provide a more efficient road network in, around, and through the city. The plan, designed for a Greensboro with multiple residential areas, numerous small shopping centers, and automobile transportation, was adopted by city council in 1954. The Babcock Plan aligned Forbis Street with Church Street, and by 1970 that historic name disappeared from the city map. Library Place became Commerce, appropriate enough as the 1906 Carnegie Public Library had been razed in 1950.

During the 1960s a revised thoroughfare plan was adopted, and Wendover Avenue, which had been a small street through the Latham property, became a major traffic artery. In 1966 Preddy Boulevard was named for World War II hero George Preddy, and in 1970 Pearson Street became Murrow Boulevard to honor the news commentator. A controversial name change took place on October 4, 1966, when the city council chose the name Friendly Avenue for a six-mile street that had been Gaston in the downtown area, Madison in the Westover Terrace area, and Friendly beyond the 1923 city limits. Friendly described the city's spirit, thought the council, and it had historic significance because the street led to the early Friends' settlement at Guilford College.

In January 1959 the Chamber of Commerce appointed a Downtown Improvement Committee to identify local problems and offer sugges-

The Sedgefield Inn, constructed in 1927, was the site of a 1953 meeting which resulted in the formation of the Atlantic Coast Conference (ACC). Eight colleges and universities located in North and South Carolina, Virginia, and Maryland agreed to join the new athletic conference. In 1954 the ACC Commissioner's office was established in Greensboro. This view of the Sedgefield Inn lobby was taken around 1935. The Inn was razed in 1993 and replaced with a new facility. (GHM)

tions for solving them. After a period of study, the committee hired the" firm of Rogers, Taliaferro, Kostritsky, and Lamb to develop a proposal for downtown. The Rogers Plan, submitted in 1963, offered six major recommendations: (1) improved access by simplifying traffic patterns; (2) construction of a city-county government center; (3) use of redevelopment funds to clear sites for new office buildings; (4) preservation of "uptown" as the retail hub of the Piedmont; (5) visual improvements; and (6) expansion of parks and plantings in and around the center city. The estimated cost was more than $100 million.

City officials, corporations, and citizens began to build upon the Rogers blueprint. A thoroughfare plan to improve street patterns was adopted in 1965, and municipal garages were opened in 1967 and 1972. The city government used its power of "eminent domain" to acquire private property for public use, and the U.S. Department of Housing and Urban Development (HUD) provided more than $6 million in grants for land redevelopment. Between 1967 and 1971 the city issued $3 million in bonds for downtown facilities and services.

On June 1, 1973, the Greensboro-Guilford County Governmental Center was dedicated by Congressman Richardson Preyer; representing an investment of nearly $15 million in government funds, it created a sense of optimism in the eroding business district. Federal redevelopment funds were spent on the Governmental Center's Plaza and the Elm Street "semi-mall," as well as a semi-mall at Tate and Walker outside the center city.

Two other downtown improvements were the removal of sidewalk signs, in compliance with a 1971 city ordinance, and the underground installation of electric lines, a project of Duke Power Company. An interesting addition to the modern skyline was Southern Bell's microwave relay tower, part of a $6.3-million expansion during the 1970s which included the preservation of an Art Deco building.

Property acquired with HUD funds was resold to private firms, including Gate City Savings & Loan, the Golden Eagle Motel, the Greensboro News Company, and Southern Life. In 1971 the First Union Bank building was completed at a cost of $2.1 million; the top floors of this skyscraper housed the City Club until 1990. The North Carolina National Bank building (now Bank of America) was constructed for $6 million in 1975.

The YWCA remained downtown, building a new million-dollar facility which opened in January 1971. Designed by Ed Loewenstein to complement the Greensboro Historical

Museum, the Y included a swimming pool, gymnasium, and cafeteria. The YMCA moved into a new building on West Market at Tate Street, and its 1925 facility was razed in 1979 to create parking spaces.

These developments were encouraging to city officials, businessmen, and many citizens, but construction at the city's core meant destruction of houses and buildings that represented the city's historical development. The Governmental Center erased Otto Zenke's studio, the original YMCA, and the first Wachovia Building; the proposed Southern

Construction of a second skyscraper on North Elm was under way by December 1964, and the site was the northwest corner of the Friendly intersection. The modern design of the Wachovia building provided an interesting contrast to that of the Jefferson building; as one columnist observed, it looked like the box in which the earlier structure was packed! The $4.6 million building was a major boost to downtown revitalization. The Banner building and corner drugstore, shown on the left, were replaced by the N.C.N.B. building. (GHM)

Right: A mayor's committee, appointed in 1975, evaluated the community's art needs, recommended a downtown center, and explored available sites. This 1924 building on Davie at Friendly (purchased for $238,000 and adapted through a federal grant of $543,377) became Greensboro's Visual Arts Center. In 1985, a bond issue provided funds to renovate this building into the Greensboro Cultural Center. It houses art and ethnic museums, arts divisions of the City Parks and Recreation Department, and offices for the United Arts Council and some of its members. (GHM)

Henry Humphreys Tate, grandson of the early textile industrialist, built Belle Meade in 1867 on Bellemeade Street at North Edgeworth. In the early 1950s the old mansion fell, despite the efforts of Mayor Frazier and J. Spencer Love of Burlington Industries. Today the Guilford County Mental Health Department occupies the site. (GHM)

Life Center required razing the O. Henry Hotel and other early buildings. Some people feared that Greensboro would become a 20th-century city cut off from its past.

The decision to spare the 1918 courthouse and maintain it as part of the Governmental Center was a victory for preservationists. In 1977 a group organized to save the Carolina Theater, raising $500,000 to refurnish the movie palace. In 1978 the city purchased Wafco Mills, a late-19th-century feed and grain mill, which was listed on the National

Register in 1979. The city later sold the building to a group of developers who converted it into condominiums in 1986. The city's temporary involvement guaranteed a stable situation in the historic College Hill neighborhood. In 1980, when the Greensboro Fire Department began preparations to abandon its Central Station, steps were taken to have it listed on the National Register. When the city sold the station to Southern Life, a condition of the sale was preservation of the building's exterior; it will remain a link to the 1920s and local architect Charles Hartmann. During 1980 Southern Railroad moved its station facilities to the Pomona Yard and donated the Washington Street depot to the city. Considered an anchor for the eastern edge of Greensboro's business district, it will soon be part of a transportation multi-modal center.

In 1975 a coalition of civic leaders, merchants, students, artists, and interested citizens organized to save the 300-600 blocks of South Elm under the name "Old Greensborough." This was a different form of preservation, as people and businesses moved into buildings that had been parts of Greensboro's early economic life. One of the first successes was the Mantleworks Restaurant, located in the former MacClamrock Mantle Company building.

The Modern Economy

For almost a century the textile industry had been the heart of Greensboro's industrial economy. In 1980 Cone Mills was still Greensboro's largest employer, with approximately 5,500 people on the payroll. J.H. Hamilton and Fred Proctor formed a new company in 1963, specializing in the production of textured-filament yarn, and in 1969 it became Texfi. Burlington Industries, the world's largest textile company, employed 2,000 people locally. In 1971 the company moved into its new corporate headquarters, a showplace for the city.

In 1955 P. Lorillard, the oldest tobacco company in the United States, built a $13-mil-

lion plant on East Market Street. Originally employing 500 people, by 1977 Lorillard had a payroll of 3,000 and was the city's third largest employer. The El Moro Cigar Company produced 125,000 cigars a day in 1955, but the new machinery required to update production would not fit in the old factory, and the company was forced to close in 1956.

Western Electric, which purchased the Pomona Manufacturing Company buildings in 1951, employed 100 people to produce coiled wire. In 1971 the company opened a Research and Engineering Center east of Greensboro employing 3,500 people; during the early 1970s, the $20-million Guilford center was involved in creating the Safeguard antiballistic missile. Greensboro's central location and transportation facilities attracted a number of other firms, including Dow Corning (1954), Gilbarco (1966), and Ciba-Geigy (1973).

Transportation, a key to industrial development, is an important industry in its own right. By 1951 Greensboro was the center of a road system that reached in 38 directions, and by 1980 it was linked to major American cities by two interstate and four federal highways. Greensboro's Pomona Rail Yard, an important crossroad in Norfolk-Southern's 10,000-mile network, serviced 7,000 trains carrying 50 million tons of goods to and from the city in 1980. By 1955 seven air routes had been established for the Greensboro-High Point Airport, and in

1958 a terminal was constructed with federal funds. Plans to modernize all airport facilities were drawn up during the 1970s, and a $60 million terminal complex, designed to serve one million passengers a year, was begun in 1980.

Since 1950 medical facilities have created a new service industry for the city, and area residents depend on Greensboro as a health center. On February 25, 1953, Moses H. Cone Memorial Hospital admitted its first patients. A memorial to Cone, who died in 1908, the $10-million facility was financed by a trust fund endowed by his wife Bertha Lindau Cone, who died in 1947, and other members of Cone's family. By 1971 Cone Hospital employed more than 1,000 people, and its existence made a municipal hospital unnecessary.

In 1959 community leaders began raising funds to rebuild Wesley Long Hospital, and a new 220-bed facility was built on Elam Avenue. In 1965 a new L. Richardson Memorial Hospital was dedicated, and in 1978 Greensboro Hospital became the city's fourth modern facility.

Educational facilities also continued to expand and change. During the presidency of Dr. Lewis Dowdy (1964-1980), A & T spent more than $30 million in construction and added a number of programs, including computer science, urban affairs, and transportation, and an African Heritage Center was established. In 1967 the general assembly created four regional universities, and A & T

Above left: In 1954 the Episcopal Church of the Redeemer was condemned as part of an urban renewal project. Constructed in 1927 at the intersection of East Market and Dudley streets, the church had been a focal point in the black community. Much of the surrounding neighborhood was also destroyed. Courtesy, Department of Housing and Community Development, City of Greensboro

Above right: East Market Street was more than a business district; it was the center of the black community. Businesses, churches, dance halls and restaurants were located along Market. One clothing store, owned by Ralph Johns, was the site of many conversations about proposed student demonstrations against segregation. Courtesy, Greensboro Redevelopment Office

became the North Carolina Agricultural & Technical State University. WCUNC continued to expand, becoming the largest women's college in the United States in 1959; during 1963–1964 it became the University of North Carolina at Greensboro, a coeducational institution. Two private preparatory schools for blacks closed, Immanuel Lutheran College in 1961 and Palmer Institute in 1971.

While manufacturing and service industries continued to grow, Greensboro's downtown retail trade became a casualty of the volatile 1960s and the more mobile, suburban 1970s. After struggling to stay in business, three Elm Street department stores closed within a three-year period: Belk's in 1975, Thalhimer's in 1976, and Meyer's (Jordan Marsh) in 1978. S & H Kress Co. also closed, leaving a fourth large building empty, and a number of small establishments folded as business dwindled. Another blow came when Sears built its new store in Friendly Shopping Center, which had grown to include more than 100 shops.

The large hotels were early casualties of the decline of downtown. In 1961 the King Cotton's occupancy rate was only 20 percent, and in 1965 the hotel closed. It reopened as a rooming house in 1967 but became a trouble spot for the police and fire departments. The O. Henry suffered a similar fate. Motels were

springing up across America, and The Oaks, built on seven acres on Summit Avenue, opened in 1953. Other motels were soon constructed on major highways leading into the city. Some favorite eating spots also closed: the Mayfair Cafeteria in 1967, the S & W Cafeteria in 1975, and Meyer's Tea Room and Coffee Shop in 1978.

The final blow for downtown as a retail center was the creation of multilevel enclosed malls surrounded by thousands of parking spaces. Four Seasons opened in 1974, and 18 months later Carolina Circle was completed. Even Friendly Center added an enclosed mall, Forum VI. The impact of the shopping centers was swift and obvious. In 1972 there were 215 retail establishments downtown, employing 2,802 people, with total sales of $93 million. In 1977 there were 139 establishments employing 926 people, and sales had dropped to $41 million, while sales at Friendly totaled $72.5 million and those at Four Seasons totaled $55.4 million. By 1980 there were 31 neighborhood centers and three regional centers competing with the Elm Street merchants.

Boosters of downtown searched for alternatives to the retail trade. Led by Mayor Jim Melvin, the city council proposed a bond issue to build a convention center, but on October 9, 1979, the $7.5-million proposal was defeated.

Below left: Anita Meares (Rivers) was photographed on an East Market Street sidewalk around 1917. The drugstore behind her is indicative of the black business district that had developed along East Market. Its growth was stimulated by the development of North Carolina A&T State University. Courtesy, Mrs. Anita M. Rivers

Below right: Solomon Monroe Hill owned a grocery store on East Market Street as early as 1906. It was a popular stop for A & T students. Mr. Hill later operated a branch of the post office from his store. When a new central post office was constructed on East Market during the 1960s, many black-owned businesses were relocated to clear the site. Courtesy, Mrs. Carrye Hill Kelley

A more promising project involved the use of public funds to stimulate private investment. Using its power of eminent domain and the last of its federal redevelopment dollars, the city purchased a tract of land that included the O. Henry Hotel and other early North Elm Street buildings, which were razed in 1979. The city then sold the land to Southern Life Insurance Company, which announced plans for a $30-million complex and began construction of the first building, completed in 1980. The Southern Life Center gave the downtown district a new focal point and the city a new source of tax revenue.

Development of City Government

In 1951 Dr. William Hampton was elected as the first black member of the Greensboro City Council; he received 54 percent of the votes cast, proving his acceptability to blacks and whites, and was reelected in 1953. Black representatives since then have included Waldo Falkener (1959-1963), Jimmie Barber (1969-1981), and Vance Chavis (1967-1971).

Hampton's election in 1951 coincided with the defeat of the first woman to serve on council. Juliette Dwiggins had been elected in 1949 and served only two years. Another female was not elected until 1967 when Mary Seymour won a council seat. Reelected three times, she ran unsuccessfully for mayor in 1975. Other councilwomen elected before 1980 include Lois McManus, Joanne Bowie, and Dorothy Bardolph.

A 1972 referendum instituted direct election of the mayor by the voters, rather than by the city council, but council members were elected at large until 1983. Proposals to reinstitute a ward system for council representation, which existed from 1870 until 1911, were defeated in 1968, 1969, 1975, and 1980, but the 1980 referendum failed by only 315 votes.

Other controversial issues submitted to the voters have included alcohol control and "blue laws." In 1951 Greensboro voters adopted the Alcoholic Beverage Control (ABC) system for liquor sales; in 1979 they approved a "liquor by the drink" proposal. Local "blue laws" were

The 1952 city council included its first black member, Dr. William Hampton. Dr. Hampton, a physician, came to North Carolina in 1938. Involved with many Greensboro civic organizations, the popular councilman served a second term and later served on the Greensboro board of education. Mayor Robert H. Frazier, fourth from right, had a special interest in historic preservation and worked unsuccessfully to save Bellemeade and successfully to save Blandwood from destruction. Courtesy, Greensboro Public Library.

The board of directors of Security National Bank of Greensboro met for the last time in May 1960. Mr. C.M. Vanstory, Jr., standing in the center, became chairman of the board of the new North Carolina National Bank (N.C.N.B.), formed when Security merged with a Charlotte bank. Vanstory served until 1966, but his efforts to establish headquarters in Greensboro were unsuccessful. Today, N.C.N.B. is the Bank of America. (GHM)

largely suspended during World War II as a concession to the Army; beer could be purchased seven days a week, and Sunday movies were legal. In 1961 Greensboro chose to exempt itself from a strict state blue law, and residents could buy almost anything after church time (1:00 p.m.) on Sunday. In 1970 voters rejected a proposal that would have increased Sunday restrictions, but the issue would not die.

Social Change

The major social issue after 1950 was, of course, racial integration. Black citizens, who made up approximately 30 percent of the city's population, finally won representation on the city council in 1951 and the school board in 1954, but segregation was practiced by a majority of institutions and establishments. The Greensboro chapter of the NAACP doubled its membership and, led by Edward Edmonds and George Simkins, attacked segregated facilities, including Lindley Park Pool, Gillespie Park Golf Course, hospitals, and schools; its weapons were lawsuits and the ballot.

On May 17, 1954, the U.S. Supreme Court ruled in *Brown v. Board of Education of Topeka* that segregated schools violated the "equal protection" clause of the Fourteenth Amendment. Greensboro had operated a segregated

system since 1875, and racial integration became the system's most significant concern. The school board immediately issued a resolution calling upon "the superintendent to study ...ways and means for complying" with the Court's decision—the first such resolution by a Southern school board.

At the state level, Governor William Umstead named an advisory committee to study the situation, but the state board of education voted to continue segregation for the 1954-1955 school year. The Catholic bishop of North Carolina ordered integration of all parochial schools, and Greensboro's Notre Dame High accepted 17 black students in 1954. In July 1956 the North Carolina General Assembly adopted the Pearsall Plan, which permitted a local school unit that had been integrated to hold a referendum on closing its schools. It also proposed a constitutional amendment that would allow parents to withdraw children from integrated schools and receive private-school tuition aid from the state; the amendment was adopted in September. Greensboro Superintendent Ben L. Smith publicly opposed the Pearsall Plan, explaining, "I should rather fail in supporting a right cause than win in supporting a wrong one." Crosses were burned in his yard, and threats were made on his life.

On September 3, 1957, five black children enrolled at Gillespie Park, which became the first integrated elementary school in the southeastern United States. The next day Josephine Boyd, an honor student at Dudley, enrolled at Greensboro Senior High, where she graduated in the top 10 percent of the class of 1958. To some these transfers seemed a positive step toward integration, but others saw them as mere tokens, designed to maintain Greensboro's progressive image while preventing wholesale integration.

In 1958 Superintendent Smith resigned, a year past retirement age; he was given the Distinguished Citizens Award by the Chamber of Commerce, and Greensboro's fourth high school was named for him in 1962. Superintendent Philip Weaver was less aggressive about integration, and the school board was growing more conservative. Two parents, refused transfers in the fall of 1958, brought lawsuits against the local and state boards of education. In response, the Greensboro board merged Caldwell and Pearson Street schools to create one integrated facility, but it reassigned 435 white pupils and every white staff person to other schools. In October 1959 the cases were dismissed because the black children were attending the school requested, but Greensboro's black population had lost faith in school officials.

During 1962-1963 Gillespie Park, with 19 blacks, was the only integrated school in the city. When the board announced that first-grade pupils could register at any school, 239 enrolled for the 1963-1964 year. By fall of 1964 there were 16 integrated schools with 500 blacks enrolled with whites. In September 1965 the board allowed "freedom of choice" for all grades, and 120 students transferred.

In 1967 the Supreme Court ruled that "freedom of choice" plans were invalid unless integration was the goal. In February 1968 the Office of Civil Rights warned Greensboro that its progress in desegregating fell below reasonable expectations and that the school board

needed to act to eliminate its dual system. In April the Department of Health, Education, and Welfare found that Greensboro had 11 schools that could be racially identified and notified the board to submit integration plans. Superintendent Weaver and other board members continued to insist on "freedom of choice" as a valid plan, and in 1969 HEW ruled that Greensboro had failed to comply with the 1964 Civil Rights Act. As a result, the city lost more than one million dollars in federal funds.

On February 24, 1970, a lawsuit filed against the Greensboro School Board charged that the "freedom of choice" plan perpetuated a segregated school system. In April 1971, following a Supreme Court decision that upheld a Charlotte integration plan based on busing, Judge Edward Stanley of the U.S. Fourth District Court ordered Greensboro to prepare a plan for complete desegregation of the school system in 1971-1972.

With Chairman Al Lineberry, who was sympathetic to black concerns, and new board members including respected black leaders Walter Johnson and Otis Hairston, the school board accepted the challenge. It prepared an integration plan similar to one prepared by the NAACP; Judge Stanley accepted the NAACP plan with the board's approval. Greensboro's elementary schools were paired, while its upper schools were assigned geographic districts. Although busing would involve 57 percent of the students, 37 percent had actually been bused during the previous year.

Opposition to the integration plan came from whites and blacks, but a majority of leaders and citizens were determined to make it succeed. "It Will Work" was the motto adopted by those favoring a smooth transition to a unitary system. On Open House Day, 30,000 parents visited the schools their children would attend, and when school opened on August 26, there were no major problems. Dr. George Simkins, a long-time foe of segregation, remarked, "I feel so proud to say that I'm from Greensboro." Years later Dudley Flood, a state assistant superintendent of public instruction and a black, reported, "Without question, Greensboro is still looked to as the prototype of how to desegregate a school system."

The movement for racial integration was not limited to the school system. On February 1, 1960, four A&T students sat down to order at the Woolworth's lunch counter after purchasing items at other counters. They were not served and left the store after closing. On the following day 31 students arrived to "sit in"; the next day blacks occupied 63 of 66 seats. A suprising event occurred on February 4th when three students from the Woman's College (now UNCG) arrived and were given seats by counter-protesters. They refused service until those there before them had been served and their statement included the black students. When closing time came black students protected the white students as they left the store and were helped into a cab. By April 54 cities in nine states had had sit-in demonstrations. According to historian William Chafe, writing in 1979,

Monday, February 1, 1960, was a revolutionary day in Greensboro. Four A&T students, Ezell Blair, Jr., Franklin McCain, Joseph McNeil, and David Richmond, sat down at the Woodworth's segregated lunch counter. Blair and Richmond were Greensboro natives. This act by the Greensboro Four encouraged others to protest, and integration was on its way. McNeil, McCain, Bill Smith and Clarence Henderson, four of 31 protesting on day two, are featured in this photograph taken on February 2nd inside Woolworth's. Courtesy, J. Moebes

The Greensboro sit-ins constituted a watershed in the history of America. Although similar demonstrations had occurred before, never in the past had they prompted such a volcanic response. The Greensboro "Coffee Party" of 1960, as one observer noted, would rank in history with the Boston Tea Party as a harbinger of revolutionary shifts in the social order.

White hecklers were present after the second day, including some members of the Ku Klux Klan, which had organized in Greensboro in 1957. Tension grew as the sit-in was extended to the Kress store, and on February 6 both stores were closed "in the interest of public safety." The A & T student body accepted a two-week moratorium which was extended, and on February 23 the lunch counters were reopened without incident. Mayor George Roach appointed an advisory committee to work out a peaceful solution, but merchants refused to cooperate, and on April 1, 1960, the demonstrations resumed. On April 12 blacks launched an economic boycott of downtown stores, and on April 21, 45 young blacks sitting at the Kress lunch counter were arrested for trespassing.

Deteriorating business conditions weakened white opposition to desegregation, and Woolworth Manager C.L. Harris indicated a willingness to integrate if other businesses would agree. On July 26, 1960, several black employees ate meals at the Woolworth counter, and within a week 300 blacks had been served. Guilford Dairy Bar, Meyer's, and Kress integrated their counters without further protest.

During the 1960s black leaders continued to press for equal representation in government and integration of public facilities. In 1962 Dr. George Simkins succeeded in desegregating Moses H. Cone and Wesley Long hospitals. A federal judge ruled that as public agencies they could not violate the "equal protection" clauses in the U.S. Constitution, a decision that affected hospitals across America.

The Congress of Racial Equality (CORE) formed a Greensboro chapter in the summer of 1962, and members participated in a national drive to desegregate interstate restaurants. When colleges reopened, students picketed the S & W and Mayfair cafeterias, and 48 were arrested in November. Black activists had a new goal.

On May 11, 1963, 30 students picketed McDonald's on Summit Avenue, and the Greensboro Men's Club, an organization of leading black business and professional men, wrote a letter supporting the students' actions. The protests moved downtown, as students demonstrated at cafeterias and theaters. By May 18 more than 900 students had been arrested, jail facilities were filled, and the old polio hospital had become a temporary prison.

On May 19, 1963, James Farmer, national CORE leader, came to Greensboro and urged black adults to participate in future demonstrations. On May 22, hundreds of students and more than 50 adults marched silently through downtown. The following day, 1,200 marched, and many were arrested. On June 5 A & T student-body president Jesse Jackson led 700 people to Jefferson Square and City Hall where they lay down in the streets. The next day Jackson was arrested for inciting to riot.

On June 7, at a meeting of business and community leaders, Mayor David Schenck summarized the city's position:

> We recognize the right under law of the property owner or business proprietor to use his property and conduct his business in any fashion he chooses, so long as public safety and morals are not violated.
>
> But how far must your city government and your fellow businessmen go to protect that right? Must the business of downtown Greensboro be disrupted ... to enforce your private business decision?
>
> I say to you who own and operate places of public accommodation in the city...

> that now is the time to throw aside the shackles of past custom.
>
> Selection of customers by race is outdated, morally unjust and not in keeping with either democratic or Christian philosophy.

By June 13, eight restaurants, three motels, and four theaters had been integrated, and on June 18 blacks were served at the S & W. By the end of August, four bowling alleys had been desegregated and a black family had moved into a "white" public-housing project. There were other positive changes for the black community. In 1967 Dr. John Marshall Stevenson (now Kilimanjaro), an A & T professor and one of the adult protestors, established the *Carolina Peacemaker* as an alternative newspaper. Its initial goals were to achieve an integrated society and to develop a strongpower base within the black community. At the Chamber of Commerce Hal Sieber worked to make that organization more inclusive, and Lewis Dowdy, chancellor at A & T, became the first black to serve on the board of directors.

In 1968 Cecil Bishop, a black minister, was appointed chairman of the Greensboro Housing Authority and Henry Frye, a lawyer, was elected to the North Carolina House of Representatives, the first black to serve in the state legislature since 1899. Frye served six terms and in 1974 became chairman of the Guilford delegation; in 1980 he was elected to the North Carolina Senate.

On April 4, 1968, civil-rights leader Dr. Martin Luther King, Jr., was assassinated in Memphis, Tennessee, on a day he planned to be in Greensboro. Three hundred students demonstrated by marching downtown. Tempers flared, and demonstrators began throwing rocks and breaking windows. The police maintained control, but Mayor Carson Bain requested mobilization of the National Guard. The next day violence erupted on the A & T campus. Shots were fired at students from a passing car, and when police and National Guards-

In 1973 Major Norman McDaniel returned to Greensboro where his wife lived during his seven-year imprisonment by the North Vietnamese. Courtesy, Jim Stratford

men arrived, snipers opened fire, wounding three policemen. The police responded with tear gas, and on April 6 Mayor Bain declared a curfew and banned demonstrations, angering many blacks who blamed the presence of the National Guard for the escalating violence.

In May 1969 an incident at Dudley Senior High erupted into another violent confrontation between black protesters and the police department assisted by the National Guard. Claude Barnes, a Dudley student who planned to run for student council president, was declared ineligible by a faculty-student committee. When he received enough write-in votes to win but was denied the presidency, Barnes approached A & T student and black-power advocate Nelson Johnson for advice. Events of the next 19 days divided Greensboro into two camps, and Mayor Jack Elam finally asked for National Guard support. On the night of May 21, 1969, Willie Grimes, an A & T student, was shot and killed. Many citizens, white and black, were shocked at the outcome of the escalating confrontation between the "extremism" of black power and the "law and order" stance of Greensboro's white officialdom.

Ten years later Nelson Johnson was a leader in the Worker's Viewpoint Organization (later renamed the Communist Worker's Party). The organization's goal was to improve the lives of workers, especially those in area Cone mills, by strengthening union groups. It chose to work with blacks.

The Ku Klux Klan was known to oppose blacks, unions and communists, and on July 8, 1979, WVO demonstrators challenged the Klan at a recruiting meeting in China Grove, NC. The following November when the WVO planned a labor rally and march, Klansmen and Nazis informed of the plan gathered to challenge the WVO. On October 30 Johnson picked up a parade permit which stated that it would begin at noon at the Everitt-Carver streets intersection in Morningside Homes, a working-class black neighborhood; it specified that the demonstrators could not be armed. WVO leaflets announced protesters should gather at 11 a.m. at Windsor Community Center, a half-mile away.

A Klan informant picked up a copy of the permit and notified Klansmen. As they and their Nazi allies formed a caravan on the morning of Novermber 3rd, a tenth car containing a police officer and photographer followed and were to stay in touch with police units assigned to the march. The police had developed a "low-profile" strategy although some local and federal officials had been warned of potential violence.

Morningside residents, joined by organizers, reporter and film crews, began gathering around eleven near the parade starting point. At 11:23 nine vehicles containing Klansmen and Nazis drove into the area and began verbally assaulting the crowd. Shots were fired from the caravan, and demonstrators attacked the vehicles with sticks. Within 88 seconds four protesters had been killed and ten wounded. Those killed, plus a fifth person who died the following day, were prominent activists. Two of the protesters fired small weapons in response to the attack. All of this happened before police officer arrived and arrested fourteen people, including Nelson Johnson and Wilena Cannon of the WVO. The demonstrators immediately charged the police with contributing to the killings. On November 5th fourteen members of the Klan or American Nazi Party were arrested on criminal charges including murder and conspiracy to commit murder. Other arrests would follow.

A peaceful funeral march was held on November 11; 400 marched while nearly 1,000 armed guards and 100 reporters watched. Another peaceful anti-Klan march, held in Greensboro on February 2, 1980, drew 7,500 participants. In April 1980 the US Justice Department exonerated the Greensboro Police Department of any wrongdoing on November 3, and in May six CWP workers, four from Greensboro, were arrested on felony riot charges. The trial of six Klan and Nazi defendants began on June 16, 1980. On November 17, 1980 all six defendants were acquitted, and on November 28 charges against the others were dropped. Since the shootings had been videotaped and shown on television, many people were shocked. Additional trials were held in 1983 and 1985; the last one resulted in a financial settlement for one victim's family.

Headlines about a Communist threat had appeared in Greensboro newspapers 25 years earlier when Junius Irving Scales, son of real-estate developer A.M. Scales, was tried under the Smith Act, which prohibited membership in an organization that advocated the overthrow of the United States government. His 1954 conviction was overturned on a technicality, but he was tried and convicted again in 1958, and in 1961 the Supreme Court, in a five to four decision, upheld the conviction, ruling the Smith Act constitutional. Scales began serving a six-year term in October 1961. Many prominent Americans, including Paul Green, Reinhold Niebuhr, Martin Luther King, C. Vann Woodward, and Saul Bellow, petitioned for his release, which was granted on December 24, 1962, by President John F. Kennedy.

Controversy and street demonstrations also surrounded America's involvement in Vietnam, where 52 Greensboro residents fought and died. Included in that number was Phill G. McDonald who moved to Greensboro from his native West Virginia and was drafted in 1967. On June 7, 1968, he sacrificed his life to save his ambushed platoon. On April 7, 1970, President Nixon presented the Congressional Medal of Honor to him posthumously, and he became the only Greensboro recipient to have won the highest-ranked and best-known decoration of the United States. Other local men were wounded or taken prisoner, and Norman McDaniel, an A & T graduate, was imprisoned for seven years. His moral and spiritual support to other POWs earned him the nickname "the chaplain of the Hanoi Hilton." Meanwhile, citizens who believed that the United States should not be involved in the war conducted weekly peace vigils at the Federal Building, lining the sidewalks at the Market-Eugene intersection to silently voice their convictions. A permanent memorial to local casualties in Vietnam stands today in the Governmental Center Plaza.

The doorway to the
Greensboro Historical
Museum is guarded
by a pair of cast-iron
lions that were orig-
inally purchased for
Bellemeade. After
Bellemeade was razed
in 1953 the lions were
relocated, and now
they complement the
museum's turn-of-the-
century facade.

Left: Three rooms from an elegant house built in Greensboro in 1867 have been re-created at the Greensboro Historical Museum. The dining room and parlor from Bellemeade, the Henry Humphreys Tate house, are furnished with original furniture, family portraits, and accessories. The Tate's son Tom was a good friend of young Will Porter, the future O. Henry. From *Southern Living,* 1980

Facing Page: Dolley Payne Todd Madison rose from her Greensboro beginnings to become the nation's First Lady. This portrait of Dolley Madison, attributed to John Vanderlyn after a portrait by Gilbert Stuart, is a focal point in the Greensboro Historical Museum's exhibit about her. A Dolley Madison Memorial Association donated the portrait, along with a number of other items, to the museum in 1963. (GHM)

Below: These watercolor paintings of John and Nancy Logan were done by an unknown folk artist in the 1820s. They reveal decorative details of the times, including wall treatments and furnishings. Logan, who lived until 1853, was a merchant and a militia officer who raised troops for the Mexican War. (GHM)

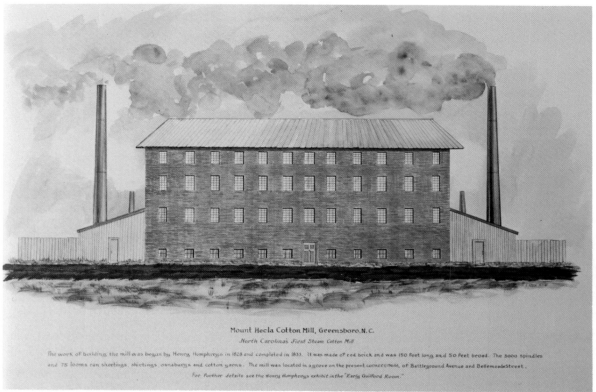

Mount Hecla Cotton Mill, Greensboro, N.C.

North Carolina's First Steam Cotton Mill

The work of building the mill was begun by Henry Humphreys in 1828 and completed in 1833. It was made of red brick and was 150 feet long and 50 feet broad. The 3000 spindles and 75 looms ran sheetings, shirtings, osnaburgs and cotton yarns. The mill was located in a grove on the present connection, of Battleground Avenue and Bellemeade Street.

For further details see the Henry Humphreys exhibit in the "Early Guilford Room."

The first steam cotton mill in North Carolina was built by Greensboro entrepreneur Henry Humphreys between 1828 and 1830. Called the Mount Hecla Mill, the building stood at the corner of Bellemeade and Greene streets from 1828 to the 1850s. (GHM)

This colored lithograph of the Johnston surrender on April 26, 1865, locates the scene "near Greensboro N.C." The generals actually met near Durham, approximately 40 miles away, which was halfway between the Union Army at Raleigh and the Confederate Army at Greensboro. (GHM)

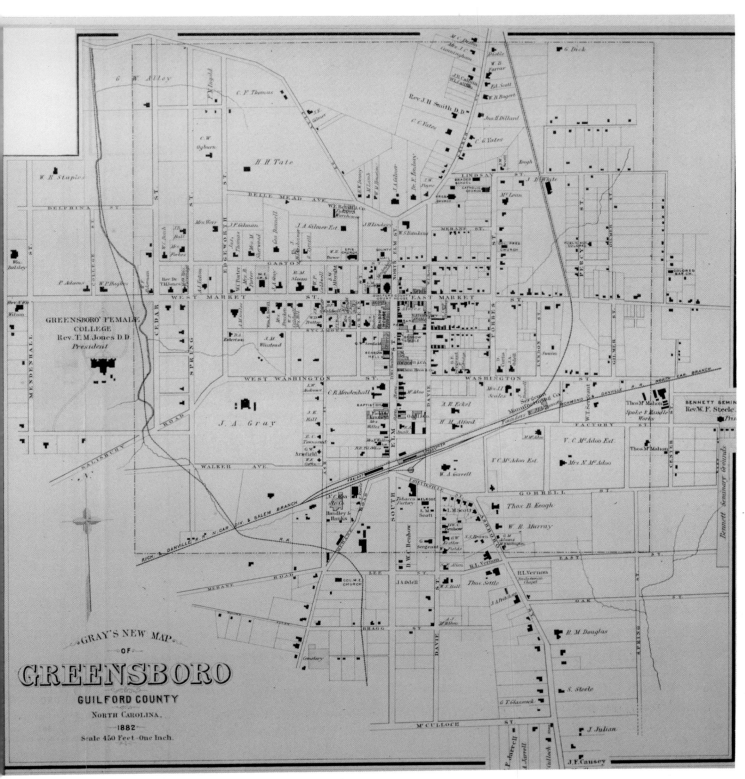

GRAY'S NEW MAP
-OF-
GREENSBORO
GUILFORD COUNTY
NORTH CAROLINA,
-1882-
Scale 450 Feet -One Inch.

By 1882 there were 30 streets within the Greensboro city limits; all were dirt except Elm, which had replaced Market as the primary business street. Schools, churches, factories, and railroad tracks are clearly indicated on this map, and the identified residences are links to early Greensboro residents. (GHM)

OCTOBER 1908
FIRST HALF

EVERYTHING

AN ORIGINAL PUBLICATION DEALING WITH THE THINGS WHICH HAPPEN AS THE BUSY WORLD SPINS ROUND

The Presidential Programme Up-to-Date—A Little Talk on Taft's Banking Ideas—The Circus Tent Fashion Business—The Ship That Never Passed—Old John Writes a Book—Other Stuff Worth While.

10 CENTS A COPY $2.00 A YEAR

BY AL FAIRBROTHER
GREENSBORO N. C.
ESTABLISHED MAY 1902

Frohn

On left
Smith Memorial Building
On right
1st Presbyterian Church.
Greensboro, N. C.

Above: In 1909 itinerant artist Harper Bond completed a 4x45-foot mural of a Southern passenger train. Bond worked where the painting was to be hung, in the Clegg Hotel Coffee Shop, while customers below watched. The mural is now on display in the Greensboro Historical Museum. (GHM)

Facing page: *Everything,* a semi-monthly literary magazine, was published in Greensboro by Colonel Al Fairbrother. (GHM)

Center: The third building used by the First Presbyterian Church from 1892 until 1928 replaced a structure on the same site which had served as a Civil War hospital. This Romanesque Revival structure stood vacant until 1937, when its conversion to a civic center was begun. (GHM)

Bottom: A & M College moved to Greensboro from Raleigh in 1893. The pictured multipurpose building and a dormitory were constructed with $10,000 from the General Assembly. The building has since been replaced, and the campus has grown into North Carolina A & T State University. (GHM)

South Elm St., from Court Square, **Greensboro, N. C.**

This postcard view of South Elm Street from Courthouse Square was taken after 1903. It shows Greensboro's transition from a village to a city. South Elm became the main business artery at the turn of the century. (GHM)

The main building at Greensboro Female College was rebuilt after a fire in 1863, only to burn again in 1904. Shown on an incline known as "Piety Hill" is the multi-purpose building. The dirt road on the left became College Avenue, which ends at McGee Street, named for Lucy McGee Jones. (GHM)

SOUTH ELM STREET, GREENSBORO, N. C.

The electric car system began in Greensboro in 1902, and these tracks divided South Elm Street. Within a decade 12 miles of track reached through the city. The tower of the McAdoo house is visible on the left. (GHM)

In April 1985 the city hosted its first O. Henry Festival, designed to honor the writer born in Guilford County in 1862. Literary, artistic and theatrical events were staged during the week. A highlight was the unveiling of a three-part bronze sculpture created by Maria Kirby-Smith. The triangle design features full-size statues of the writer and a dog with an oversized open book. It is located near the intersection of North Elm and Bellemeade streets in a plaza adjacent to the U.S. Trust Building. Courtesy, City of Greensboro

Right: The "new" First Presbyterian Church in Fisher Park, built in 1928 with Gothic features, is the fourth building the congregation has used. The third building now houses the Greensboro Historical Museum. (Windsor)

Left: *The Student*, a life-size bronze statue, commemorates the young men who attended David Caldwell's Log College between 1767 and 1800. It stands in the David Caldwell Memorial Park (established in 1976), which includes approximately 20 acres of the Caldwell's 18th century plantation. (GHM)

The Francis McNairy log house was built around 1780, and moved to the Mary Lynn Smith Richardson Memorial Park in 1967 and restored. Its furnishings and exhibits cover a century, from 1762-1862. From *Southern Living,* 1980

Center left: The William Fields house on Arlington Street has been restored to its former Gothic Revival glory. It is a rare Greensboro structure, built before 1879. Once the parsonage for Centenary Methodist Church, it was preserved by a local antique dealer. (GHM)

Center right: The Gatekeeper's House at Green Hill Cemetery was built during the 1880s. Listed on the National Register of Historic Places, it is North Carolina's only surviving Victorian gate keeper's residence. The house was to be torn down, when it was purchased in 1978 for $23,000. Restoration, which cost over $70,000, saved this singular building. (GHM)

Blandwood, residence of Governor John Motley Morehead, was purchased by the Greensboro Preservation Society in 1968, restored as a house museum, and formally dedicated in 1976. Located at 400 West Washington Street, the house resembles a Tuscan villa; its arcades were designed to blend two dependencies with the mansion. (GHM)

Left: This postcard view of Elm Street in 1955 captures the bustling spirit of the decade. Shoppers, businessmen, and office workers filled the sidewalks, and traffic clogged the principal streets. Neon signs advertised stores, theaters, and restaurants. Courtesy, Greensboro Public Library

Right: A bust of Edward R. Murrow is located on the southwest corner of Friendly Avenue and Murrow Boulevard. Murrow, born in Guilford County in 1908, became famous as a radio and television commentator. His on-the-scene reports during World War II and the Korean War brought those conflicts into America's living rooms. Pearson Street was renamed for Murrow in 1970. (GHM)

This 1990 view of Green Valley Office Park, taken from the northeast, shows Green Valley Road with the Medical Arts Center and Women's Hospital on the left and the new Prudential and Piedmont Natural Gas buildings on the right. By 1997 the park was a top commercial real estate location as Starmount partnered with and sold to other firms for new buildings. (GHM)

Left: On February 1, 1980, a state historic marker was erected on North Elm Street, two blocks from Woolworth's. The four men who as students had begun the "sit-ins," returned to participate in the ceremony. Ezell Blair, Jr., David Richmond, Franklin McCain, and Joseph McNeil took a risk and began a movement toward integration. Courtesy, Jim Stratford

Right: The new Central Library opened on October 31, 1998, three years after the Glenwood branch was completed for $1.4 million. At Central "The Tree of Knowledge," created by sculptor William Donnan and centered under the skylight dome, is a focal point, as is Michael Brown's mural of historical figures. Central Library was designed by Patrick Deaton of J. Hyatt Hammond Associates, Inc. Courtesy, Aerial Photography Services

The Washington Wall Street Mural Park was a downtown feature from 1981 until 2000. This crowd is part of the 1984 Fun Fourth Festival. The mural was painted on a brick surface that was originally an interior wall, and continued to deteriorate. The owner of the adjacent building purchased the wall and park from the City and created shops and Liberty Oaks restaurant. The park remains as a condition of the sale.(GHM)

Top left: The Greater Greensboro Open Golf Tournament, a project of the Greensboro Jaycees, began in 1938. It has been played at Sedgefield and Starmount country clubs, but in 1977 the GGO was moved to Forest Oaks. Lanny Watkins, shown here, is a popular and regular participant. Courtesy, Greensboro Jaycees

Top right: Each September the Historical Museum sponsors "5 by O. Henry," a dramatic presentation of stories by one of Greensboro's best known authors. The series began in 1987 with a grant from the Grassroots Arts Program of the NC Arts Council to coincide with the 125th anniversary of O. Henry. Joe Hoesl has been the writer/producer from the beginning. The 2000 production features many characters including (left to right) Matthew Bradshaw, Kathy Andren and John Collier. (GHM)

Bottom: Greensboro Country Park, in the northwest section of the city, was built with WPA funds during the Depression. A series of man-made lakes for swimming, boating, and fishing were included (swimming has been prohibited since the 1950s).

The Southern Life building on North Elm Street was completed in 1980 at a cost of $11.8 million. It has been called "a mural of Greensboro's skyline," with the 3,000 panes of glass that cover the structure reflecting color and light. Primary occupants of the building are Southern Life Insurance Company and Northwestern Bank. Courtesy, Southern Life Insurance Company

Bottom left: Green Hill Center for North Carolina Art, incorporated in 1974, is located in the downtown Greensboro Cultural Center. Established to showcase North Carolina arts, the gallery changes its exhibits frequently. Green Hill also sponsors ArtQuest, a unique interactive gallery to educate children in the visual arts. Courtesy, Green Hill Center for North Carolina Art

Bottom right: The Greensboro-Guilford County Governmental Center, designed by Eduardo Catalano, covers two blocks. This interior view of the Municipal Office Building features the interior courtyard and the exterior of the city council chamber, which is at the building's center. Courtesy, Public Information Office, City of Greensboro

A former car dealership building with 50,000 square feet of space and ample parking now houses the Greensboro Children's Museum. The logo, created by Graphica and fabricated by Carolina Steel, represents the infinite possibilities available inside. Designed by J. Hyatt Hammond Associates, the building was renovated by Lomax Construction with Moser Mayer Phoenix as engineering consultants. Courtesy, Greensboro Children's Museum

Bottom right: The Millennium Gate, an interactive bronze and steel sculpture standing 18 feet high, features icons designed by 17 area artists to represent major developments and people in world, national and local history. Designed by Jim Gallucci and constructed in his studio, the gate was dedicated in a community event on December 30, 2000. Courtesy, Charles Lowe Photography

Bottom left: The Greensboro Symphony Orchestra, conducted and directed by Stuart Malino since 1996, is a valuable cultural resource. It began as a college-supported orchestra in 1939 and became an independent community orchestra in 1963. Concerts are staged at the War Memorial Auditorium. Courtesy, Greensboro Symphony Orchestra

This aerial view of downtown Greensboro taken from the northeast shows the develop-ment that took place in the 1980s. In the left corner the Historical Museum with its new wing is visible, the new office towers are in the center and the Marriott Hotel is on the right. Courtesy, City of Greensboro

Chapter Nine

A BRIDGE TO
THE MILLENNIUM
1981 - 2000

*D*uring the last two decades of the twentieth century the face of Greensboro changed in many ways. Physically it almost doubled in size, growing from nearly 61 to more than 113 square miles. The population increased from nearly 155,000 to more than 213,000 residents. The composition of its citizens was altered by a massive influx of people from many countries who chose to make the city their home. Leadership also emerged from non-traditional sources as a result of political action and development programs. Less positive was the shift from a manufacturing-based to a service-based economy, only because external factors dealt heavy blows to the textile/apparel, tobacco and furniture industries—the traditional employers in the region. The acquisition of old local companies by national and international firms presented additional challenges.

The city welcomed new and expanded business, cultural and entertainment facilities in its downtown area and throughout its boundaries. The airport drew firms to the northwest, Grandover Resort & Conference Center and Adams Farm attracted people to the southwest, Rock Creek Park and Stoney Creek made the southeast and northeast more viable for business and residential investors. Yet, there were issues about growth and a lack of growth, employer-employee relations and equality of treatment for all quadrants, and

Members of the 1983 City Council, the first elected under the 5-3-1 plan, included, left to right, Dorothy Bardolph, Jim Kirkpatrick, Earl Jones, Joanne Bowie, Mayor John Forbis, City Manager Tom Osborne, Lois McManus, Lonnie Revels, Katie Dorsett, and Cameron Cooke. Dorsett and Jones represented the two black-majority districts, and Revels, a Lumbee Indian, represented District Five. Courtesy, *News & Record*, Greensboro, NC, Dave Nicholson

a public education system forced to deal with merger, redistricting, bond issues and a changing enrollment.

These decades required new ways of looking at situations, communicating in open forums and distributing public and private funding. As the millennium approached Greensboro endeavored to transform itself.

Changes in City and County Government

In 1981 Councilman Jimmie Barber resigned after serving six consecutive terms, and an all-white council governed the city for the first time since 1969. Concerned citizens formed the Greensboro Dialogue Task Force and resurrected the idea of a district or ward system to ensure minority representation. Voters had rejected the district plan five times since 1968. This time proponents insisted on a city ordinance, and on December 16, 1982, the council voted on a district system to become effective in 1983. The 5-3-1 plan required the election of five representatives from districts with three representatives and the mayor elected at-large. Two of the established districts would have black majorities. This was the first fundamental change in city government since 1911 and the third major change in the twentieth century. Greensboro, now the third largest city in North Carolina,

was the state's last major city to adopt a district plan. On December 5, 1983, a new council was sworn in with black representatives from two districts and a Lumbee Indian from a third. Mayor John Forbis was reelected for a second term, and the other representatives had served one to four previous terms.

A second major change took place a decade later when Carolyn Allen became Greensboro's first female mayor, winning 59 percent of the vote. Running for the first time in 1989, she led the ticket to gain an at-large seat and was re-elected in 1991. She served three mayoral terms, retiring in 1999, the same year that Yvonne Johnson became the first black mayor pro tem. Johnson also had become the first black elected to an-large seat under the district plan in 1995.

Greensboro, continuing to operate under the city council-manager plan, had three managers during the 1980s and 1990s. Tom Osborne, appointed in 1973, served until 1984; Bill Carstarphen served from 1984 until 1995; and current manager Ed Kitchen was selected in 1996 after serving as assistant/deputy manager for a decade.

Voters also responded to bond issues proposed between 1981 and 2000 in ways that reflected increasing awareness of political power. In 1985 they rejected expanding the

Sylvester Daughtry, police chief from 1987 to 1998, also served as president of the International Association of Chiefs of Police (1993-1994). Greensboro was the first major NC city to appoint a black police chief. Daughtry, who joined the force in 1968, worked to place officers in neighborhood centers and in schools. Courtesy, City of Greensboro

complemented those of the Chamber of Commerce: Leadership Greensboro (1976), Leadership Seniors (1992) and Other Voices (1994). The application was strengthened by other facts, including the appointment of Greensboro's first African-American police chief (1987) and fire chief (1991).

As the county seat and largest city, Greensboro faced a number of controversies with neighboring towns, including expansion. Several decided to incorporate to prevent annexation, and disagreements were settled with Summerfield (incorporated 1996) and Pleasant Garden (incorporated 1997). Negotiations with High Point, Guilford's second largest city and NC's eighth, were also required, since the

two cities, once divided by sixteen miles. now had common boundaries.

Greensboro also shared some of its most-qualified leaders with the state, when Governor Jim Hunt appointed county commissioner Katie Dorsett to his cabinet and Senator Henry Frye to the supreme court. Dorsett, the first African-American female to serve in a cabinet position, became Secretary of the Department of Administration, and Frye became the first black to serve on the NC Supreme Court.

Economic Development

Both positive and negative changes occurred between 1981 and 2000. Downtown revitalization earned high marks and new projects included: the Sheraton Hotel ($26.5 million); First Citizens Bank ($3.5 million); SouthTrust Bank Plaza (approximately $7 million); Greensborough Court at Center Square ($20 million); Wrangler; a new general building; and three parking decks in 1998 groundbreakings were held for three skyscrapers: Renaissance Plaza, the Jefferson Pilot Building and First Union Tower. Their combined cost was $198 million, and the result was a new Greensboro skyline.

From left to right, Mayor Keith Holliday and mayors Carolyn Allen (1993-1999), Jim Melvin (1971–1981) and John Forbis (1981-1987) met for a joint interview in 2001. Vic Nussbaum (1987-1993) was too ill. All identified education as the most important current issue and listed earlier challenges as comprehensive planning, rezoning, wastewater treatment, district elections and the coliseum expansion. Courtesy, *News & Record*, Greensboro, NC, H. Scott Hoffmann

In 1993 Wrangler, the largest division of VF Corporation, announced plans to build a new four-story headquarters at North Elm and Lindsay streets. J. Hyatt Hammond designed the building to connect to the former headquarters building, and Matteson Construction Company was the general contractor for the 60,000 square foot building. The landscaped park area adds beauty to downtown, especially at Christmas. Courtesy, Mark Wagoner Productions

Greensborough Court was a three-phase undertaking by First Home Federal, Jefferson-Pilot and JMD Inc. with some federal funding for preservation. The initial plan was to renovate existing buildings along South Elm and Davie streets as apartments, but a 1985 fire required adding new units. In 1986 tenants moved into Phase 1, 46 apartments on Elm. Weaver Construction Co. managed the second phase that involved reconstructing three large buildings on Davie Street. The planned third phase, to convert the Guilford Building to high-rise apartments, never took place, and in 1988 the principal investors gave the building to the county. After considering several uses for the structure, the county sold it to an individual who has worked to convert it from the ground up.

This renovation project and others were a quick response to the 1982 listing of much of Greensboro's "main street" on the National Register of Historic Places. The historic district extends southward from the 100 block of North Elm to the Lee Street intersection and includes buildings on Davie, Washington and Greene streets. Historic designation is an honor, but it also provides tax credits for restorations. Renovation projects between 1982 and 2000 included a hotel and apartments, office buildings, entertainment centers and restaurants. In 1981 there were four families living downtown under the "night watchman"

clause of a 1977 ordinance. This number soon increased as new apartments were created over old buildings—21 by 1996. These residential projects and future ones were aided by zoning changes and an improved economy.

In 1982 investors purchased the old Greenwich Hotel at 111 West Washington Street with plans to create a first-class hotel emphasizing service. A chain purchased the restored hotel (1983) and changed its name to The

Construction of the Jefferson-Pilot Building began in 1988 and ended in 1990. The company moved 600 people from its Sedgefield building to join 900 already working downtown. The new building joins the 1923 structure and houses the City Club on the top two floors. It has been described as one of the great new buildings in America. The biggest downtown spending period in decades ended in 1991 with the completion of this building plus the Renaissance Plaza and First Union Tower, three parking garages, $1 million in streetscape projects, and renovations to the Carolina Theatre, Cultural Center and Historical Museum. (GHM)

The Greenwich (now Biltmore) Hotel, built in 1903 as headquarters for the Cone Export & Commission Company, became a rooming house after the original owners moved to new headquarters on Greene Street in 1924. It was first restored in 1983 and is still a popular specialty hotel with 25 rooms and a long history. (GHM)

Biltmore in 1992. Other buildings took on new identities and avoided destruction. The 1927 train station became a teen and then special event center managed by non-profit groups; current plans are to use it as part of a modern multi-modal transportation center. Belk's, empty since 1975, was refurbished as a bank and office complex in 1983, and the J.W. Scott Building (1902) became office condominiums in 1987. Another 1987 transformation took place when VF Corp. sold the 1916 Blue Bell Plant No. 1 at South Elm and Lee to investors who converted the facility into The Old Greensborough Gateway Center. It houses a variety of businesses and non-profit groups. The First Union Bank Building went through a $2 million renovation to become the Greensboro Public Interest Center in 1993, and a 1926 Atlantic service station became Macado's restaurant in 1994.

In June 1982 much of downtown, including the 100 block of North Elm and South Elm to Lee Street and appropriate structures on adjacent streets, was listed on the National Register. The Old Greensborough Preservation Society prepared the application approved by the NC Department of Cultural Resources. The state department said that the area "contains a number of excellent examples of the different types of commercial architecture that were popular from 1895 to 1930." Among the buildings was the Salvation Army headquarters at 500 S. Elm built in 1928 and renovated by Broach and Company in 1986. The former chapel now houses the Broach, a non-profit professional theatre. (GHM)

In 1983 Preservation Greensboro reconstructed the Blandwood Mansion dependencies, completing the restoration begun in 1967. The house is one of two National Historic Landmarks in Guilford County.

There were downtown losses also, as firms closed and buildings were razed. In 1983 Blue Bell purchased the Bishop Block (1951) and eventually removed it. Maxwell's Furniture, Wright's Clothing and the Greensboro Coffee Shop, all on South Elm, closed in 1983, and the Mantleworks Restaurant, opened in the 1970s to encourage downtown revitalization, closed in 1985. The 1990s brought the closings of Woolworth's (1994) and Southside Hardware (1995).

In 1985 the Chamber of Commerce urged the City to hire a professional to focus on downtown concerns, but a consulting firm was hired instead. It recommended that the mini-mall on Elm Street (1973) be removed and that two-way traffic and parking be restored. In 1986 business leaders formed Downtown Greensboro Incorporated (DGI), donating $300,000 in seed money. The first president of the non-profit was hired in 1997 to develop a long-range plan for revitalization and coor-

dinate support between private enterprise and local government. During Ed Wolverton's tenure, downtown gained 27 businesses, 72 jobs and $26 million in real estate development. In 1999 Ray Gibbs became president, and his agenda includes encouraging private investments, more residential, restaurant and commercial options, and stabilizing existing office space.

Two other groups working to improve specific areas are SEEDS (SouthEast Economic Developments, Inc.) formed in 1995, and the East Market Street Development Corporation (EMSDC) formed in 1997. In 1996 Greensboro voters approved a $1 million redevelopment bond for the East Market corridor, and EMSDC oversees the use of those funds. Two firms, Graphica and Moser Mayer Phoenix, have restored buildings in the 300 block of East Market, and the unsuccessful Cumberland Shopping Center has been razed. The space will be developed by Project Homestead, a non-profit community development corporation formed in 1991 to assist low-income families.

The efforts of the Greensboro Merchants Association (founded in 1908), the Greensboro Area Convention and Visitors Bureau (established in 1985), and Forward Guilford (created in 1993) promote downtown and the Greensboro region as good places to do business. Positive developments occurring across the city and county also impacted downtown.

In 1985 Starmount opened a spacious office park, replacing the Green Valley Golf Course (1928-1985). IBM was the first occupant, and other firms followed, including Lorillard Tobacco Co. In a reverse move SouthTrust Bank moved its Triad headquarters from Green Valley to a new building downtown in 1998.

The Koury Corporation created an even grander park and residential area in 1996. The Grandover Resort and Conference Center covers 1,500 acres in southwest Guilford County and includes golf courses, a $5 million clubhouse, a country club and a variety

Joe Bryan (1896-1995), an outstanding Greensboro philanthropist, is shown carrying a torch for the 1971 Special Olympics that he supported. Bryan came to Greensboro in 1931 after his marriage to the daughter of Julian Price who headed Jefferson Standard Life Insurance Co. He launched Jefferson's broadcasting division and is considered a founder of NC public television. In 1971 the City of Greensboro named a 1,500-acre park for Joe and Kathleen Bryan and half of his ashes are buried there. The Joseph M. Bryan Foundation, established in 1984 to handle his personal assets, is charged with caring for the park as well as promoting programs to improve economic, cultural and recreational enhancements for local residents. Courtesy, News & Record, Greensboro, NC

of housing options. When completed it will have 1,600 houses in 16 communities. Founder Joe Koury (1925-1998) transformed a vision into reality here and at Four Seasons with a mall and hotel in the 1970s and a convention center in 1990.

Shopping centers and residential areas, including Brassfield, Adams Farm and Benchmark Square, reflected Greensboro's growth in many directions. Another growth factor was the regional airport located in the northwest. A new airport terminal, six times larger than its predecessor, was completed in 1983 for $65 million, and the major runway was extended to 10,000 feet making it the longest in NC. The same year the Marriott Airport was completed on airport property, and in 1989 Embassy Suites was built nearby. In 1987 the facility was renamed Piedmont Triad International (PTI). In 1998 the airport was selected over five other locations for a Federal Express national hub. The debate over that decision continues, but not debated is the role that Ceasar Cone II and Stanley Frank played in developing the airport for Guilford County.

A drastic change in the local economy was reflected in the shift of jobs from manufac-turing to service-provider companies. Traditional apparel and textile companies were forced to restructure to meet competition, and in 1982 Cone Mills closed its Revolution plant (1898) and laid off 400 workers. When Cone, the fifth largest textile company in the U.S., was faced with a hostile takeover bid in 1984, it converted to a privately held company. In that same year Blue Bell managers and employees bought out the publicly held stock to end speculation about a takeover. In 1986 VF Corporation purchased the company, consolidated plants and laid off workers.

In 1987 Burlington Industries, the largest textile company in the world, became the target of a takeover attempt. Like Cone and Blue Bell it warded off the takeover by going private which required a $2.4 billion loan, selling off properties and divisions, and layoffs. Weakening hosiery sales due to imports and casual dress codes further hurt both Burlington and Kayser-Roth. During the 1990s Cone modernized its White Oak Plant and built a new corporate headquarters, but in 1998 Burlington, Cone and Guilford Mills suffered losses and looked to Mexico for new opportunities.

Joe Dudley, a self-made millionaire, still enjoys giving tours of his multi-million dollar complex in Kernersville, west of Greensboro. Born into poverty in eastern NC, he worked his way through NC A&T State University by selling Fuller's ethnic cosmetic products door-to-door. In 1967 Joe and Eunice Dudley opened a Fuller distributorship in Greensboro and in 1970 a beauty supply company on South Elm Street. They sold Fuller products as well as ones they manufactured. Joe Dudley was selected for a "Point of Light" award by President Bush in 1991 and for the prestigious Horatio Alger Award which recognizes people who have risen from modest circumstances to great success in 1995. He wrote his autobiography *Walking By Faith* in 1998. Courtesy, *News & Record*, Greensboro, NC, John Page

In 1934 Joe Bryan of Jefferson Standard Life Insurance Company acquired radio station WBIG. This was the first step toward creating Jefferson-Pilot Communications. First housed in the Jefferson Building, it operated at the O. Henry Hotel from 1934 until 1956 when it moved to a new building on Battleground Avenue. The decision to close the station in 1986 was based on its inability to compete with the more powerful FM stations in the region. The street entrance to the hotel studio is featured in this photograph. (GHM)

On September 8, 1996, a Town Meeting was held at the Greensboro Cultural Center—260 people anxious to discuss issues concerning the working poor and local working conditions attended. Panelists included the mayor, a representative of the Pulpit Forum, businessmen, and union and non-union workers. US Army Colonel Charles King was the facilitator. Members of the audience had an opportunity to ask questions and make comments, and selected spokespeople reflected on the discussion. The meeting ended with many hoping similar sessions would follow. Courtesy, *News & Record*, Greensboro, NC, James Parker

The tobacco industry was involved in a national struggle against new FDA regulations and lawsuits, but Lorillard's financial impact on Greensboro was positive. In 1995 the company built an $11 million distribution center here, and in 1997 moved its corporate headquarters to Greensboro from New York. It is still a major employer with more than 2,000 employees.

The 1980s attracted new companies. AB Volvo Truck Corporation came in 1981 and later constructed a permanent research and testing headquarters building. After forming a partnership with GM, Volvo built a communications and technical center in 1990. In 1982 Twinings Tea built a $6 million plant, and in 1985 American Express opened a credit card center that employed 2,500. Konica built a modern plant on Interstate 85 in 1988 and expanded it in 1996.

In 1991 the VF Corporation acquired Health-Tex, a children's apparel company with a good reputation and financial troubles. Wrangler's president took over at Health-Tex and relocated its headquarters to Greensboro. The company tripled in size after its acquisition. In 1998 VF, a Fortune 500 company, moved its headquarters to Greensboro.

RF Micro, started here in 1991, manufactures microchips for portable telephones. Sales increased to $17 million within four years, and the company built a $70 million plant near the airport in 1997. Lucent Technologies, formed in 1996 when AT&T restructured to form three companies, also manufactures communication devices. Another local firm Replacements Ltd., begun by Bob Page in 1981, is the largest supplier of obsolete china, silver and crystal in the world.

Other new firms include: Shionogi & Co., a major pharmaceutical manufacturer (1994); Highland Tank & Manufacturing Co. (1994); and Dana Corporation (1996). Existing companies expanded: Proctor & Gamble and Allen-Bradley built new plants; Halstead Industries moved its headquarters from Pennsylvania; and K-mart built a distribution warehouse.

New owners acquired old companies: Carolina Steel Corporation, Richardson-Vicks, USA (by Proctor & Gamble), Gilbarco and Dillard Paper Company.

Liberty Life Insurance Company purchased Southern Life in 1986 and transferred many of its employees to SC. The company skyscraper became the NC Trust Center, named for its largest tenant, a company founded in 1983 to offer comprehensive services to investors. U.S. Trust acquired North Carolina Trust in 2000.

In 1986 WBIG, one of NC's oldest radio stations, went off the air and in 1987 the Gannett Company purchased WFMY-Channel 2 for $155 million. Financial changes included the startup of a dozen new banks, BB&T's acquisition of Gate City Savings & Loan, Southern National's (now BB&T) acquisition of Community Bank, and the 1993 dissolution of First Home Federal Savings & Loan Association, Greensboro's oldest financial institution.

Friendly mergers occurred when Jefferson Standard (1907) and Pilot (1903) life insurance companies joined to become Jefferson-Pilot Life Insurance Co. in 1987, and when Moses Cone Memorial and Wesley Long Community hospitals combined to create Moses Cone Health System in 1996. The system included The Women's Hospital (previously Humana), purchased and converted by Cone in 1988.

There were many changes for area shoppers. The Fresh Market opened in 1982, Four Seasons Mall added a third floor in 1987, Friendly Shopping Center began a transformation in 1994, Sears closed its catalog merchandise center, the State Street shops opened in 1983, and downtown retail stores closed.

The most troublesome economic issue originated at the Kmart Distribution Center that opened in 1992. In 1993 workers voted to unionize but contract negotiations stalled. Neither a sit-in during the 1994 Kmart GGO nor a strike resulted in a contract. In 1995 the Pulpit Forum, an organization of black ministers, threatened a regional boycott of Kmart facilities if wage and working conditions were not addressed. When evidence that

local workers were paid less than workers at other centers was presented, Kmart responded that its pay equaled that of other local companies and was partially based on longevity. Demonstrations and arrests at Kmart's Super Center followed. By February 1996 the city had spent more than $40,000 in overtime pay for police and there were 125 people to prosecute, including ministers, state representatives and white college students. Only after the Chamber of Commerce released a Triad wage study placing Kmart at the low end of the scale did negotiations resume.

In an interesting twist, the national NAACP met in May and recognized Kmart for two decades of support through seeking out black suppliers and purchasing $800 million in goods. When made aware of the local situation, the NAACP recognized eight of the Kmart protesters.

In June, when the NLRB hearings were held, Kmart decided to settle before a ruling was made rehiring workers and paying back

Mayor Pro Tem Yvonne Johnson cut the ribbon to open the International House in September 2000. It was a project of Faith Action's Multicultural Unity Group, established in 1999. The headquarters for both organizations is a house provided by First Presbyterian Church at 705 North Greene Street. Courtesy, Faith Action

This photograph, taken at Dr. Gloria Scott's inauguration on October 9, 1988, includes two former presidents. Dr. Isaac Miller, who served from 1966 to 1987, is shaking the new leader's hand, while Dr. Willa Player waits behind him. Dr. Player, Bennett's first female president, served from 1955-1966 and was a strong leader for the students during the civil rights protests of 1960 and 1963. Dr. Althia Collins is the new president at Bennett. Courtesy, Bennett College

Pat Sullivan was inaugurated as UNCG's ninth chancellor in 1995. Since her arrival the NC General Assembly has increased UNCG's annual share because of long underfunding and a capital campaign exceeded a $43 million goal. Here Chancellor Sullivan participates with students in a Tate Street "plant and clean-up day." Courtesy, *UNCG Publications*

wages. In July a contract was adopted that provided a pay increase, two additional holidays and eight hours of compensatory time as well as an extra vacation week for 15-year employees. The immediate increase to a minimum of $7.75 an hour met Kmart's national average, and the wage increase would mean $5.5 million for Greensboro's economy over three years.

During this struggle a discussion group, the Pulpit Forum/Business Work Group, began meeting to better understand the conflict. Businessmen explained some of Kmart's decisions and ministers explained that entry-level jobs were the best some people would ever do under current circumstances. A question debated by the group became the theme for a town meeting: "At what point do work place issues become community issues?"

Snapshots of Social History

The religious climate changed drastically in the late twentieth century, as immigrant groups brought in new beliefs and traditions. Today Greensboro has an Islamic Center where Muslims from more than 30 countries gather, a Baha'i community established in 1943, a Buddhist Temple built in 1986 and a Hindu Center in 1995, a Korean church and Native-American churches of several denominations, as well as a new Beth David Synagogue completed in 1982. The population includes followers of Jainism and Sikhism; Jews; Mormons; Pentecostals; Roman Catholics; and mainline Protestants. This diversity is reflected in religious festivals and holidays, as well as lectures and demonstrations. The Piedmont Interfaith Council, established by Dr. Jim and Jo Hull in 1983, stages an ecumenical Thanksgiving Service each November and sponsors the Triad Tapestry Children's Chorus. This nonprofit, volunteer organization works to strengthen understanding of ethnic and religious diversity. The mission of FaithAction, organized in 1997, is to provide training and support to regional communities as they establish programs to assist immigrants. In 1999 it began a Multicultural Unity Group to develop understanding and trust between blacks and Hispanics in Greensboro. That group recognized the need for a place where people could gather to work on issues and the International House was established.

The Beloved Community Center is defined as a neutral place where equals meet to dis-

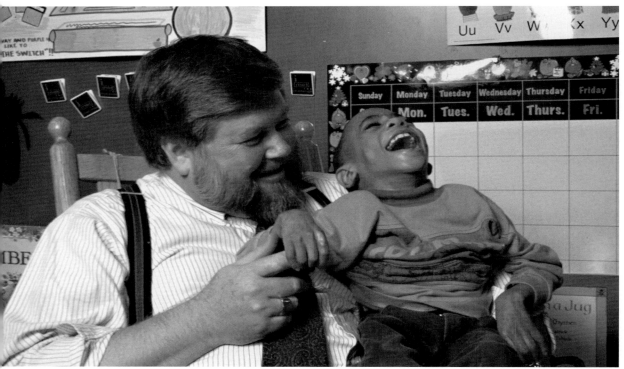

cuss divisive issues and to learn to understand people shaped by different life experiences. Located on Arlington Street, it was the starting place for the Servant Leadership School and the meeting place for the Pulpit Forum/Business Work Group that met during the Kmart crisis; it is also headquarters for the Poor People's Association. The name comes from Dr. Martin Luther King who impacted founders Z. Holler and Nelson Johnson. These ministers realized the need to address issues of race relations and the poor in a systematic manner in the aftermath of 1979. An original goal was to bridge the racial gap and another was to bring the powerful and poor together. The Beloved Community Center and the Pulpit Forum/Business Work Group sponsored the 1996 Town Meeting as a model for community building. Former staff member Jeff Thigpen is now a county commissioner.

There were many educational changes during these decades, as new leaders were chosen for the colleges, universities, public schools and private schools. At Guilford College Dr. William Rogers who served from 1980 to 1996, was replaced by Dr. Don McNemar, a Quaker with a doctorate in politics. In 1993 Dr. Craven Williams became president of Greensboro College, following Dr. William Likins (1984-93), Dr. James Barrett (1981-84) and Dr. Howard Wilkinson (1972-81). Both GC and Bennett College are affiliated with the United Methodist Church and Bennett is one of two historically black colleges for women in the U.S. Dr. Gloria Scott served as Bennett's 12th president (1987-2001). At NC A&T State University Dr. Lewis Dowdy was chancellor from 1964 until 1981, followed by Dr. Edward Fort (1982-1999) and Dr. James Renick, inaugurated as the eighth chancellor in 1999. At UNCG Dr. Patricia Sullivan became the first female chancellor in 1995, succeeding Dr. William Moran (1979-1994). Both GC and Guilford celebrated their sesquicentennials in the 1980s, while Bennett celebrated its 125th year and A&T and UNCG celebrated centennials in the 1990s.

Another important transition occurred in 1983 when Guilford Technical Institute became Guilford Technical Community College. Dr. Donald Cameron has led the school since 1991, following Ray Needham (1980-1990) who served during the transition years. With its mission to train a work force, GTCC is considered a tool for attracting industry.

The most significant educational develop-

Gateway began as the Greensboro Cerebral Palsy and Orthopedic School in January 1950. The Junior League hired the first physical therapist and contributed thousands of dollars and volunteer hours to the growing school. The United Way, foundations and community organizations also gave support. In 1982 the school became part of the Greensboro Public School system, and today it is funded by Guilford County Schools and the Greensboro Cerebral Palsy Association. Housed in a $5 million facility, it is considered the most advanced institution of its kind in the Southeast. Dale Metz (pictured with a student) has been principal since 1983, succeeding Mrs. Bennie Inman. He was named NC Principal of the Year in 1987. Courtesy, Mark Wagoner Productions

ment for the community was the 1993 merger of the city and county public schools. By 1990 the county schools were 81 percent white, the Greensboro system was 49 percent white and the High Point system was 50 percent white. Voters approved a consolidation referendum in 1991 seeing merger as a way to integrate the public system and eliminate some administrative costs. Jerry Weast arrived in 1993 as superintendent of the countywide system that included almost 58,000 students. In 2000 Terry Grier became superintendent.

In 1996 the school board announced that it was necessary to redraw county attendance zones and that a committee of community representatives would perform the task. In another announcement the county manager stated that the system was currently $700 million behind in repairs and new construction. The two issues were related, and a large bond proposal was defeated 2-1 in 1994 due to the redistricting question. The completed redistricting process was to be phased in beginning in 1999, and a $200 million school bond referendum was successful in 2000.

Gateway Education Center which educates children with multiple disabilities was com-

pleted in 1983, the only project of the decade. Pilot (1996), the first new elementary school in the county in 18 years, Jesse Wharton Elementary (1998) built near the Lake Jeanette residential area, and Jefferson (1999), located on a New Garden Road site donated by developer Jefferson-Pilot, were all built in areas of new growth. The middle school that opened in 2000 is named for John Kernodle who was chairman of the Guilford County School Board from 1992-1995.

The first charter school approved for Guilford County opened in 1998. The Imani Institute, a middle school for at-risk students, is located downtown and integrates use of neighboring facilities: the public library, YWCA, and museums.

Existing private schools continued to expand. Greensboro Day School, incorporated in 1970, is the largest with more than 800 students; Vandalia Christian School (1971) has more than 500. Canterbury, organized in 1993 to offer a strong academic program, religious values, and a diverse student body, completed its first building in 1997; Caldwell Academy, another Christian school, designed its curriculum around a classical model. Guilford

Habitat founder Millard Fuller visited a Greensboro site in 1997 during one of the blitz campaigns. Habitat volunteers build houses for working low-income families and family members participate in building Habitat homes. The 1997 blitz used 500 volunteers daily for four days to build 10 houses. Courtesy, *News & Record*, Greensboro, NC, Jerry Wolford

Dancers from the Guilford Native American Association perform throughout the year, especially during fall pow-wows. The GNAA, incorporated in 1975, is a nonprofit organization that assists Indians to achieve social and economic self-sufficiency. Ruth Revels served as director of the association for 21 years, retiring in 1998. The number of Native Americans in Greensboro increased from 779 in 1990 to 989 in 2000, a 27 percent gain. The city's population shifted from 66 percent white, 33 percent black and one percent other in 1980 to 55 percent white, 37 percent black and eight percent other in 2000. (GHM)

Day School continues to accommodate students with special learning needs. A regional Catholic high school and Jewish boarding school are planned to supplement the lower schools operated by both religious groups.

A number of human service agencies were established or relocated between 1981 and 2000. Hospice, established as a grassroots organization in 1978, hired Pam Barrett as its first fulltime executive in 1985. In 1991 it moved to new headquarters on Summit Avenue and later developments included residential care at Beacon Place and a special program for children. Greensboro Urban Ministry, established in 1967, relocated to Lee Street in 1993, but its mission remained the same—serving people in need through practical action. HealthServe, a medical clinic and pharmacy sponsored by GUM and Cone Hospital, moved into an adjacent building. The American Red Cross and United Way also got new headquarters during the 1990s.

Project Uplift began in 1986 when former congressman Robin Britt decided to create a non-profit organization to work with disadvantaged pre-school children and their parents. A later move for Britt was starting a child devel-

A & T graduate Dr. Ron McNair, a victim of the 1986 Challenger disaster, is shown on his first Challenger mission in 1984. McNair earned his doctorate in physics from MIT in 1976 and was one of 35 chosen from approximately 11,000 for shuttle crew training in 1977. Today at A & T there is a bust of McNair near a building named for him and there are McNair Fellows on scholarship. (GHM)

opment center at Ray Warren Homes. One of the best known organizations working with low-income families is Habitat of Greater Greensboro that started building houses in 1988. It is one of several groups addressing the problem of affordable housing.

Greensboro residents can enjoy sports activities of many kinds. Through the Parks & Recreation Department they can visit 13 recreation centers with programming, 91 playgrounds, 115 tennis courts, more than 4,000 acres of parks and 3 reservoirs. New parks include the Barber facility dedicated in 1989 and Bur-Mil acquired in 1989 that join Country, Hagan-Stone, Bryan, and Hester parks to serve all quadrants of the city.

The Greensboro Jaycees with corporate sponsors present a golf tournament each year that is the second oldest PGA event. Much of the money raised is used for community projects, including the annual holiday parade. The Jaycees have been selected the best chapter in the US several times, and a number of Greensboro mayors (Melvin, Forbis and Holliday) have received training as Jaycees.

The Greensboro Prowlers (football), the Greensboro Generals (hockey), the Greensboro Dynamos (soccer) and the Greensboro Bats (baseball) represent professional sports. Only the Bats have been involved in an issue

that blended political, economic and social history. In 1993 the owners of the Greensboro Hornets, a Yankee farm team playing in the South Atlantic League, decided to make some changes. The Hornets became the Bats in 1993, and in 1995 team owners agreed to help fund a new $15 million stadium and to purchase a Double-A franchise if the City would provide $10 million. At the same time the N.C. Baseball Committee was attempting to gain a Triad major league franchise that would require a $200 million stadium. A two-county vote to approve a special tax if a major-league franchise was awarded failed, so the Triad dropped out of the competition. A third factor, an offer by the Brame family to give the City or the Bats 50 acres of land in northwest Guilford for a stadium, was refused by both.

Throughout this controversy the City tried to be objective and a $2 million improvement bond for War Memorial Stadium was put before voters in 1996. It failed by 60 percent due to confusion about the facts and reaction to the cost of the Coliseum project. The City did spend $50,000 on necessary repairs to keep baseball at the stadium. In 1999 a group of local investors (Greensboro Baseball LLC) purchased the Bats, which continues as a Class-A Yankee farm team in the South Atlantic League. In 2001 the stadium, believed to

On February 2, 1990, a new exhibit at the Historical Museum featuring four of the stools used during the 1960 sit-in opened as part of a five-day 30th anniversary celebration. Three of the "Greensboro Four" were present to unveil the stools that had been donated by the Woolworth Corporation. Standing left to right are Joseph McNeil, Franklin McCain and David Richmond. Ezell Blair Jr. (now Jibreel Khazan) was in Greensboro but missed the ceremony. Blair and Richmond were Greensboro natives. (GHM)

be the oldest active minor-league stadium in the U.S., was listed on the National Register. This was Greensboro's 47th NR property.

New cultural organizations, events and sites expanded opportunities for people of all ages and interests. In 1980 the Greensboro Opera Company was organized, and its first production was *La Traviata* in 1981. A ribbon cutting for the Greensboro Cultural Center (formerly the Arts Center) was held in 1990, and people poured through the 120,000 square foot complex created by renovating five buildings. The GCC houses many tenants, including the City Arts Division of the Parks & Recreation Department, the United Arts Council, plus offices and studios for the Symphony, Eastern Music Festival, Civic Ballet, Community Theater, and Creative Arts. There are five art and ethnic galleries: Green Hill Center for NC Art with its interactive ArtQuest; Greensboro Artists' League; a branch of the Mattye Reed African Heritage Center, the Guilford Native American Association Art Gallery; and the African American Atelier. In 1989 the Anne and Benjamin Cone Building at UNCG opened and the Weatherspoon Art Gallery moved into a space five times larger than its previous home. In addition to art there are many theater offerings in

the City, and Triad Stage will inaugurate its first season in January 2002.

Among the events impacting the city were the explosion of the Challenger spacecraft in 1986 and the 30th anniversary of the Greensboro Sit-ins, both involving A & T students. Ron McNair (Class of 1971) was one of seven killed in the explosion, and three of the Greensboro Four (Class of 1963) participated in the dedication of Woolworth stools at the Greensboro Historical Museum.

Two other happenings especially important for the black community occurred in 1997. A completed Hayes-Taylor YMCA reopened after six years of work and fund-raising drives in 1985, 1989 and 1993. The $6 million raised created a full-service family facility. Union Cemetery, founded by three black churches around 1880, was listed on the National Register of Historic Places in 1992. In 1994 a marker was erected, and in 1997 Delta Sigma Theta sorority adopted the cemetery as a restoration project. Union is one of four cemeteries owned and maintained by the City.

Other sites were developed or opened in the 1980s and 1990s. The state of NC purchased the Palmer Institute property in eastern Guilford County and dedicated it as the Charlotte Hawkins Brown Memorial State Historic Site in 1987. It was the first site to honor an African-American or a woman. A number of buildings, including Brown's home and Stone Teachers' Cottage, have been restored and others stabilized but many need to be renovated when funding is available.

In 1988 Tannenbaum Park, adjacent to Guilford Courthouse National Military Park, opened as another Revolutionary War site. Eight acres of land including the Hoskins House had been purchased by a new Guilford Battleground Company (1983) and donated to the city to operate. Fund raising continued and the city and county contributed to help build the Colonial Heritage Center (1992) which has user-friendly exhibits. Tannenbaum hosts living history groups and battle reenactments during the year. In 1990 the His-

On February 4, 1983, Henry E. Frye was sworn in as NC's first African American Supreme Court justice. William Person is assisting him with his official robe. Frye served in the NC House from 1968–1980 and in the NC Senate from 1980–1983. Governor Jim Hunt appointed him to the court in 1983 and appointed him Chief Justice in September 1999. Frye ran unsuccessfully for the office in 2000 and retired in 2001. Now practicing law in Greensboro, he and wife Shirley are outstanding civic leaders. Courtesy, *News & Record*, Greensboro, NC, Duane Hall

The Arboretum, dedicated in May 1991, covers 17 acres in the historic Lindley Park neighborhood and contains more than 2,500 trees and plants. The Parks and Recreation Department, Greensboro Beautiful and the Council of Garden Clubs worked together to create the Arboretum which is funded by the City with contributions from civic groups, businesses and individuals. Here Jenny Moore (Green Hill Center for NC Art), Bonnie Kuester (Parks & Recreation Department), and Roger Halligan (Tri-State Sculptors) cut the ribbon for a 1993 sculpture show. Courtesy, City of Greensboro

toric Jamestown Foundation opened Mendenhall Plantation to the public. The house that dates back to 1811 is associated with the Underground Railroad, and the complex is a National Register property.

In 1998 the "cultural block" containing the YWCA (since 1920), the Greensboro Historical Museum (since 1939) and the Greensboro Cultural Center (since 1979) acquired a new neighbor, the Central Library. The $14 million building includes 100,000 square feet designed to provide accessible materials, state-of-the-art technology and customer comfort. The Community Foundation, established in 1983, awarded the largest grant in its history to the Greensboro Public Library system to install Internet access at all nine locations.

Two new museums were proposed in the 1990s, one for children and the other to commemorate the history of international civil rights. The idea of a children's museum began with Jerry Hyman who donated the Montgomery Ward Building on South Elm

Street. In 1995 Cynthia Doyle formed a steering committee to plan and raise funds for a museum to open in 1999. In 1998 the Bryan Foundation provided a different building, larger and better located, and the museum board quickly responded. The new museum opened on May 15, 1999, on Church Street across from the cultural block, so the new designation became the "cultural district." The Elm Street building will soon become the home of Triad Stage.

The civil rights museum board purchased the famous Woolworth's store on Elm that closed in 1994, and since that time founders Skip Alston and Earl Jones, other staff and volunteers have been planning and raising money. Recently the board has teamed with NC A&T State University to complete fund-raising and open the facility as soon as possible.

So, a future promise concludes Greensboro's history as recorded from prehistoric times through 2000.

"The Spirit of St. Louis" and its pilot Charles A. Lindbergh are shown at Lindley Field on October 14, 1927.   Courtesy, Dr. T.E. Sikes, Jr.

Chapter Ten

CHRONICLES OF LEADERSHIP

Greensboro's commerce and industry began where they usually began—in the home. Like other pioneers, early Guilford settlers produced most of their necessities.

The city's first important recorded industry was North Carolina's first steam cotton mill, begun in 1828. Henry Humphreys built Mt. Hecla Steam Cotton Mill at the corner of Bellemeade and Greene. The four-story brick mill had 2,500 spindles and 75 looms by 1840 and produced sheeting, shirting, osnaburgs and spun cotton yarns for home weaving.

In an 1826 copy of *The Patriot*, a weekly local newspaper that was converted to a farm weekly in the 1950s, there were ads for Greensboro-made hats; coaches, gigs and carryalls; saddles and harnesses; and chairs and bedsteads. By 1860 local manufacturers produced cigars, snuff, chewing tobacco, men's clothing, plows, castings and tools.

By the late 1800s Greensboro firms processed large quantities of dried fruits, shipping them all over the United States, to Canada and abroad. Two Greensboro firms made cooking and heating stoves. When the surviving one devoted its buildings to warehousing after World War II, no one dreamed a group of oil-rich nations would revive this industry later in the century.

Woodworking and metalworking machines made in Greensboro since the turn of the century are internationally known. The old Porter Drug Company, marked by plaques beside a law office, was home to both an acclaimed short story writer (O. Henry) and a little blue jar of medicine (Vicks VapoRub) that became the foundation of a chemical company that is now a part of Proctor & Gamble.

Greensboro is home to Burlington Industries, Inc., one of the largest textile manufacturers in the world, and Cone Mills Corporation, one of the world's largest producers of denim and corduroy. Cone played a large part in turning denim from an overall fabric into a high-fashion cloth. Blue jeans woven or assembled in Greensboro are popular around the world.

Another internationally known firm headquartered in the area is Gilbarco, part of Reliance Electric, maker of gas station lifts and pumps and pipeline pumps. A smaller, highly mechanized local company manufactured end caps that protected segments of the Alaskan Pipeline until they were installed. Volvo-White Trucks is quartered here also.

This area is home to a major life insurance company and to an agricultural chemical research facility. Local products include toothpaste, toilet items, electrical switchgear and tea bags. Variety, industry, initiative and progress have always been a part of the Gate City, a nickname created in 1891 because of Greensboro's superior transportation network. These same qualities guide the city as it enters yet another century.

ADA COMPUTER SUPPLIES, INC.

Jerry Fox is a man who will not be denied. Against obstacles that would have stopped many in their tracks, Fox's vision for his future fueled the drive that has steered his company, ADA Computer Supplies, Inc., to the pinnacle of success. Self-reliant, resilient and totally focused on his goal, Fox has consistently formulated innovative strategies to overcome every possible stumbling block since the very beginning of his career.

After majoring in mechanical engineering at North Carolina A&T (where he now serves on the Advisory Board of the School of Education), Fox spent three years developing data processing and computer programming skills before starting work in the computer department at Burlington Industries. In 1968, his desire to grow professionally and personally spurred him to take his life savings—less than $500—get in his old Pontiac LeMans and drive north to the city of opportunity—New York City. There he found a room in a low-rent hotel and confidently applied to work for what was then the leading computer company in the world, IBM. In just two weeks, he was hired as a computer operator in their offices in Westchester County. Although the

Jerry W. Fox, president.

starting salary was meager, he saw the potential to rise through the ranks of the company, gaining valuable experience at every rung of the corporate ladder.

And climb the ladder he did. During his 11 year stay with Big Blue, Fox's talent and drive did not go unnoticed; he steadily rose through the ranks from Computer Operations Technician and Procedures Analyst to Programmer, Systems Analyst, Shift Computer Operations Manager and, finally, Data Processing Manager at the company's offices in Sterling Forest, N.Y. IBM's operated each department as an independent "profit center," and it was in this position as manager that Fox gained first-hand knowledge of how to run a business, including the overall responsibility for employees, equipment and production, and administration of a $14 million annual operating budget.

This knowledge was all Fox needed to ignite his entrepreneurial spirit as he came to understand that his future was in running his own business, not IBM's. Again he decided it was time to move on, but when he submitted his resignation, it was refused. He was so valuable an employee that IBM instead granted him a one-year leave of absence to pursue his dream, with the offer of an open door for his return at the same salary and level if his new business should fail.

In 1978, Jerry Fox became the owner and sole employee of ADA Computer Supplies. His mission was clearly defined: to pursue large corporations along with local, state and federal government agencies through direct face-to-face marketing to DP managers, systems managers and purchasing agents, fluently speaking the "language" of computers that was so rare a skill in those early days of corporate automation. Up at 4:00 a.m. to respond to quotes from the previous day, he hit the streets for direct sales in the morning, wrote orders and placed purchase orders in the afternoon and checked, boxed and shipped merchandise long into the evening.

More obstacles caused Fox to shift strategies, but never once to stumble. While he could easily "talk the talk" with potential clients to establish credibility with his customer base, it took time to convince major vendors that his fledgling company could effectively represent their products. Again, his can-do attitude served him well, eventually earning ADA a well-earned place as an authorized dealer for a full line of products from such respected names as Hewlett Packard, Compaq, Verbatim, 3M, Xerox, Imation and Lexmark. From sales locations in North Carolina, South

ADA's shipping and receiving area.

Carolina and Virginia, the company now has direct access to virtually anything in the computer and office supplies industry.

Fox has achieved his initial goal to list major corporations and government entities on his client roster. Today ADA's customer portfolio includes such global leaders as American Express, Glaxo-Wellcome, Proctor & Gamble, United States Postal Service, Dow Corning, City of Greensboro, Sara Lee, Michelin Aircraft Tire Corporation and Caterpiller. Indeed, even Fox's old employer-turned-customer IBM has awarded ADA its "Dealer of the Month" honor numerous times over the past years. Consistently providing exceptional customer service along with superior products and effective information technology solutions has made ADA a valuable vendor partner for these and a multitude of other major corporate leaders. Plus, with ADA's alliance with Vision Business Products, Inc., a consortium of 73 independent computer/office products suppliers across the country, the company has further strengthened its ability to better solicit and service national accounts.

ADA Computer Supplies, Inc. currently employs 17 people, a dedicated team of highly-trained professionals who reflect Fox's commitment to responsive customer service. Offering a complete line of computer supplies, network supplies, hardware, software and peripherals, word/data processing supplies, furniture and office supplies, the ADA team works tirelessly to respond immediately to every customer request. On line with major suppliers for instant pricing and product availability, ADA stands ready to accept orders via the Internet at their website (www.ada-computersupplies.com), by phone, 24/7 fax line or 24/7 EDI (Electronic Data Interchange) line with delivery

Meeting of the minds.

to virtually any destination in the continental United States through its national warehousing network within 24 hours. Yet, even more impressive than the broad spectrum of products the company offers and the speed of its delivery system, is Fox's unwaver-

Warehouse supervisor Ferris Evans leads his crew.

ing commitment to being the supplier of quality support for each and every product sold.

For Jerry Fox and ADA Computer Supplies, the pursuit of excellence continues. With respect for the dignity and right of each person within the organization, ADA continues to achieve its mission to exceed its customers' expectations through its adherence to the fundamental principles that have guided ADA management since the company's founding. These principles are to serve its customers as effectively and efficiently as possible while enlarging the capabilities of employees through job development, job satisfaction and equal opportunity for all.

Still a 100 percent minority-owned, independent distributor/wholesaler, ADA Computer Supplies, Inc. is one of the fastest growing businesses in the south. All because one man, Jerry Fox, had the vision, dedication, talent and work ethic to leap over obstacles to achieve a dream.

ADAMS KLEEMEIER HAGAN HANNAH & FOUTS PLLC

Today, Adams Kleemeier Hagan Hannah & Fouts PLLC is a multi-specialty law firm headquartered in Greensboro, with an office in Asheboro. The present day firm, now employing 100 people, had its beginnings in collegial friendships that evolved into a powerful business alliance. The founders' desire for a professional career and a balanced life is still evident today. Through the years, the members of the firm have held public office, sat on city and state boards, and actively sought ways in which to serve their community.

"The way that we do business has come to be just as important to us as the business that we do," says Walter L. Hannah. "It becomes a question of way of life versus the bottom line."

The formation of the firm was a natural consequence of a need to re-establish their disrupted professional lives after years of military service. In October 1954, Huger S. King

The firm's original offices were located in the Jefferson Building at 101 North Elm Street.

persuaded John A. Kleemeier, Jr. and Charles T. Hagan, Jr. to form a firm. They met only a few brief times before working out the terms. Kleemeier and Hagan already shared a single office space and secretary in the Jefferson Building on Elm Street in downtown Greensboro along with Hannah. Quarters were so cramped, one of them would leave the office

whenever a colleague held a meeting. To their relief, Hagan was out of the office much of the time trying cases, and they maneuvered around one another's desks, frequently skinning shins on the furniture.

On January 1, 1955, the men moved into five offices on the Jefferson Building's sixth floor. They chose Walter L. Hannah as their first associate. All were World War II veterans, and the public responded warmly to them. King had commanded a Navy vessel. Kleemeier had accompanied Roosevelt to Yalta and served in Naval Intelligence. Hagan participated in the Pacific campaign at Saipan, Tinian, and Iwo Jima. Hannah had been stationed in Europe and the Asiatic-Pacific theater. The four men were not only warriors, they were lawyers who shared an easy comradeship and even attended the same church —First Presbyterian in Fisher Park. King served as the president of the Community Chest (now the United Way) and the Empty Stocking Fund; Hagan was a former 12th Judicial District Solicitor; Kleemeier was a former interim judge.

The three founding attorneys from left to right: Charles T. Hagan, Jr., Huger S. King and John A. Kleemeier, Jr. The latter two are deceased.

Postwar America was experiencing a resurgence of building and an industrial boom. An expanding infrastructure and highway system were moving Greensboro much closer to its business markets. A variety of manufacturing giants moved into town, including Western Electric, P. Lorillard, and Gilbarco. Only six months after the firm's beginning they moved into a suite of offices formerly occupied by Jefferson executives. King brought a silver coffee pot and eight bone china cups and saucers from home. The circumstances of the war had forced them all to begin their law careers anew, and they marveled at their growing good fortune.

King was now 48 years old. In 1940 he became Greensboro's youngest elected mayor at age 33, later resigning from his post as mayor to enter World War II. Kleemeier, now age 43, had practiced briefly with a Charlotte firm before creating a solo practice before the war years. After the war he returned to his native Greensboro, where he resumed his practice. Hagan, 41 at the time of the formation of the new firm, had graduated from law school with a reserve commission in the Marine Corps. When Hagan returned to Greensboro he served two terms as a Solicitor (an elected position equivalent to what is now known as a District Attorney) for Guilford and Davidson Counties. Throughout his career Hagan remained active in the Marine Corps Reserve, attaining the highest possible rank of Major General.

Prior to joining King, Kleemeier, and Hagan, Hannah worked as an adjuster for U.S. Fidelity and Guaranty Company from 1950-1953. Hannah, the youngest member of the firm at 28, had opened a solo practice before the invitation to join the firm.

The evolution of the firm was swift. Their client base soon grew to include

notable firms such as Duke Power, Southern Life, Carolina Steel, and American Tobacco Company.

William J. Adams, Jr. joined the firm as a partner in King Adams Kleemeier and Hagan in 1956. Adams practiced law for six years before joining the North Carolina Department of Justice. He was assistant attorney general of the state until 1945, when he formed a partnership with D. Edward Hudgins until Hudgins accepted an appointment as general counsel for the Jefferson Standard Life Insurance.

In 1958, King left the firm to join the Richardson family businesses. King later became chairman of Richardson's board. A year later, Daniel W. Fouts joined the firm. Fouts had spent a year following his law school graduation with the North Carolina Supreme Court clerking for Supreme Court Justice Carlisle W. Higgins. His father knew Hudgins and arranged for Fouts to be introduced to principals at Jefferson Standard and to Adams. Both offered Fouts a job, but Fouts accepted the position at Adams Kleemeier.

In 1966, Adams Kleemeier moved from downtown Greensboro to their present modern headquarters at 701 Green Valley Road.

The firm known as Adams Kleemeier Hagan Hannah & Fouts by 1964 would grow to include second-generation employees and fourth-generation clients. The principals were fond of saying they were most proud of the fact that they had been able to grow the firm with like-minded professionals, both respected and respectful.

Another distinction has endured: a passionate civic-mindedness transcending duty. At this writing, William J. Adams, Jr., John A. Kleemeier, Charles T. Hagan, Jr., Horace R. Kornegay, and Daniel W. Fouts each have served as presidents of the Greensboro Bar Association. William J. Adams, Jr. also served as president of the North Carolina Bar Association. Robert G. Baynes is a former president of the North Carolina State Bar. Three members of the firm have served as president (now Chairman) of the Greensboro Chamber of Commerce.

CONE MILLS CORPORATION

The story of Cone Mills Corporation began in the late 1800s, when Moses and Ceasar Cone were salesmen for their father's wholesale grocery firm in Baltimore.

The brothers traveled throughout the South, taking orders from the "general stores" of that day. Many of the small southern textile mills of the time also operated stores—called "company stores"—for the benefit of employees and their families. This gave the Cones their first contact with the cotton mills of that day.

As the brothers moved through the largely rural South, they recognized the need for textile development and diversification, a realization that eventually led to the establishment of Cone Mills Corporation. In their first step, the brothers established a firm to sell textile goods produced in southern textile mills. This venture, the Cone Export and Commission Company, opened in New York City in May 1891.

Above: Moses Cone, co-founder and first president of Cone Export and Commission Company.

Ceasar Cone, co-founder and first president of Cone Mills Corporation.

Below: Cone Mills' company picnic, July 4, 1910, with Ceasar Cone standing in the center.

It still operates as the selling and merchandising division of the firm and is now known as the Cone Textile Group.

In 1895 the first Cone manufacturing plant was built in Greensboro. That early plant was for the specific purpose of producing blue denim, and it was from that small beginning that Cone Mills grew to be one of the world's largest and best-known textile manufacturers.

Over the next several decades new plants were built and others purchased. During these years, some plants operated as independent companies. A reorganization of the corporation occurred in 1948, with all subsidiaries merged into the parent firm. In 1951, for the first time, the stock of the company was listed for trading on the New York Stock Exchange.

Cone has successfully combined a tradition of producing high-quality fabrics with a heritage of good relationships with its employees and the communities where plants are located. Against this background, Cone Mills has emerged as one of America's leading textile manufacturers.

Today the company operates in three principal business segments: Denim & Khakis; Commission Finishing; and Decorative Fabrics for upholstery, draperies and bedspreads. Cone Mills is the largest producer of denim fabrics in the world and the largest commission printer of home furnishings fabrics in the United States.

Chief executive officers of Cone Mills have been community leaders as well as textile men. Ceasar Cone was chief executive officer from 1895 to 1917; Bernard M. Cone held the post from 1917 to 1938; Herman Cone, from 1938 to 1955; Ceasar Cone II, 1956 to 1965; Lewis S. Morris, 1965 to 1980; Dewey L. Trogdon, 1980 to 1990; J. Patrick Danahy, 1990 to 1998; and John L. Bakane, since 1998. Serving as chairman of the board were Bernard M. Cone, 1938 to 1950; Herman Cone, 1950 to 1955; Benjamin Cone, 1956 to 1965; Ceasar Cone II, 1965 to 1972; Lewis S. Morris, 1972 to 1980; and Dewey L. Trogdon, since 1981.

When Herman Cone moved from Bavaria to America in 1845, he was lonely. A letter from his brother-in-law, Joseph Rosengart, has been dutifully read by succeeding generations of the family. Its advice is timeless.

"You may shed tears, because you are leaving your parents' house, your father, brothers and sisters, relatives, friends, and your native land, but dry your tears, because you may have the sweet hope of finding a second home abroad and a new country...a real homeland where you as a human being may claim all human rights and human dignity...."

"If you should be lucky enough to become wealthy in that distant land, do not let it make you proud and overbearing. Do not think that your energy and knowledge accumulated that wealth, but that God gave it to you to use it for the best purpose and for charity. Do not forget that you are also under obligation to assist your relatives and to help them get ahead...."

Members of the Cone family have been noted for their concern for others. One early example of this occurred during the Banking Holiday in 1933. The family had chartered the Textile Bank in 1911 at White Oak Mill village for the convenience of their

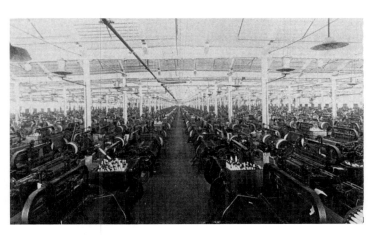

An early 1900s photo of the weave room at White Oak, the world's largest denim mill.

employees. The bank was later sold to another banking institution. In 1933 the bank closed its doors, as it was unable to pay depositors in full. As a tribute to the memory of Ceasar Cone, members of his family paid the difference between the amount the bank could pay and the full amount of company employees' deposits, thereby ensuring that there would be no loss to their employees.

The modern Nissan Air Jet looms in the present-day White Oak weaving department.

ELECTRIC SUPPLY & EQUIPMENT COMPANY

It was 1935 and Franklin D. Roosevelt was president, Social Security had just been born and "I'm in the Mood for Love" was in the top ten. It was also the year Electric Supply & Equipment Company first opened it's doors at 228 East Sycamore Street in Greensboro. The company was owned and operated by Howard M. Sutherland, president, Mrs. Howard Sutherland, vice president and Ray Fogleman, secretary/treasurer. B.I. Sherrill was also an original employee and stockholder. After one month of operation sales totaled $3,142.27.

Although the country was still feeling the effects of the Great Depression and unemployment was as high as 25 percent, Electric Supply & Equipment Company was expanding. In 1936 two new employees were hired, including its first female employee, Janet Fox. By 1938, in order to accommodate expanding business, the company moved to a larger building at 213 Bellemeade Street.

In 1941, as the United States entered World War II, Electric Supply & Equipment Company also went to war, as three employees were granted leaves to serve in the Army and the Navy. The employees who served during the war included Howard Sutherland, R.S. Hunt, Jr. and W.A.

The warehouse at 213 Bellemeade Street.

Lancaster.

With the war over, Americans were feeling optimistic about a bright future. The company's future was also bright as many changes and expansion took place during the 1950s. Sadly, before much of the expansion, in February 1952 the president of Electric Supply & Equipment Company, Howard Sutherland died. The company was reorganized and Ray Fogleman became president. In March 1954 a branch was opened in Burlington to better serve its customers in Burlington, Durham, Fayetteville and Southern Pines, and in 1955 a lot was purchased at 1812 East Wendover.

The building contract was awarded to King-Hunter Construction Company and plans were under way to construct a 25,000 square foot building. The completion of the building came in on schedule and employees were able to move in on July 4, 1957.

To celebrate the new location an open house took place on September 23, 1957. Customers and friends were invited and Allen Bradley's band and orchestra performed during the event. According to a history written by Paul Boone in 1975, the band's performance "is still remembered with pleasure to date."

During the turbulent sixties as Americans watched the assassination of three young leaders and the escalation of the Vietnam War, business at Electric Supply & Equipment Company underwent a few changes. The most eventful change was the announcement of Ray Fogleman's retirement in 1964. However before he announced his retirement he took a week's vacation to visit a lawyer and the bank. Without anyone's knowledge he put the plans together for a buyout. The following

Electric Supply & Equipment Company's employees in 1947.

Monday morning Ray Fogleman walked in and instructed Adrian Lancaster, Paul Boone, Rector Hunt, Otis Deese and Bud Whitcomb to head to the bank to sign the papers. This represented the third successful change in ownership since the founding of the company. Another bit of company history took place in the sixties as Dana Smith came on board in May 1967.

January 1970 ushered in a new decade and a new employee by the name of Eli Whitaker. Shortly after Eli joined the Greensboro ranks another well-known figure came on board when Jim McCormick was hired on February 23rd.

The decision was made to sell the Burlington location and in 1973 a new branch was opened in High Point. With a new location additional employees were needed, and Herb Davis had his first day on March 27th. Fresh from high school, Liz Quinn's first day as an employee was September 19th and four months later William Joyner began the start of his career on January 18, 1974. As of December 3, 1974 the number of people on the payroll totaled 31.

By 1976 Adrian Lancaster and Paul Boone were ready to hand the company over to younger hands. Just like Ray Fogleman before them, they selected three employees and offered them ownership of the company. Those three employees were Bill Holt, Dana Smith and Jim McCormick. On April 1, 1976 the transfer of ownership took place. At that time sales totaled 2.6 million. By the early eighties Bill Holt had elected to retire and Jim and Dana became sole owners. Under their leadership many changes began to occur. Perhaps the biggest change and the one that still impacts the organization today was the decision to position themselves not as a contractor supply house, but to market and go after industrial automation.

In 1978 a new location was opened on the coast of North Carolina. New Bern was selected as a result of heavy business with Weyerhaeuser, Hatteras Yachts, and Texas Gulf. In October 1980 a young man, named Mike Skinner entered a training program in Greensboro and in 1981 headed to Rocky Mount to assist with the opening of a new location. The Rocky Mount branch successfully absorbed responsibility for the sales generated in New Bern and as a result the New Bern location was closed. Also during the eighties a location in Wilmington was opened. However, when Allen Bradley offered the APR in Raleigh, Jim and Dana traded New Bern and Wilmington for Raleigh. In 1987 the Morrisville branch was opened to serve RTP and the north central part of the state.

Electric Supply & Equipment Company, born during the Great Depression, also lived through what Jim and Dana have described as the toughest time they have experienced during their ownership. In the mid eighties sales were excellent and the customer base solid. However, all that changed when

From left to right, Dana Smith, Jim McCormick and Herb Davis.

RJ Reynolds and Burlington Industries underwent a leveraged buyout. These buyouts still represent some of the biggest takeovers in history. Business that the company relied on dried up. Jim and Dana, along with the 65 employees, dug deeper. They went after business and customers they had never considered calling on before. A five year plan was devised to provide cost saving programs to its customers while at the same time provide superior service. The commitment was also made in this plan to offer developmental programs to employees and to maintain excellent data processing systems. The company also spent wisely or not at all. This program, in a nutshell, was the company's commitment to partner with its customers and to be its customers' preferred provider. At this time the commitment was also made to make Electric Supply & Equipment

Company one of the best operated distributors in the electrical industry.

In keeping with this new direction the company pursued ISO certification. This was achieved in November of 1995 under the leadership of Andy Collins. In addition, the Automation Group was formed and engineers with software expertise were recruited. John Russell was tapped to lead this specialized group in December 1995. The company soon outgrew its Morrisville location and in 1996 a 15,000 square foot facility was built in Apex North Carolina.

In 2001, Electric Supply & Equipment Company continued in the spirit of its founders with Dana Smith and Jim McCormick at the helm. With their leadership the company enjoys the benefits of an excellent reputation and a formidable position in its chosen market. As it celebrates the richness of its past, Electric Supply & Equipment Company looks forward to the future. Although they cannot tell what the future holds they do know that the future is guided by its heritage and the business practices that are the foundation of the company will be its foundation in the future.

Electric Supply & Equipment Company's current location at 1812 East Wendover Avenue.

DOW CORNING CORPORATION

Greensboro, North Carolina was the site of Dow Corning's first manufacturing operation established outside Michigan. In 1954 the company decided that it could better serve its textile industry customers by locating a plant in closer proximity to those customers. In 1957, the first building was constructed at the Greensboro plant's present site on Patterson Street. Then, in 1959, additional buildings housing manufacturing, laboratories and offices were added, allowing all of the company's operations in Greensboro to be consolidated at one site.

Dow Corning Greensboro quickly developed into a center for producing and packaging the company's specialty silicone products and related high performance materials. Plant expansion continued in the 1970s and 1980s with construction of additional laboratory, production and warehouse space. A technical service center on site is in the heart of the U.S. textile industry; a Dow Corning sales and customer service office is also located on site. Today Dow Corning's specialty materials operations at Greensboro are among the most versatile and productive in the company.

The site employs approximately 120 people in a work force that consists of trained plant operators, engineers,

A street level view of Dow Corning Greensboro's administration and laboratory facilities.

technicians, supply and distribution coordinators, maintenance and administrative personnel. "The consistent strength of the Greensboro site over the years has been the flexibility and competency of our work force," says plant manager Jim Whitlock. The high caliber of people employed at Dow Corning Greensboro is one of the company's key strengths.

Dow Corning was founded in 1943 as a joint venture of the Dow Chemical Company and Corning Glass Incorporated. It is the leading developer, manufacturer, and marketer of silicones. Silicones are man-made materials produced in a complex and technically demanding process. They are based on the chemistry of the element silicon, one of the world's most abundant elements. Environmentally safe and ecologically sound, silicones are moisture resistant, thermally stable, and provide excellent electrical insulation.

Dow Corning's product line from Greensboro is wide-ranging. It includes: popular silicone sealants used in residential and commercial construction, sealant coating primers, silicone greases and lubricants for industrial applications, silicone brake fluid, material to defoam solutions of many kinds, silicone-based textile coatings, fabric finishes and various automotive applications. Dow Corning Greensboro produces approximately 165 distinct products. Another expertise on-site is small packaging. Dow Corning Greensboro packages over 660 products,

A Dow Corning operator and set-up person examine production on one of the plant's tubing machines.

in containers bearing Dow Corning, distributor, and private label names in various forms including tubes, cartridges, blisters, pails, bottles, cans and two-part kits.

The Greensboro site has worked hard to achieve one of the best personnel safety records in Dow Corning and in its industry. The site maintains an attitude that places safety first and emphasizes practicing responsible work habits. At Greensboro, this shows through injury-free work. North Carolina OSHA recently renewed the Greensboro site with the Carolina Star award, which is given to North Carolina manufacturing sites that qualify in Safety and Health. The site first received the Star award in 1997 and has renewed two times since. Dow Corning also participates in the Chemical Manufacturers Association's "Responsible Care" program, which encourages companies to keep their communities well informed about the processes they use and the products they make.

At Dow Corning Greensboro, there is an ongoing commitment to provide an environment that promotes employee excellence, customer satisfaction, and community relations.

GREENSBORO HISTORICAL MUSEUM

The Greensboro Historical Museum is a place filled with the stories of people and events that have shaped the community, and a membership organization made possible through the efforts of volunteers. On opening day November 11, 1925, visitors could see 200 items in a basement room of the Carnegie Public Library; today their descendants can tour 12 exhibit galleries, four restored buildings, and a gift shop. The museum operates under the direction of the City of Greensboro and Greensboro Historical Museum, Inc. City monies fund staff salaries and building maintenance, and the membership is responsible for the collections (now numbering over 25,000 objects and 400,000 archival items), programming, and traveling exhibitions.

An important anchor in downtown's cultural district, the museum's home since 1939 has been a facility that began as First Presbyterian Church. The main building is actually four structures: an 1892 sanctuary, 1903 Sunday School, 1939 connecting addition and a 1990 wing made possible by a municipal bond. It was listed on the National Register of Historic Places in 1985. Four historic buildings moved to adjacent Mary Lynn Smith Richardson Park are used to interpret 18th and 19th centuries: the Francis McNairy House, Christian Isley House, Hockett Blacksmith Shop, and Hockett Woodworking Shop.

Current exhibits highlight significant events such as the 1960 sit-ins and 1781 Battle of Guilford Courthouse, famous people such as First Lady Dolley Madison and the writer O. Henry, and historical trends such as transportation and urbanization. Additional exhibits, focusing on Native Americans, early immigrants, and community life enable visitors to appreciate other aspects of Greensboro's heritage. Special col-

Located downtown at 130 Summit Avenue, the museum occupies a Victorian structure that was formerly First Presbyterian Church.

lections on exhibit include decorative arts, Confederate firearms, and photographs. As a place to learn about the community, state, and nation, the museum offers many services: tours for adults and children, research information on local history, picture or object identification, advice on preserving family heirlooms, lectures for clubs, hands-on activities for young-

sters, and badge work for Scouts.

The museum was accredited by the American Association of Museums in 1984 and re-accredited in 1996, a designation which indicates adherence to professional standards for operations. Volunteers continue to provide invaluable support by donating their time and service in every area of operation, including tour guides, collection assistants, shop clerks, and board members. Open six days a week with no admission charge, the museum today is an important educational and leisure resource for current and future Greensboro citizens and visitors. To learn more, visit www.greensborohistory.org.

Imagine traveling dusty roads in this 1906 Cadillac, which cost $750 and had a top speed of 35 miles per hour. Visitors can learn how people have lived and worked in Greensboro in the museum's many galleries and restored buildings.

HiLCO TRANSPORT, INC./LONG BROTHERS

HiLCO Transport/Long Brothers is a full service transportation company specializing in Dump, Tank and Solid Waste Operations.

The future was set when Doc Long's father started in the grading business in the early twenties. His father, James Gurney Long, brother John, and partner John Pearman, graded roads primarily in Rockingham and Guilford counties. Their equipment consisted of drag pans, wheelers, horse-drawn road graders and stump pullers. They would set up camp on the job sites and there they worked, slept and fed their help. Because it was costly to move and mobilize, they did not like to venture far from home.

Doc's fascination with trucks, particularly dump trucks, grew as he watched them travel the crooked and hilly US Highway 220 from the Stokesdale Quarry to Greensboro. He remembers tales of Mr. Leon Ellis as he would stand between the two bridges below Doc's house (now Lake Brandt) with hat in hand waving the trucks on. Dump trucks back then came with no cab or seat. Drivers used a box as a seat and a pillow for a

LONG'S Service Station and Grill was built in 1947. It was located on Highway 220 North at Lake Brandt in Summerfield, North Carolina.

The Long Brothers, left to right, William H. Doc, George, and James.

cushion. As a backrest they leaned against the dump body. These pioneer truckers were some rugged individuals.

Doc finished school in 1941, the same year the nation was at war with Germany, Italy and Japan. In 1943, he was drafted into the Army and was placed in the 79th Infantry Division as a foot soldier. One cold November afternoon in 1944, while in France, he was wounded and lay on the battlefield for 18 hours. The next day, after being picked up, he spent 23 months in the hospital. He was awarded the Purple Heart and the Oak Leaf Cluster for wounds received in combat. On one occasion the 79th Infantry Division received accreditation for the fastest opposed march by any infantry division in the history of warfare, advancing 180 miles in 72 hours.

The war ended in 1945 and Doc's brothers were discharged shortly after. In that same year, Doc married Doris Westmoreland while he was still in the hospital. After Doc was released from the hospital, he and his

brother, James, bought their first truck, a used 1935 Ford. George, the youngest brother, soon joined them and they were on their way.

In 1947, LONG'S Service Station and Grill was built. A tea room and jukebox were included which attracted many college students looking for a night of fun and dancing. In 1948, the first New Ford dump truck was purchased for $2,000. It rented for $2.50 per hour on their first job, hauling dirt from the Ellis Stone Department Store's new building on Elm Street in Greensboro to Overseas Replacement Depot (ORD). In 1954, they went into the well drilling business. They were young and energetic, working day and night. About this same time they gave up the service station and grill. They stayed in the well drilling business until the industry revolutionized and began using air drills. These were expensive so they had to choose between trucking or well drilling. In the end, they gave up the well drilling business.

In 1952, with the continued success of Long Brothers, the three men founded a second company named Asphalt Paving Company of Greensboro. Then, in June of 1977, the family suffered through the untimely and devastating loss of George, who was killed in a private airplane crash.

The company structure changed again in 1983. James chose to remain with Asphalt Paving Company of Greensboro (APC) and Doc stayed with Long Brothers (of Summerfield). At this time, Doc joined with his sons, Charles and Gurney, at the intersection of US 220 and NC 65 where they operated for three years. Doc's daughter Patty joined them in 1984. Long Brothers relocated to Kernersville in 1986. One year later, Patty started her own company, HiLCO Transport, Inc. and shortly thereafter her husband Bruce came to work for Long Brothers.

HiLCO/Long Brothers executive team, left to right: Gurney Long, vice president; Bruce Hill, vice president; Doc Long, founder and chairman; Patty Hill, president; and Charles Long, vice president.

The next few years were very exciting for the Long family. Their businesses continued to grow and expand geographically. On December 31, 1990, HiLCO purchased Southern Oil Transportation Inc. and Tidewater Fuels, Inc. The two companies were merged to form a terminal in Wilmington, NC. It was the start of a perfect corporate marriage. This location was, and still is heavy in hauling asphalt, black oil, gasoline, bulk fertilizer materials and salt.

Acquisitions and mergers continued to pave the way for HiLCO's tremendous growth. Its yellow trucks have become a significant icon in the trucking industry.

On July 1, 1998 Long Brothers of Summerfield and HiLCO Transport, Inc. merged to form one of the largest transportation companies in North Carolina. The bonding of this family-owned company allows it to offer a wide range of services specializing in dump, tank and solid waste operations. This strategic marketing of integrated services and dedicated employees has been HiLCO's recipe for success.

In 1998 the company also purchased 31 acres of land off of Highway 68 in Greensboro. A new 34,000 square foot, state-of-the-art facility was built in 1999 to service approximately 200 employees and 150 trucks.

Today HiLCO/Long Brothers has three terminals in North Carolina located in Greensboro, Troy and Wilmington.

Another key component of HiLCO/Long Brothers success has been an emphasis on safety. The company is dedicated to the concept that all accidents are preventable. This philosophy has enabled HiLCO/Long Brothers to maintain an excellent safety reputation. Safety remains a cornerstone of the HiLCO/Long Brothers vision.

The company's contributions to the community through volunteerism and support of charitable organizations are an important part of its identity. The family and its employees share a special interest in the Rotary Club, Masonic Fraternity, Special Olympics, Northwest School District, Summerfield United Methodist Church, North Carolina Dump Truck Association and

a host of other worthy organizations. And one can find Doc driving his restored 1935 Ford red dump truck and his employees proudly walking by his side during the annual Kernersville Fourth of July, Christmas and Summerfield Founders Day Parades.

With focus on leadership, Patty Hill, the president of HiLCO/Long Brothers was chosen in 1999 to serve as president of the Kernersville Chamber of Commerce.

Three generations are represented at HiLCO/Long Brothers. Doc Long, the father and founder, still comes to work everyday. His children, Charles, Gurney and Patty, manage the daily operations. Charles' daughter Wendi Long Brewer represents the third generation of Longs in the business.

Doc's strong work ethics have played a powerful role toward the mentorship of his children. Together they continue to be a leader in the transportation industry. Doc's children mirror the image of their dad. They respectively believe, as Doc does, that, "Anything we have accomplished...has been done by the help of our family, friends, associates, and by the grace of God."

HiLCO/Long Brothers is committed to its valued reputation and adopted motto: Quality and service are always in season.

JEFFERSON PILOT FINANCIAL

Although the brand name, Jefferson Pilot Financial, was first introduced in 1998, the organization's history actually dates back to 1903. Today's Jefferson Pilot Financial features companies that together offer both traditional and variable universal life insurance as well as annuity products and group life and disability products. If they had been ranked as a single entity in the year 2000, JPF's three primary insurance companies combined would have ranked third nationally in the production of universal life insurance.

The evolution of what is now Jefferson Pilot Financial began with the combining of two namesake companies, Jefferson Standard Life Insurance Company and Pilot Life Insurance Company.

Jefferson Standard Life dated back to August 7, 1907, when it opened for business in Raleigh, NC. Joseph Gill Brown was the company's first president. *The Raleigh News and Observer* hailed Jefferson Standard as the biggest corporation ever to have been launched in the state, with half a million dollars paid in the day after the firm was licensed. Half this sum was set up as surplus. The founders of the company did not select a name at random. Thomas Jefferson—third President of the United States, author of the Declaration of Independence, the nation's greatest exponent of liberty and independence—was made the company's namesake. Officials adopted the slogan, "A Jefferson Standard Policy Is A Declaration of Independence For The Family."

Beginning as a small local operation, the new company was a success from the start—first in North Carolina and, within a few years, throughout the South. When the company made its first annual report, after only five months of operation, Jefferson had almost a million dollars of insurance

Julian Price, president of Jefferson Standard Life Insurance Company from 1919-1946.

in force—a very large number in those days.

On September 20, 1912, Jefferson Standard merged with two Greensboro-based companies, Security Life and Annuity Company and Greensboro Life Insurance Company, moving its operations to Greensboro. In 1919, Julian Price was elected president, and his hand guided Jefferson Stan-

dard through more than a quarter of a century of increasingly successful operations.

Howard Holderness, after long service as vice president and treasurer of the company and a member of the board of directors, was called to the presidency in May 1950. Mr. Holderness served in that capacity for 17 years before being named chairman of the board, a position he held until his retirement in February 1978.

W. Roger Soles, CLU, became the sixth president of Jefferson Standard in February 1967, succeeding Mr. Holderness, with whom he had worked closely for many years. Mr. Soles assumed the duties of chief executive officer in July 1967.

In the following year Jefferson-Pilot Corporation, a holding company, was incorporated, and Mr. Soles was elected president and chief executive officer. During his time as chief executive, Jefferson Standard grew its life insurance in force from $3 billion to over $7 billion.

Pilot Life Insurance Company—1953 photograph of the company's headquarters from 1928-1987.

W. Roger Soles, CLU, was named president of Jefferson Standard Life Insurance Company in 1967. He retired as chairman of the board and chief executive officer of Jefferson-Pilot Corporation and Jefferson-Pilot Life Insurance Company in 1993.

Pilot Life Insurance Company, then known as Southern Loan & Trust Company, entered the life insurance business in July 1903, and changed its name to Southern Life & Trust Company in 1905. By year-end, the new company had $1 million of insurance in force. In 1924, the company changed its name to Pilot Life Insurance Company. A new trademark was developed—a pilot behind the wheel—and "Pilot to Protection Since 1903" became the company slogan.

The year 1928 brought an unprecedented move to "the country" where magnificent new buildings had been constructed on 132 acres of land in Sedgefield, seven miles from downtown Greensboro. The company reached $100 million of insurance in force several times in 1930. Because of the depression, it took two more years to again surpass that figure.

Jefferson Standard bought controlling stock in Pilot Life in 1931, with Pilot buying this stock back in 1940 to once again become an independent life insurer. Jefferson Standard purchased Pilot stock again in 1945, and merged the company with Gate City Life, also a Jefferson-owned company. The merger began a period of formidable growth for Pilot. With the merger came the addition of group insurance, making Pilot Life a multiple line company. In 1948, Pilot pioneered scholastic accident insurance for schools.

By 1955, the company reached $1 billion of insurance in force. The next year, Pilot Life became a major regional television advertiser by being first, sole sponsor and, later, the major sponsor of Atlantic Coast Conference basketball on television.

In 1968, the year Jefferson-Pilot Corporation was formed, Pilot hit $4 billion of insurance in force. After another 10 years, the insurance in force had reached $11 billion.

Seven Pilot Life presidents provided 83 years of capable leadership. E.P. Wharton, a prominent Greensboro businessman, was the first, A.W. McAlister served the longest number of years (1908-1932), and Louis C. Stephens Jr. was serving as president when Pilot Life was merged with Jefferson Standard in January 1987 to become Jefferson-Pilot Life Insurance Company.

The joining of two history-making insurance companies during Roger Soles' tenure was a logical decision. Both companies had been wholly owned subsidiaries of the Jefferson-Pilot Corporation since 1968 and had been ably managed since 1945 by management teams that worked closely together. Both were well-known, successful companies with complementary operations. At the time of the merger, Jefferson-Pilot Corporation assets totaled $3.8 billion. By the end of 1992, they had grown to over $5.2 billion.

In March 1993, David A. Stonecipher, FSA, succeeded Mr. Soles as president and chief executive officer of both Jefferson-Pilot Corporation and Jefferson-Pilot Life Insurance Company. In the years since, Jefferson-Pilot Corporation and its subsidiaries have experienced explosive growth, highlighted by a number of key strategic initiatives. Since 1994, Jefferson-Pilot has completed four major acquisitions including Chubb Life Insurance Company in 1994 (since renamed Jefferson Pilot Financial Insurance Company) and its subsidiary now named Jefferson Pilot LifeAmerica (1997), Alexander Hamilton Life (1995), Guarantee Life (1997) and the in-force life insurance of Kentucky Central Life. Effective in August 2000, Alexander Hamilton Life and Guarantee Life were merged into Jefferson Pilot Financial Insurance Company.

The additions brought total assets to more than $27 billion and positioned the companies that make up

The Jefferson Building (circa 1985), listed in the National Register of Historic Places.

David A. Stonecipher, FSA, was named president and chief executive officer of Jefferson-Pilot Corporation and Jefferson-Pilot Life in March 1993. He became chairman of the board in 1998.

Jefferson Pilot Financial among the top life insurance organizations in the U.S. Together, the companies have more than $210 billion of life insurance in force.

The companies' product offerings, already among the broadest in the industry, continue to expand and JPF has extended its franchise to people across the country. Jefferson Pilot Financial companies are licensed to operate in all 50 states, the District of Columbia, Puerto Rico, the Virgin Islands and Guam. Jefferson-Pilot's stock is traded on the New York, Midwest and Pacific Stock Exchanges under the symbol JP.

In Greensboro, Jefferson Pilot Financial's home office staff is housed in two beautiful and historic buildings in the center of downtown. They stand, side by side, as permanent proof of the company's commitment to the community and to Jefferson-Pilot's policyowners and shareholders.

Built on the site of the old Guilford County Courthouse, The Jefferson Building was ready for occupancy in October 1923. It had cost $2.5 million, but was debt free the day it opened. Considerably more than that has since been spent to renovate and modernize the building.

At the time, the *Greensboro Daily Record* wrote, "White, immaculate and imposing, guarding Greater Greensboro by night and day, as it were, this great shaft, milestone of progress, marks a new and greater era in the history of this metropolis."

The late Charles C. Hartmann, Sr. designed the 17-story building which has 313,410 square feet of floor space. It took 23 carloads of marble to line the corridors. The U.S. Department of the Interior in 1976 declared the Jefferson Building a national landmark. It is now included in the National Register of Historic Places, the first business or commercial structure so designated in North Carolina.

Designed by the Atlanta architectural firm of Smallwood, Reynolds, Stewart and Stewart and Associates, the Jefferson-Pilot Building was dedicated in August 1990. At 375 feet, the 20-story structure is the tallest in Greensboro. As was intended, the building has a timeless appearance, both inside and out, which is entirely compatible with the historic Jefferson Building. An adjacent, 860-space parking deck was also built to complement the decor of both buildings.

The Jefferson-Pilot Building features a three-story rotunda resplendent with rich-hued mahogany and polished Italian marble from the same quarry Michelangelo used for his Renaissance masterpieces. The rotunda lends an air of spaciousness, stability and grace to the building, which is capped by a 75-foot tall, copper-clad roof. Company employees may enjoy breakfast or lunch in the 360-seat cafeteria on the third floor. The private City Club, for members from the Greensboro business community, is located on the top two floors of the building.

The officers and staff of Jefferson Pilot Financial are rightfully proud of their heritage, which is the foundation from which the company builds for the future. The City of Greensboro has certainly benefited from the corporate citizenship of Jefferson-Pilot since the early 1900s. Conversely, the financial giant has gained much from its association with the "Chosen Center."

The Jefferson-Pilot Building (left), alongside the Jefferson Building.

A.P. HUBBARD LUMBER CORPORATION

While on an aircraft carrier during World War II Ainslie Hubbard decided when the war was over he wanted to start his own business. He was a native of Virginia but chose North Carolina as centrally located. He came to think of Greensboro as an ideal place to live and work. His first venture after the war was a cement block factory. This was financed by money he had saved and family loans. Due to being undercapitalized he was forced to close this plant, so he called and wrote everyone he owed money to tell them they would be paid in full. Although it took years no creditor lost a cent. He realized it would be difficult to pay these debts working for a salary so he talked to many people in the business about starting a lumber company. They all told him without experience and substantial financing it would not be possible. In later years Hubbard said it would have been better had he worked for someone else first so that he might gain knowledge and experience but instead he borrowed money on his car, his only remaining asset, and sold his first lumber order. He started A.P. Hubbard Lumber Corp. in 1950.

The first office was in the Overseas Replacement Depot (ORD) section of Greensboro. Fifty-one years later the present location is still in the ORD area now on Arnold Street. The company started selling softwoods to building contractors. In a few years laminated beams and arches were added to the sales of the company which now represents Structural Wood Systems of Alabama.

Later a hardwoods division was added and this became an important part of the company. The late Jay Doty was vice president in charge of hardwoods for many years. Now his son Skip Doty holds that position. Cypress, poplar and oak are specialties of the hardwood sales. Bill Griffin is vice president in charge of white pine sales. The company ships lumber all over the United States and Mexico. A.P. Hubbard was an early believer in the ability of women and gave them much responsibility and opportunity to advance. Vicki Weaver is the office manager as well as being involved in sales. This is a business where all of the stockholders are women.

A.P. Hubbard, founder.

Many people showed extraordinary confidence in A.P. Hubbard and great generosity in giving him help in the early days of his business, among them George Efird, Allen Mebane, the late Arza Milliken and his son Jerry Milliken.

Marion Hubbard became president when her husband died in 1997. This has always been a family business with Fred Hubbard, a brother, working in the Roanoke, Virginia office until his death. Edward Cosby, a son-in-law, is vice president in charge of the Richmond office which also sell windows as well as engineered wood and gluelam beams and arches.

A.P. Hubbard Lumber Corp. continues the basic philosophy of the founder who was known for his integrity, fairness, high standards, and his ability to motivate others.

Marion Hubbard, president.

KAY CHEMICAL COMPANY

Food safety is becoming increasingly important, and Kay Chemical Company is at the forefront of developing the products and services needed to clean surfaces where prepared foods are sold.

Kay is among the world's leading suppliers of cleaning and sanitation products and programs for fast food restaurants, grocery stores and convenience stores. The company's customer list includes some of the world's largest chains in each of these categories.

Customers rely on Kay for cleaning products that are specially formulated for food service environments. The types of foods prepared, the high volume of customers, and the surfaces in the food prep and dining areas create unique cleaning needs. By focusing its research and development on these cleaning needs, Kay has experienced tremendous growth since its humble beginnings in 1932.

Harry Kaplan started Kay in his High Point, North Carolina garage with a barrel of T.N.T. (Takes No Time) All-Purpose Cleaner that he ordered from a manufacturer in another state. When it arrived, he repackaged the powder into one-pound bags and sold it to local gas stations. Soon afterward, Harry added Kay Shine Metal Polish.

Kay's early years were marked by rapid growth. In 1937 the company moved out of Harry's garage and into a 1,200-square-foot building in High Point that Harry rented for $23 a month. The company moved again in 1942 and by 1945 was manufacturing several of its own products.

Harry's son Leonard joined Kay in the summer of 1948. Leonard began his career by walking the streets of downtown High Point demonstrating the company's products to local businesses. These demonstrations proved to be an effective selling tool and

Leonard soon found himself taking orders for the company's growing list of products.

Leonard assumed the role of CEO in 1954 and transformed a company that was already successful into a national player, by leading Kay into the foodservice industry. It was a move that would prove to be a turning point in the company's history.

The entry into the foodservice industry in 1958 led to the development of cleaning programs. With the advent of these programs, Kay's customers saw how a comprehensive

Kay moved into its Capital Drive facility in 1987. Since then, the building has been expanded to 275,000 square feet.

approach to cleaning could have a positive impact on their restaurants' appearance and reputation. These programs fueled sales as customers learned proper cleaning procedures.

The company's cleaning programs have evolved to include training, instructional materials, technical advice, research and development, customer service, and field support. This comprehensive approach helps Kay's customers protect their patrons and their reputations, by maintaining clean, sanitized facilities.

Field support is one component of Kay's cleaning programs and is an important part of the company's comprehensive approach to food safety. Field representatives are in restaurants and stores every day. These frequent visits give the Kay team firsthand knowledge of customers' needs.

By being in the stores and restaurants daily, field service representatives see the cleaning challenges that come with new equipment, leading

Kay manufactures products that are shipped around the world. Labels are often printed in several languages to accommodate the growing number of countries where Kay products are sold.

Kay to develop new products or modify existing ones. Customers count on Kay to find ways to keep equipment looking new and make cleaning easier. Often Kay is consulted when new stores are being designed. By doing so, stores are designed with easy cleaning in mind. As a benefit to its customers, Kay can test floor and counter surfaces, seating, and fixtures for ease-of-cleaning.

In addition to examining interior surfaces, Kay's research scientists study the soils and bacteria associated with the foodservice industry, and develop products that will clean without harming the surface or the employee. Kay's lab is one of only a few in the nation that is certified by the Council for Antimicrobial Quality (CAQ). In order to achieve this rating, Kay must maintain strict adherence to laboratory research practices.

Kay's scientists, research team and regulatory staff have familiarized

themselves with international laws and guidelines since the company began international sales in 1991. Today, Kay operates from a 325,000-square-foot facility on Capital Drive in Greensboro and has customers in over 90 markets around the world.

Kay's international presence is leveraged as a wholly-owned subsidiary of Ecolab, Inc. Ecolab is the leading global developer and marketer of premium cleaning, sanitizing, maintenance, and pest elimination products and services for the hospitality, health care, and light industrial markets.

Ecolab, Kay's parent company since 1994, appears on several exclusive lists. Ecolab was named as one of *Industry Week*'s 100 Best Managed Companies, based on financial performance, philanthropy and safety. The Calvert Social Index, an exclusive listing of socially responsible U.S.-based companies, included Ecolab after reviewing the company's performance in the environment, workplace issues, product safety and impact, international operations and human rights, weapons contracting, and indigenous peoples' rights.

Ecolab has also been selected as one of *Business Ethics* Magazine's 100 Best Corporate Citizens following a review of the company's local community relations, service to international stakeholders, customer

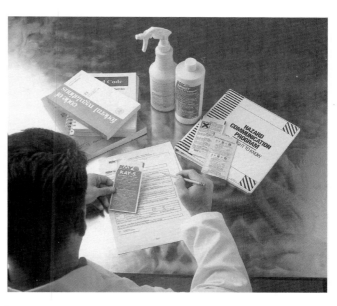

Product safety information is provided to all of Kay's customers.

relations, product quality and innovation, employee relations and diversity, environmental protection, and financial returns for stockholders.

Ecolab's commitment to corporate social responsibility can be felt at Kay. The company takes its role as a responsible corporate citizen very seriously. Each year, Kay employees award grant money to nonprofit agencies and schools in the area. The company gives employees time off to volunteer for community projects, such as Kids Voting, Habitat for Humanity and Days of Caring. Also, each year, Kay conducts a United Way campaign that is among the largest in Greensboro.

Whether it's product innovation or community funding, Kay is aggressively looking for solutions to the needs of others. Kay's commitment to its customers and the community guide every decision. With these as its guiding forces, Kay is poised for continuing growth in sales and community involvement.

Kay offers a complete line of cleaning and sanitation products for quick service restaurants, food retail establishments and convenience stores.

KNIGHT CARR & COMPANY

Linda Knight Carr entered the interior design business world through a back door. The Page Private School where she had been teaching closed unexpectedly in 1979, leaving her unemployed. As a segue into her next job, Carr sublet her apartment in Greensboro and headed to the beach for the summer. Unbeknownst to her, her tastefully decorated apartment was being greatly admired by Bill Johnston, a guest invited by the tenant. Johnston was so impressed with her work that he invited Carr to join the staff of his new furniture store.

Carr's degree in interior design from the University of North Carolina at Greensboro, and her previous four years of freelance decorating experience while teaching, prepared her well for her job of designing and executing showrooms at Johnston & Mitchell. Here she also honed her customer skills by offering free consultations.

In September 1985 Carr opened a door for herself. She rented a single room in a house at 406 West Fisher Avenue in Greensboro where she and a business partner founded Knight & Elliott Interior Direction, funded only by a combined savings of $800. By the end of their first year, Knight & Elliot had spilled over to all rooms in the house and hired their first employee.

The next two years witnessed further dramatic events. In October 1994 the partners moved their business into a larger base at 909 North Elm Street, as space was needed to match their continuing growth. The following year when Paul Elliott set out to pursue other opportunities, the business partnership dissolved. Finding herself suddenly a sole proprietor, Carr moved beyond the break-up and her dependency on a partner and summoned her energies to successfully lead the business into the future. By December 2000 Carr had moved

Linda Knight Carr.

her burgeoning company into yet a larger facility at 703 Hill Street where it is located today. She changed the name of the full service design firm to Knight Carr & Company. At this site Carr hopes to expand into retail sales with the advantage that the new showrooms offer.

The accomplishments of Knight Carr & Company may be attributed to several key factors. The personal touch and sense of style of its founder and owner are major elements, and Carr remains the driving force behind her successful business. Yet Carr believes that the final rendition must reflect the lifestyle of the client and she keeps their needs foremost throughout the design process. The heritage of the region and a building's distinct architecture and locale are

also considered. Carr is an artistic designer who approaches each project as individual and unique.

Topnotch service is another hallmark of Knight Carr & Company. The seven employees, who range from designers and design assistants to a business manager and installers, form a competent staff. This innovative and talented team prides itself on assisting clients throughout the decision making process, giving advice on basic tasks that range from faucet selection to more complex ones such as working with contractors. They remain involved every step of the way until the last picture is hung and the house-warming gift purchased.

Also setting Knight Carr & Company apart is their extensive selection of textiles, furniture and accessories. Their library of high-end fabrics imported from New York, Atlanta, and foreign sources are renowned in the area. The prominent furniture market of North Carolina provides a fabulous selection of quality outfittings and antiques from England, France and Italy. In-house made reproductions are kept on hand to be ready for a client's choosing.

One of Carr's unique decorating techniques is layering. Each project, whether a single room or entire home, is approached through multiple dimensions: furniture, draperies, wall coverings, accessories, and lastly art, books, and finishing touches. All are balanced through color and proportion with the emphasis on a welcoming and comfortable feeling.

Carr's insightful solutions and fresh ideas have made her work stand out above the rest. For this she has received extensive recognition in illustrated articles by both *Southern Living* and *Renovation Style* Magazines, as well as the Greensboro *News and Record*.

Early in 2000 Carr was chosen to renovate one of Greensboro's most notable homes, a Georgian Colonial revival in an historic district. For this major renovation and design work she was invited to appear on the Joy Philbin Show. Yet, her most recent triumph was being chosen the designer for the 2001 Idea House in Advance, North Carolina, by the editors of *Southern Living Magazine*, a lifestyle magazine published in Birmingham, Alabama. The three Idea Houses built throughout the South showcase products, designs, innovations, landscaping and ideas to readers.

Over the years Knight Carr & Company has served clients from as far away as Las Vegas, NV, Boston, MA and Naples, FL, and has successfully approached renovations from tiny beach houses to former embassies. Meeting challenges is *de rigueur* for Carr, who has shown her considerable talents by mastering the unusual design spaces of yachts and private jets. But most satisfying are the frequent customers who return again and again for Knight Carr & Company's services, and who recommend them to their friends, as well. With the past successes and bright future of Knight Carr & Company, Linda Knight Carr continues to open beautiful doors for others.

Greensboro, North Carolina, family room designed in 1998.

LAUGHLIN-SUTTON CONSTRUCTION COMPANY

Laughlin-Sutton Construction Company, established in Greensboro, North Carolina in 1958, was founded by Curtis L. Laughlin and Alex D. Sutton as a general contracting firm serving clients in North Carolina, South Carolina and Virginia. The company started in a rented office on Carolina Avenue. In 1965, land was purchased and an office/warehouse complex was built at 2210 North Church Street, which served its needs until 1989 when the present office/warehouse complex was built at 5855 Rudd Station Road near Bryan Park.

Laughlin-Sutton's reputation is mainly built upon an extensive industrial construction background in textile mills and in the construction of water and wastewater treatment plant work. The bulk of the repeat business comes from the many relationships built over the years in this field. Most of these relationships started with the textile and apparel manufacturers in the Carolinas and Virginia. With Greensboro-based home offices of textile companies—Burlington Industries, Cone Mills and

Main office located at 5855 Rudd Station Road.

Guilford Mills—Laughlin-Sutton started doing construction projects for these businesses at their plants in and around Greensboro. Of these companies, there are no plants in Greensboro that Laughlin-Sutton has not worked in over the years. At one particular plant, construction ranging from small maintenance work to multi-million dollar projects has been continuous for over 35 years. As Laughlin-Sutton grew, so did its area

base. Soon work was being performed at textile plants owned by these and other textile companies around North Carolina, the southern part of Virginia and the northern part of South Carolina. As the industrial base diversified, so has the client list, which also includes producers of furniture, chemicals, plastics, machinery, electronic components, power tools, cosmetics and construction products. Most of their customer base comes from repeat clients, or new clients who were recommended by a former client, or architects and engineers they have worked with in the past.

Specialty construction of water treatment and wastewater treatment plants is a big part of Laughlin-Sutton. Greensboro's Lake Townsend and Mitchell Water Treatment Plants, as well as North Buffalo Wastewater Treatment Plant, have been projects of Laughlin-Sutton. Also, several water and wastewater pumping stations have been constructed around the Greensboro area.

Clarifier amd aeration structure in a waste water treatment plant.

An office and manufacturing building for a textile plant built in 1993.

Laughlin-Sutton Construction Company is owned by a group of managers and field superintendents who are all active in the day-to-day operations of the company. Curtis Laughlin and Alex Sutton's philosophy was to offer stock ownership in the company to key employees, both as an incentive and as a means to retain key employees. Most were trained by the founders, who instilled in these employees/stock holders their high standards of competence, ethics and performance, insuring that the customers got a good value for a good price. Their hands-on leadership assures the company's ongoing strength and success. Laughlin-Sutton's administrative and clerical staff is structured to provide its clients with optimum service. Each client works with a management team member who is both an estimator and project manager, insuring continuity, accountability and simplified communications. Most of the management personnel have degrees in civil engineering or related fields, and all are well versed in the latest construction techniques, including the utilization of up-to-date computerized estimating, scheduling, and cost control systems.

Laughlin-Sutton's field superintendents are highly experienced builders, with an average of over 20 years in the construction industry. Four of the field superintendents have over 30 years experience and two have been employed by Laughlin-Sutton for 36 years. The field superintendents are supported by their core group of field employees including carpenters, concrete finishers, equipment operators and steel erectors. Laughlin-Sutton's employee turnover rate is quite low, which assures a continued high performance of field operation.

Over the years, Laughlin-Sutton has developed a fleet of construction equipment, cranes, trucks, tools and concrete forming systems, which is maintained in-house. This inventory allows for self-performance of many critical elements of construction projects which expedites scheduling, assures tighter quality control, maintains a competitive edge and helps to handle emergency needs which arise from time to time for their customers.

For over 40 years, Laughlin-Sutton has built a reputation among engineers and municipalities around North Carolina for performing quality work in a timely manner.

An office complex in Burlington, North Carolina built in 1990.

LUKE JOBE CONSTRUCTION

It is not uncommon for Greensboro real estate agents to advertise a house built by Luke Jobe Construction Company as simply, "a Luke Jobe home." Like Jacuzzis, fireplaces, skylights or pools, Luke Jobe's name sells homes.

Luke Jobe Construction has built over 1,000 homes in Greensboro, many of which are showcases, since Jobe stepped out on his own in 1954 at the age of 21. These homes grace fine neighborhoods such as Irving Park, Starmount and Grandover.

A typical Jobe home may cost $1 million or more; some elegant homes top $2 million. "Jobe is a southern boy who personally prefers the traditional Georgian colonial style," his wife Barbara says, "but he's also built an English castle, Contemporary and Country French styles, and Federal types."

It is not unlikely that a Jobe client is a repeat customer. Luke Jobe Construction has built second homes for many clients. People are looking for

someone they trust, and they trust Luke Jobe Construction, primarily because Jobe is adamant about quality. "It's got to be right," Barbara Jobe says. "If it's not right, you have to tear it out and do it again. We're successful because of what Luke believes in—craftsmanship, individual style, and long-lasting beauty."

Jobe began working for his father, a Greensboro builder, as soon as he was old enough to do cleanup at the job sites. Jobe's four sons learned construction as he did—from the basement up—at their father's side; they too got their start picking up scrap lumber.

At one time or another all the Jobe sons—Steve, Michael, Robin and Luke—have worked in the family business. Daughter's Shaila and Barbara Marie have helped their mother in the company office. Like many wives of building contractors, Barbara Jobe is the motor that keeps the office running smoothly, performing the legwork, paperwork and office management.

Barbara Jobe is as essential as nails to Jobe's business. Typically, she and Jobe design the house, then take the designs to a draftsman, who draws it to scale. Jobe and his sons build the house. Barbara then decorates it and sells it. She has moved nine times in 50 years of marriage, because

Luke and Barbara Jobe.

people keep making offers for the family's own solidly-built and stylishly decorated homes.

Anyone who is ready to build their "dream house" must find a general contractor who values built-in dreams. Luke Jobe is such a man. Responsive to the wishes and aspirations of his clients, Mr. Jobe and his staff work closely with their clients to create the kind of home they have always wanted—one designed specifically for their unique, individual lifestyle. Luke Jobe Construction is solidly experienced in the business, as well as in the art of building beautiful, lasting homes. Each Jobe home incorporates the features most important to homebuyers: design, location, realistic price, craftsmanship, and resale value—all adding up to quality. Growing with Guilford County for more than four decades, the Luke Jobe Company combines the best of the old and new in every home that it builds.

A Luke Jobe home—that says it all.

KINDRED HOSPITAL GREENSBORO

The history of Kindred Hospital Greensboro (formerly Vencor Hospital Greensboro) dates back to the original L. Richardson Memorial Hospital short-term acute care established in 1966. Kindred Hospital Greensboro, in conjunction with its parent Kindred Healthcare, Inc., is a pioneer in the industry of acute long-term care services. Kindred Hospital Greensboro was the first and remains the only acute long-term provider in North Carolina. Kindred's goal is to provide the highest level of care in the most cost-effective environment, and to strive to enhance patients' quality of life. The hospital's expertise in respiratory care is essential to its strong emphasis on ventilator-dependent patients. The hospital has an average of 65 ventilator patients per day; there have been occasions when the hospital has had up to 83 ventilator patients, along with other very ill patients.

The hospital is a four-story brick building on a 16-acre campus at the crossroad of Highways 85 and 29, midway between Raleigh and Winston-Salem, on the south side of Greensboro in Guilford County, North Carolina. The facility is unique because it has

Front view of Kindred Hospital, Greensboro.

both Acute Care and Skilled Nursing Unit in the same building. The facility is considered a center of excellence with high scores in JCAHO and deficiency-free surveys from HCFA.

The hospital provides the following services: Intensive Care, Critical Care step-down with Telemetry, Skilled Unit, Dialysis, Surgery and PACU, Inpatient and Outpatient Rehabilitation, Outpatient Treatment Area, Laboratory, Radiology, CT Scan, ECHO Cardiogram, EEG, Sleep Center, Occupational Medicine, Pharmacy, and Recreational Therapy.

The hospital employs many disciplines and specialists providing care to multisystem failure patients. Specialized equipment is needed to care for this type of patient. The hospital is the largest user of a special artificial intelligence computerized ventilator in the United States, enabling the staff to wean patients from the ventilator who would otherwise live on one for the rest of their lives.

Kindred Hospital Greensboro receives patients from 97 facilities' intensive care units in North and South Carolina and Virginia. They are known as the hospital to go to when a patient

needs to be weaned off the ventilator or has critical care needs. Its number one referring hospital is Wake Forest University Baptist Medical Center in Winston/Salem. Kindred is well-known to referring facilities throughout North Carolina and Virginia, and has been recognized in articles that have appeared in the business journals and local newspapers.

The hospital also has a small outpatient department, and recently added a Sleep Laboratory in a separate building on campus to help diagnose sleep disorders that may be contributing to 97 various conditions or serious illnesses.

Kindred Hospital is very fortunate to have 350 hard working employees taking care of a very difficult population. The staff takes its mission and vision to heart. Kindred seeks to be the leading provider in the Carolinas and Southern Virginia of quality care to acute medically complex and skilled level patients, as well as of compassionate support to their families. Its value statement says it all, "Kindred Hospital Greensboro is driven by the uncompromising belief in the value, dignity and intrinsic worth of every individual."

Operating room being prepared for a patient to have surgery.

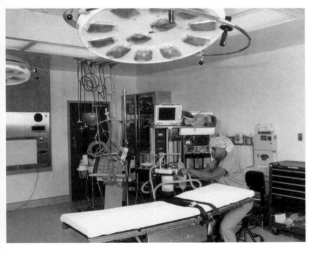

MOTHER MURPHY'S LABORATORIES, INC.

Mother Murphy's Laboratories, Inc. was started in Greensboro in the mid-1900s by two unlikely associates—Dr. Richard Stelling, a physician who worked his way through school by making and selling food flavorings, and Kermit Murphy, a sales agent for Jefferson Standard Life Insurance Company. Starting out in the small back room of a drug store in 1945, the two partners installed a mixer and manufactured food flavorings on nights and weekends. By the end of 1947 they had created a formal corporation, Southern Laboratories Company, and both men devoted their full attention to the business.

By 1948, the Company had outgrown its small back room operation so a new plant on Arnold Street in the southeastern part of Greensboro was built. When the new plant was operational, the Company boasted of annual sales of $56,000. There were still only two full-time employees, Kermit Murphy and a secretary, with Dr. Stelling assisting as a supervisor. Due to the growth of the business and the many requests of its customers for new flavor ingredients, they hired their first full-time chemist from a large competitor in New York. In 1958 the Murphy family involvement

Kermit Murphy, founder and chief executive officer.

increased when L.M. "Pete" Murphy resigned as president of a Greensboro paper company to join his brother Kermit in the growing flavor business.

By 1955 the Company changed its name to Mother Murphy's Laboratories, Inc. and in 1962 they moved into their present plant at 2826 South Elm Street. The headquarters are still located there some 40 years later. After numerous expansion projects, the Elm Street facility has grown from an original 22,000 square feet to over 60,000 square feet of production and warehouse space. A new distribution center was opened in July 2000 on Industrial Avenue.

Mother Murphy's now employs upwards of 60 people in Greensboro and throughout the United States and has annual sales in excess of $20 million.

Over time, the Company's product line has expanded from basic food flavorings, such as vanilla extracts, to include drink bases, fruit flavors, meat and seafood flavors. Its food flavors can be made in the form of liquid, powder or spray-dried products.

Mother Murphy's boasts an impressive list of customers, including some of the largest food companies in the world, who operate in the baking, dairy, tobacco, and beverage industries. However no customer is too small as Mother Murphy's also supplies smaller companies such as entrepreneurs who bake wedding cakes and your local neighborhood bakery.

The late L.M. "Pete" Murphy, former chairman of the board.

The Company's growth has come from focusing on the development of new and different flavors. Its salesmen, chemists and production personnel work jointly to custom-design flavors for specific customer needs. So whether its a new fruit filling in your favorite donut, a different sourdough flavor for your favorite delivered pizza or that special sweetness in your next cookie or bowl of ice cream, there's a good chance that Mother Murphy's Laboratories, Inc. had a hand in the development of that good taste.

The home office of Mother Murphy's Laboratories, Inc.

NEESE COUNTRY SAUSAGE, INC.

It was in 1917 that James Theodore Neese, a farmer living in eastern Guilford County, began to market his popular country sausage. By 1920 the population of Greensboro reached 19,861 and that of High Point 14,303—so there were eager customers for "Mr. Thede's" special recipe. Actually, it was his wife, Annie Smith Neese, who developed the recipe until it was just the right proportion of ham to other pork cuts, and just the right seasoning of salt, sage, and pepper.

Samuel D. Smith, an attorney in Hickory, North Carolina, remembers very closely those early days. "I saw, on many occasions, Mr. Thede peddling ham, sausage, and occasionally beef from a buggy long before any plant was ever established. I can very vividly recall the last time I ever saw him. I was with my father, Bob Smith, and we were coming from Greensboro, down what we called the Alamance Road. We met Mr. Thede just below where Arthur Sharpe was living and he asked my father if he wanted a beef roast for the weekend, and Dad said, 'Yes.' I think he paid him 50 cents for it."

Mr. Thede operated a "Trade House" and also butchered hogs and cattle for his neighbors, concentrating on this work after cold weather set in. He began making sausage with a hand-operated grinder. Gradually he built a trade in town, making deliveries in a "prairie schooner" (covered wagon), the kind that crossed the western plains. By 1925 the company had acquired a Dodge screen-sided truck. Since refrigeration was in its infancy, everything from slaughtering to packaging was done at night. By daybreak the truck would head for town.

In the 1920s "Miss Annie" stirred up still another Neese recipe—liver pudding. She ground the pork livers and other pork cuts, seasoned the mixture with herbs and spices, and added just enough cornmeal to hold it together. She never used chemicals or preservatives in either sausage or liver pudding, and the same recipes are still faithfully followed.

The original plant in eastern Guilford County, about 1915, with, (left to right) James Theodore Neese, Raymond Coble, Jake Coble, John Neese, Al Coble, Milt Allred, and George Hubbard.

In 1925 Mr. Thede's son, Tom, graduated from high school and went into sausagemaking full time. Mr. Thede turned the business over to him, as he was already an experienced sausage maker. Tom and his brothers, Homer and Robert, later became partners. The firm is still family owned and operated, with Tom Neese, Jr. as president. Ernest Huffine and great grandchildren Andrea Neese Pegram and Tommy Neese III are vice presidents.

The company moved to its present site on Alamance Church Road in 1936. First there was a wooden structure, then one of brick, which is the nucleus of several additions. Neese Country Sausage's principal sales area is North Carolina.

The Neese Country Sausage Plant, circa 1945.

RUCKER ENTERPRISES

One dusty August afternoon in 1905, a 20 year-old Southern youth left his home in Columbia, South Carolina to seek his fortune in more distant climes. Shortly after the "Late Unpleasantness" his father, a Confederate veteran, had also left his home in the Lynchburg, Virginia area for a brighter future. However, Lee's warrior was finding it nearly impossible to raise a family on the meager living he made selling mill supplies and lubricating oils to the emerging but impoverished Southern manufacturers. As independent commission men were gradually being displaced by the rapacious agents of the Oil Trust and other combines, Houston Rucker earnestly advised his sons to try other lines of work. Thus, after two years at the University of South Carolina, necessarily terminated by strained financial circumstances, Pierce Christie Rucker sought his future and fortune beyond the restricted confines of Richland County, South Carolina.

Having apprenticed as a cotton broker during his summer recesses,

Pierce Christie Rucker, founder of Rucker Enterprises.

Pierce had made contact with several buyers and warehousemen in the Greensboro, North Carolina area and chose to make his way there. Shortly after arriving in Greensboro, he established Rucker Cotton Company and became a significant factor in the cotton trade of the Upper South. Always optimistic and forward-looking, he next built a cotton warehouse that was then joined by a general mer-

Bryan Park Facility.

chandise warehouse. He then started a drayage business.

In due time Rucker's business interest had expanded and he acquired substantive holdings in local real estate, banking and insurance. As the 1920s were halcyon days for the South and the entire country, he felt secure about the future and sought to expand his interests. Alas, his economic euphoria was not justified, and the advent of the 1930s saw an end of many a bright dream. The economic quake that followed may have only shaken the financial centers of the country, but it annihilated the economies of the burgeoning cities in the South.

By dint of hard labor and perseverance, Pierce Rucker managed to retain his primary calling, cotton brokerage, but all of his peripheral holdings were swept away in that debacle known as the Great Depression. Ever alert to the new opportunities presenting themselves, he made his way back by sheer persistence. By 1940 concern with diversification had replaced survival as the order of the day. The end of World War II found Rucker in distribution, storage, trucking and real estate, and a substantial corporate structure had been erected on the old foundations. By 1950 the complex of companies now functioning were recognizable and emerging in their present form. At this juncture he chose to turn the direction of the business over to the next generation.

In 1937 Pierce Rucker Jr. had joined his father in manage-

Walker F. Rucker.

upgraded and greatly expanded. A real estate company was incorporated and a trucking line initiated. Having served in the business for over 45-years Walker, as his father before him, had trained his successor.

James G. Rucker, a grandson of the founder and graduate of Wake Forest University class of 1986, joined the family business that year. Jim will guide the companies into the 21st century. Rucker Enterprises faces the new century with confidence.

In memory of Mary Fry and Pierce C. Rucker Sr. the family committed to financing the Emergency Wing of the new Wesley Long Hospital. The original hospital had been the Rucker's neighbor for several decades. The dedicatory remarks are summed up in the inscribed plaque personifying Mary and Pierce Rucker's humanitarianism:

"Not unacquainted with disaster, we have learned to aid the unfortunate." (Virgil)

James G. Rucker.

Inside the Greensboro facility.

ment of the business. Pierce Jr. was inducted in the Army in 1941. In 1945, after service in the Philippines, he was mustered out and returned to the family business. Pierce Jr. found his niche in managing the distribution operations. He worked effectively and successively in distributing beverages, automotive supplies and lastly household appliances.

In 1940 Mr. Rucker's only daughter Mary Lewis joined the company as a bookkeeper, after graduating from college. She served effectively therein until 1946 when she married Robert Edmunds, a Virginian, and moved to Halifax, Virginia.

In 1951, after service in the Army Air Corp. as a navigator and graduating from the University of North Carolina, Chapel Hill, Mr. Rucker's younger son Walker assumed management of the plant properties. Under his aegis the older properties were

RF MICRO DEVICES, INC.

In 1991, William J. Pratt, Powell T. Seymour and Jerry D. Neal put a high-tech spin on manufacturing in the Triad when they founded RF Micro Devices®.

RFMD® manufactures a type of integrated circuit known as "radio frequency." These radio frequency integrated circuits process signals transmitted and received by wireless communication devices.

While the company's primary success evolved from its power amplifiers, RFMD also manufactures a broad array of chips from mixers and modulators to receivers and transceivers. These components are used in wireless handsets, wireless infrastructure, cable television modems and personal communication systems. RFMD is also targeting developing markets such as wireless local area networks and *Bluetooth*™ wireless technology.

If you've used a cell phone, personal digital assistant or two-way data pager, chances are you've had an RFMD chip in your hand.

The company takes pride in its customer relationships and is aligned with many of the leaders in the industry such as Nokia, QUALCOMM, Siemens, Ericsson and Motorola.

RFMD specializes in multiple process technologies—gallium arsenide heterojunction bipolar transistor (GaAs HBT), silicon germanium, silicon CMOS, silicon BiCMOS and GaAs MESFET—that address a wide range of applications. The company leads the wireless market in manufacturing GaAs HBT semiconductors which offer better performance than conventional silicon-based semiconductors, making them ideal for wireless communications applications. Demand for RFMD's revolutionary GaAs HBT chips grew quickly, and in 1997 RFMD sold its stock publicly to help build its first fabrication facility.

Today, the company continues its pursuit of adopting new technologies

in advance of the marketplace. In May 2001, RFMD formed a strategic alliance with Agere Systems, within which it owns silicon semiconductor manufacturing equipment in Agere's Orlando manufacturing facility. This alliance provides a framework for both companies to cooperate in the development of new wireless products and next-generation silicon processes.

As the industry continues its global expansion, RFMD is prepared to expand with it. Over the past decade RFMD has grown from a single office with a handful of employees into a 1.2 million square foot campus with offices located worldwide, employing over 1,000 people. The company owns and operates two fabrication facilities, a multi-chip module research and development assembly facility, five design centers and has plans to construct a test and tape and reel facility in China in 2001.

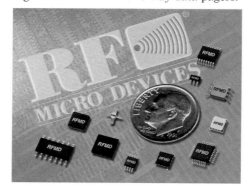

Since 1991, RFMD has introduced more than 200 circuits, most no bigger than a dime, that amplify and process signals transmitted by wireless communication devices such as cellular phones, personal digital assistants and two-way data pagers.

Since its inception, RFMD has grown from a small design house into one of the biggest players in the wireless market. Greensboro is home to RFMD's corporate headquarters as well as the world's largest GaAs HBT fab, where RFMD manufactures state-of-the-art components for wireless applications.

RFMD employees play a key role in the company's successful growth and future development. Dave Norbury, RFMD president and CEO said, "We believe good ideas come from the people who are actually doing the work, and they're also the ones who keep the Company competitive."

RFMD combines cutting-edge talent and revolutionary technology with its ability to design and manufacture state-of-the-art components to establish itself as a leader in the wireless industry. Looking forward, the company plans to continue this trend by supporting its corporate vision—to dominate the RF and related sections of high-volume wireless devices. "By focusing on that vision and by capitalizing on our fundamental strengths—strong customer relationships, technology, research and development, high-volume manufacturing and testing capacity, and innovative and dedicated employees—RFMD will continue to be a premier player in the wireless communications industry," said Norbury.

SOUTHERN BUILDING MAINTENANCE CO.

Southern Building Maintenance Co. Inc., the oldest janitorial service in Greensboro, was founded in 1959 by James S. Ray, Sr., an Industrial Engineering graduate from Georgia Tech. Ray's experience had been with an Atlanta janitorial firm, conducting studies to evaluate and select the most efficient methods, equipment, and production techniques for the business.

SBM opened it's first office in Greensboro in 1959. By 1970 its assets had grown to $900,000, and offices had been opened in Charlotte, Raleigh, Durham, Winston-Salem, and High Point. In 1975 annual sales had grown to $2,000,000. In 1977, SBM bought Colonial Building Maintenance, Inc. of Columbia, SC, and the next year Dr. Clean. By July 1980, SBM's annual sales had grown to $3,000,000, had 700 employees, and was operating out of four regional offices covering two states. Annual sales continued increasing to $4,000,000 in July 1981.

Because of health and safety concerns of the interior building air, Southern Building Maintenance changed its name to Environmental Consultants, Inc. in 1973. Environmental concerns were not sellable to building service markets in the 1970s, and after two years it was decided to do business again as Southern Building Maintenance Co. because of the name recognition.

In August of 1980, James S. Ray, Sr. retired, giving up majority ownership of the common stock. SBM had a fine reputation based upon good cleaning and great service. For the first year or two after Ray's retirement, the company continued to prosper. After that, it went into a tailspin due to poor management. In November 1988, Mr. Ray regained the stock and management. SBM had gone from 700 well-trained employees with an excellent reputation to 200 poorly trained employees with a bad reputation.

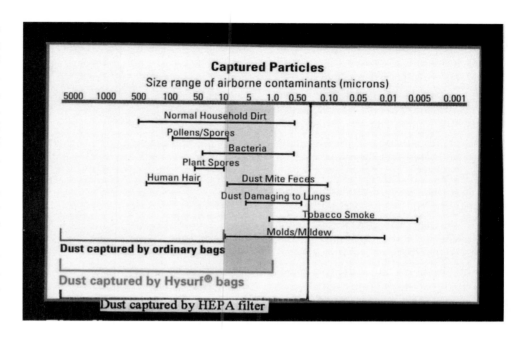

Southern Building Maintenance Co. uses only the finest bags to trap the finest dirt.

The focus was immediately changed back to the basics of good cleaning and great service, to "treating our customers and employees just as we would want to be treated." The concept of partnering with customers, cleaning for health and safety, as well as appearance was reinstalled. Full disclosure contracts were offered.

Vacuums used today have filters that capture over 99 percent dust particles one micron and larger with the HEPA filter capturing 99.997 percent dust particles of .3 microns and larger. Removing the visible and the invisible dust from the building is far

These photos demonstrate that "the proof is in the bag."

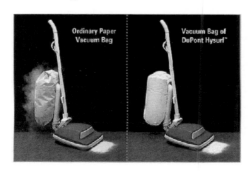

superior to leaving it inside the building. Better chemicals have reduced VOC's and improved cleaning effectiveness. Better tools, equipment, and methods have increased productivity making this better service cost effective. Training has been emphasized at all levels. Managers answer cell phones 24 hours a day, 7 days a week. Comments have been made that our quick response is outstanding. Computers have increased administrative efficiencies.

SBM has attained the high revenue level enjoyed prior to Ray retiring while maintaining a good reputation in all respects. The company expanded into Virginia in 1992 and has plans for the most exciting further expansion in its history, expecting to be in at least two more states by 2002. Although clients include offices, plants, educational institutions, malls, and churches, most of the business is with plants and offices.

SOUTHERN PAINT AND WATERPROOFING COMPANY

Life was hard in the cold mining section of West Virginia. R.C. "Dick" Doutt left school after the seventh grade. He took assorted jobs with logging companies to feed himself and help his family survive. By word of mouth, he had heard that they were hiring at a furniture manufacturing company in Pulaski, Virginia. When he arrived, the superintendent told him that they needed another person to spray the furniture. While he had never seen a spray operation in his life, his reply of course, was, "Sure, I can do that." Trying to be inconspicuous, he watched the other workers for a little while. Then, with more determination than skill, Dick Doutt began his life career as a painter.

Most jobs were short-lived during those depression years, but his brother had found work in Greensboro, NC. Being the ambitious young man he was, he hopped on a freight train and hoboed his way to find the promise of work. There he learned a new skill—caulking with Deatherage Stone Company. Mr. Deatherage took

R.C. Doutt, Sr. at the 50th anniversary celebration.

a liking to this determined young man. At night he taught him to read blueprints. There was not enough caulking work to give Doutt full time work, so Mr. Deatherage helped him start contracting for other construction companies and along the way Doutt developed other paint related skills. Doutt joined forces with another relative, Pete Poe and concentrated on wa-

terproofing. Mr. Deatherage sold Mr. Doutt an older panel truck, which he painted black and lettered: SOUTHERN WATERPROOFING CO., WATERPROOFING AND PAINTING CONTRACTOR, GREENSBORO, NC. This was the birth of Southern Paint and Waterproof Inc. Company in 1939, along with the birth of his son Richard Doutt, Jr.

The war years arrived and the government needed housing and training facilities. H.L. Coble Construction Company had already been using Doutt's services and became his major source of work. Since he was so busy getting his work accomplished, Doutt did not know that he needed licenses to operate a company until 1944. His motto was, "Get the job done." He had already decided early on, that if he couldn't make money doing one type of work, he would learn to do something else.

Southern Paint & Waterproofing has always been a true family business. Richard Doutt Jr. and Dick's son-in-law Paul Childress took over the field operation. Richard Doutt had always known that he would continue on with the painting business; he had no desire to do anything else. In 1980 he purchased the company and recruited his wife Jane from her job at an accounting firm to run the office side of the company. Richard and Jane's son John joined the company in 1984. Unlike his parents, he had been unsure of his future in the family business.

When John went to college, he took an empty five-gallon paint bucket to use as a trash can to remind himself he never wanted to wash out another paint bucket for the rest of his life. He wanted nothing to do with the dirty old paint business—computers were definitely the way to go. But alas, genes definitely get passed to the next generation. Being as ambitious

Papa Doutt's Southern Paint Company truck.

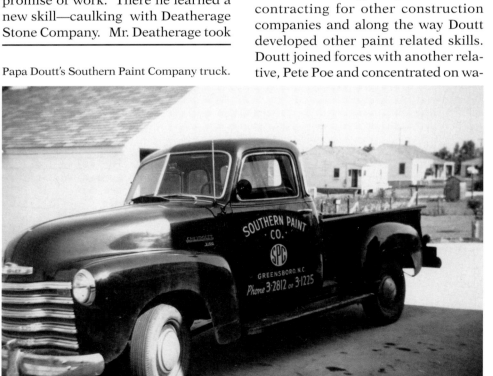

Richard, Jane and John Doutt. Photo by
William Jarrett

as his granddad, he started a funnel
cake business in college. With this
experience, he realized that someday
he wanted to have his own business.
In his senior year he finally came to
the conclusion that it would be fool-
ish not to carry on the tradition that
his grandfather had begun and his father had continued.

In 1986 Richard moved the company from a commercial warehouse
located near the center of town to a
28-acre plot of land that was previously used as a dairy farm. Barns,
sheds, silos and other structures on
the farm have been converted to
handle the company's various operations. In a building where cows were
once milked, estimators bid new
projects. Painters now gather to obtain
spray equipment and materials before
they head out on a job, in a structure
that was previously filled with straw
and feed. Beside old concrete silos,
Southern's fleet of trucks is parked in
place of tractors and combines. This
did not interfere with growth. It ac-

tually afforded additional space to
venture into other areas of the painting business. Since Southern already
employed skilled painters and owned
most of the equipment necessary,
they began to refinish furniture, sand-
blast metals and apply finishes to
metal products.

John took over the field operation
for Southern after his father was
seriously injured in an accident that
forced him to be bed ridden for nearly
a year. Jane and John have progressed
Southern into a company that is licensed
to do business in seven states: North
Carolina, Virginia, South Carolina,
Georgia, Tennessee, West Virginia and
Alabama, performing painting services
for the commercial and industrial
markets with a satellite office in
Durham, NC. Southern has revitalized
the waterproofing aspect of the business while still striving to give reliable,
personal service that most remember
from the past.

"Diversification has been one of the
keys to our success," explains John
Doutt. "My father and grandfather
believed it was important not to put
all your eggs in one basket, and we

still employ this same strategy. It just
makes good sense. When one market
is down, we switch our attention to
other areas to keep the business on
an even keel."

Southern Paint and Waterproofing
Company has made an impact on the
landscape of Greensboro. R.C. Doutt
Sr. painted offices in the Jefferson-
Standard Building and even changed
light bulbs on the tower above for
many years. When an addition was
built to include the City Club, Southern was there again. Across the street
First Citizen Bank created a new
building with Southern's help. Southern painted the interior and exterior
of the first high rise apartment building in Greensboro, The Towers, now
the Hampshire. They did the painting
and wallcovering when the Governmental Center was built. Painting,
wall-covering, staining and special
crackle finishes to the renovation
of the Sedgefield Country Club was
completed with pride, which resulted
in being asked to do the painting renovation to the Hotel Roanoke in Virginia. More recently Southern enjoyed color-coding the new Greensboro
Children's Museum and even applied
an Italian faux finish to the exterior
of the Kayser-Roth Building. In addition to numerous projects in Greensboro, Southern has also impacted
other locales: Kenan-Fagler School of
Business at UNC-CH (UNC-CH is John's
Alma Mater), the UNC-CH Dental
School, Paul J. Rizzo Conference
Center in Chapel Hill and various
hospitals, schools and industrial
buildings across the southern states.

Richard, Jane and John have led
active civic lives, as well. Richard is
past president of the Pleasant Garden
Jaycees. John was president of the
Junior Civitans in high school, Alpha
Kappi PSI Business Fraternity in
college and an active member of the
Greensboro Jaycees.

STARR ELECTRIC CO., INC.

Starr Electric Co., Inc. was founded in 1928 by Raymond Starr, in a small office at 205 North Greene Street in Greensboro. The business was started as a one man, one truck operation, which struggled but endured during the depression era. After several years Raymond invited his brother John W. Starr (J.W.), who was working for the Greensboro fire department, to join the business. John started by working in the field and by managing the growing labor force. As the business grew another brother, Roy Starr, joined the company as a field employee. Soon Raymond brought J.W. and Roy into the office to help manage the company.

North Carolina began licensing contractors in 1937, and on May 7, 1937 the company obtained license number four. The company became incorporated in the state of North Carolina

The Moses H. Cone Memorial Hospital in Greensboro is one of the finest health care facilities in the region and Starr Electric has performed much of the work at this hospital through the years.

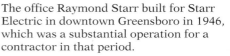

The office Raymond Starr built for Starr Electric in downtown Greensboro in 1946, which was a substantial operation for a contractor in that period.

on July 22, 1942. They soon outgrew their small office and in 1946 Raymond built a new office at 231 North Greene Street. Later, in 1946 at a board of directors meeting, the company realized they needed the services of an electrical engineer, and authorized the hiring of Mr. Joe Guill who was then employed by Duke Power. In July 1948 the board decided to lease their building, and bought five

lots at 1421 Battleground Avenue for $6,875, on which they built an office later that year. In 1950 the company expanded by building a motor shop at the same location.

The company continued to grow and expand and in 1951 surpassed $1 million in gross revenues. The "Motor Repair Shop" was sold in 1955 to William H. Morrison of Electric Service and Sales of Greensboro. Upon Raymond Starr's death on September 10, 1956, J.W. assumed the roles of president and treasurer of the company. Joe Guill was also elected vice president and a director and Roy remained the secretary of the corporation. Raymond's daughter, Iris Starr Harris inherited all of his stock in the company; in 1958 the company elected to buy all of this stock from Iris.

In 1959, Jack Shoffner was recognized as one of the key employees and was allowed to purchase stock. Starr Electric purchased additional property in 1960 at 1406 Battleground Avenue for $29,000 with the intent of constructing a new office. Tom Nance was elected assistant secretary and assistant treasurer and made a director in 1961. In 1962 Joe Guill was elected first vice president with Jack Shoffner assuming the role of second vice president.

In 1962 J.W. had brought his son John D. Starr into the business while John was attending Guilford College. John D. worked in many facets of the company, including the service department, estimating and project management. On February 20, 1963 Roy Starr passed away and Roy's wife Martha became the assistant secretary.

In 1965 the State Highway Commission began work on relocating Battleground Avenue, which took back a portion of Starr's property. This meant that they would again need to construct another building. They elected to build an office and warehouse on the property they had purchased previously and in 1966 moved into this office at 1410 Battleground Avenue. In 1967 Starr Electric reached an agreement with Roy's estate to purchase his stock and at this time John D. Starr was invited to a board of directors meeting and was made vice president.

In 1968 four long time employees—Richard A. Kennedy, Roger Brown, Eugene Shelton, and Harvey Lee Starr—were welcomed into the company as stockholders. The company purchased four additional adjacent lots from the city of Greensboro in 1970, for $35,000, and in 1972 built a tool, repair and maintenance shop on that property. The company at this time was impacted by the economic recession and in 1974 suffered a severe loss when a local contractor declared bankruptcy while Starr Electric was the subcontractor on three of its major jobs, including the Four Seasons' Mall. The company

Above: First Union Tower in downtown Greensboro is one of many examples of the diverse commercial installations that Starr Electric has risen to the occasion to perform.

Below: The RJ Reynolds World Headquarters building in Winston Salem was a large and complex fast track project. RJ Reynolds recently donated the building to Wake Forest University for their use.

had to use over $500,000 in reserve to stay afloat.

In 1975, J. W. assumed the role of chairman, Joe Guill was elected president, John D. Starr became executive vice president, and Jack Shoffner became vice president with Tom Nance as the secretary. At this time the Company had surpassed $5 million in sales and was growing rapidly. Following his excellent service for over 20 years, Richard A. Kennedy was elected vice president in 1978 and in 1980 John D. Starr became the president as Joe Guill contemplated retirement after 33 years of service and resigned his position as president. The company was now doing nearly $12 million in sales and Dennis Norris was hired in 1979 as an electrical engineer in anticipation of Mr. Guill's retirement. Ed Lyndon, an employee of 10 years, joined the list of stockholders in 1982 and in 1983 Dennis Norris also joined as a stockholder. J. W. Starr passed away in 1985 leaving the bulk of his estate to his wife Katherine B Starr. The following year the company surpassed $20 million in sales for the first time and remained prosperous. In 1992

Ed Lyndon and Dennis Norris became vice presidents of the company as Jack Shoffner and Tom Nance had announced their retirement. In 1997 Dennis Norris became senior vice President and John D. Starr became CEO and chairman of the company. Richard A. Kennedy, employed for over 40 years, became president in 2000.

The company's headquarters has always been in Greensboro, although through the years it has performed work throughout the Southeast with licenses in eight states. In September 1983 a company known as SECON was founded in Fayetteville by Don Harrison, an organization in which Starr Electric had an interest and an affiliation. On January 1, 1995 Starr Electric Co, Inc. acquired a major interest in SECON and the name was changed to be part of Starr Electric Co, Inc. Don Harrison is now an executive vice president in the corporation. The company opened an office in 1994 in Charlotte under the direction of Phil Hargett. In 1996 the company acquired an electrical contractor in Charlotte, IND-COM Electric Company, and merged the existing office with IND-COM's operation. Phil Hargett continues to manage that office and is now a senior vice president of the corporation. IND-COM Electric Company had been in business since 1956 and this acquisition vaulted Starr to new heights. The company opened offices in Raleigh and Southern Pines in 1999.

Starr Electric has been involved in many types of work throughout the years. During World War II they experienced large growth, due to a significant amount of construction for the military, particularly at Fort Bragg. They were also involved in the construction of three missile plants in Charlotte during the Cuban missile crisis in 1962, and have performed work and been involved in the construction of many prominent buildings and businesses in the area. These include: Greensboro College, Guilford College, Bennett College, Women's College (UNCG), Wake Forest, UNC-CH, NC A&T and East Carolina. The industrial sector has included work for P. Lorillard, RJ Reynolds, Union Carbide, Goodyear, Burlington Industries and AMP, as well as many others. The company has always aggressively pursued work in the health care industry and has performed work at many hospitals including Moses Cone, Wesley Long, Women's Hospital, Moore Regional, Charlotte Memorial, Annie Penn, Martinsville Hospital and High Point Hospital, to name a few. Starr Electric was involved in the first major furniture showroom in High Point, known as the Southern Furniture Exhibition Building, and was involved in the construction of the Greensboro Coliseum, the Smith Center at University of North Carolina, Chapel Hill and one of their greatest accomplishments, Ericsson Stadium, home of the Carolina Panthers. Starr Electric has twice been selected by the Carolinas Associated General Contractors to receive the Pinnacle award as the "Best Subcontractor of the Year."

Starr Electric continues to thrive today and remains a privately-owned company with stockholders consisting of family and other long time, key employees. The company has now surpassed $60 million in sales and has over 700 employees, 15 percent of whom have been with Starr for over 10 years each. The Starr family treats its employees well, and in fact thinks of all of its employees as family. Starr Electric has an intensive in-house apprentice-training program and strives to uphold its reputation for providing quality work through skilled employees. Starr Electric has figured prominently in the electrical contracting industry in the area for many years. Quality, service and integrity are common words used in describing the employees and the work of the company. Starr Electric continues to seek new opportunities and expand its customer base while continuing to serve its long list of satisfied customers.

Ericsson Stadium in Charlotte was one of the most challenging adventures undertaken and it was an opportunity of a lifetime to be involved in this impressive facility.

GUY M. TURNER, INCORPORATED

Two brothers, Frank and Guy Turner, founded Turner Transfer in September 1927. Few details surrounding the inception of their company or about the early years remain. But it is known that they got their start in the specialty business of heavy transportation by moving full fashioned knitting machines all the way from New England to the Carolinas.

The textile industry grew up in New England where the fast moving streams generated the power for the weaving mills. By the end of the World War II, however, when the widespread utilization of electricity overcame that advantage, an effort was made to bring the mills closer to the raw materials source, the southern cotton. Also, labor was cheaper as unions had not yet been established there.

By the late 1940s this movement was fully underway and Turner Transfer helped to relocate a large portion of the textile industry. During this time the company was also directly involved in preparing machinery and equipment for overseas shipment to Europe.

Turner Transfer was reorganized in the early 1960s under the new name of Guy M. Turner, Incorporated. They continued to move textile machinery as their core business, but also transferred such massive equipment as printing presses and metal working machinery.

In 1974 Guy M. Turner, Inc. was purchased by Carolina Crane and crane service was introduced. By now, interplant moves became important since the displacement of the textile industry from the North was over. Today the crane service is the largest in central North Carolina, operating as a separate company. A modern fleet of 30 hydraulic and conventional cranes with capacities from 20 to 365 tons. The business includes lifting and placing precast bridge sections and manufactured housing units, hoisting roof trusses, and erecting communications towers.

Congress passed the trucking deregulation bill in 1980. This legislation allowed Guy M. Turner to re-enter the for-hire trucks business that had been sold in the early 1960s. Now the Transportation Division operates nationwide, in Canada and Mexico, hauling payloads up to 400 tons. Their turnkey service offers loading and unloading from railcars, trucks and barges. They are also primed to transport power generation equipment, transformers, plastic injection molding machines and presses.

Ownership changed again in 1982, and through the leadership of Jimmy

Guy M. Turner, Inc. corporate offices located in Greensboro.

A turnkey rigging job in the 1940s.

Clark, Michael Hoggard, Douglas Gilliam and Jeanette Landreth, Guy M. Turner began a systematic rebuilding, heavily investing into cranes, trucking and rigging equipment.

The new leadership oversaw steady growth in the nineties that led to the opening of more than eight additional offices in neighboring and mid-Atlantic states. They fully integrated the resources of the transportation and crane services with the contracting arm of the business, so Guy M. Turner Inc. can offer customers a well-coordinated turnkey plant relocation service anywhere in the United States.

The more than 300 employees at Guy M. Turner, Inc.'s three branches have matured into a strong team. Their motto "safety is our business—without it we are out of business" illustrates the commitment to the company and the industrial community they serve with competitive pricing and customized service.

UNITED GUARANTY CORPORATION

United Guaranty Corporation, which counts among its subsidiary companies one of the nation's largest private mortgage insurance companies, can trace its beginnings to a small group of Greensboro businessmen who shared a dream. The group, led by Marvin Legare, in association with William Hemphill and Sidney Stern, believed that they could establish a business that would help people in the region buy homes for their families. That business—mortgage guaranty insurance—enables families to purchase homes they might not otherwise be able to afford. Many home buyers are creditworthy and have enough earning power to handle the day-to-day cost of owning a home, but are faced with the major obstacle of accumulating the cash required up front—a 20 percent down payment. With mortgage insurance, a lender can lend up to 97 percent, 100 percent, and even 103 percent of the value of a house instead of 80 percent (maximum loan-to-value ratios are determined by individual state insurance departments and vary from state to state).

Established in 1963, United Guaranty Corporation today employs more than 800 underwriters, salespeople, and support staff in its home office and regional underwriting offices located throughout the United States. Since it was established, United Guaranty has insured home loans for more than 2.5 million households.

The original Greensboro company merged with two other small companies to become United Guaranty in 1973. In 1981, United Guaranty was acquired by American International Group, Inc. (AIG) the leading U.S. based international insurance and financial services organization, and the largest underwriter of commercial and industrial insurance in the United States.

United Guaranty Corporation's Domestic Residential Insurance Group includes the flagship subsidiary company United Guaranty Residential Insurance Company, which provides mortgage guaranty insurance on single-family homes and generates most of the company's business. Other companies making up this group include United Guaranty Mortgage Indemnity Company, providing coverage for high loan-to-value mortgages, and United Guaranty Services, Inc., which delivers loan review and contract underwriting services to financial institutions, mortgage bankers, and investment banking firms.

United Guaranty's Credit Insurance Companies include United Guaranty Credit Insurance Company and United Guaranty Residential Insurance Company of North Carolina, which provide coverage for property improvements, second mortgages, and home equity lines of credit. In 1999, United Guaranty established its newest subsidiary company, San Francisco-based Centre Capital Group, Inc., as a conduit to secondary capital markets for unique mortgage products.

As U.S. financial and mortgage companies continue to expand into the global market, United Guaranty stands ready to support new ventures. In 1998, United Guaranty established its first international operation, Ezer Mortgage Insurance Company, Ltd., in Jerusalem. This step was followed in 1999, when United Guaranty began operations in Hong Kong.

United Guaranty is committed to quality, and through United Guaranty's QualityQuest℠—a total quality management program— every employee strives to assure that the company offers the finest financial products in the market, backed by even better service.

Although less than one percent of United Guaranty's business is generated in Greensboro, the company works with others to make the community a better place to work and live. This includes a company-wide program of community support that encourages United Guaranty employees at every operating level to get involved. This commitment to community quality was also reflected in United Guaranty's decision to join with others in building Renaissance Plaza in 1989, creating one of the downtown's finest office facilities. The company's operations now use all, or part of, 11 of the building's 19 floors.

The founders' dream is not only still alive at United Guaranty, but it has grown much bigger. Today's commitment is to help people across America—and now in other parts of the world—to enjoy the benefits of home ownership.

Renaissance Plaza in downtown Greensboro—home to United Guaranty Corporation since 1989.

THE UNIVERSITY OF NORTH CAROLINA AT GREENSBORO (UNCG)

Chartered in 1891, The University of North Carolina at Greensboro (UNCG) began life as the first state-supported school dedicated to the education of women. It was first known as the State Normal and Industrial School.

Charles Duncan McIver, the first president of the institution, led the battle to establish the school. "Educate a man and you educate an individual; educate a woman and you educate a family," he said.

As the University's mission changed through the years, its name changed as well. After 1896, the School became the State Normal and Industrial College until 1919. During the period 1919 to 1931 it was known as the North Carolina College for Women. It was the Woman's College of the University of North Carolina from 1932 to 1963 and is warmly remembered as "the WC" by many of its alumnae to this today.

By 1964, the University became coeducational, and its name changed from Woman's College to the current name The University of North Carolina at Greensboro.

Now, more than a century after its founding, the University has evolved into a multi-disciplined resource that not only provides an exceptional education for students but also provides invaluable service for the community.

As students explore the more than 150 graduate and undergraduate programs offered in liberal arts and pre-professional programs, they frequently apply classroom learning to real life situations through internships and practica. Greensboro reaps the benefits, as education students hone their craft in area classrooms, nursing students provide wellness clinics to serve the elderly, music and theatre students offer performances, science students conduct research, and business students bring their global expertise to area industries.

Outside the classroom, UNCG takes seriously its motto of service. The Center for Social Issues is helping revive the West Macedonia neighborhood of High Point by guiding residents to resources. Faculty and students at the School of Nursing coordinate an award-winning teen pregnancy prevention program. And the University has spearheaded an effort to create the Center for New North Carolinians, designed to offer support to the state's newest residents and provide research in immigrant and refugee issues for the state.

The University also leads the way in groundbreaking research. Faculty members are working a myriad of projects, including an at-home cancer test; guidelines for teaching hearing-impaired infants; an invitational school model that teaches trust, respect, intentionality, and optimism in schools; genetically engineered alfalfa to inoculate cattle against ecoli bacteria; and "sentinel" plants that may guard against bio-terrorism attacks.

As Greensboro has evolved, so has UNCG. As the University looks toward the future, it will continue to strengthen its academic excellence while working to be a leader in economic, cultural, and social development in the Piedmont Triad.

Foust Building, constructed in 1891-92 as one of two original campus buildings, is a familiar landmark for students and alumni.

Students and faculty engage in cutting-edge research that serves the larger community.

Music School students perform the spring opera *Orpheus in the Underworld*. UNCG has consistently won first-place awards from the National Opera Association for its opera performances.

WEAVER COOKE CONSTRUCTION LLC

Weaver Cooke Construction was originally founded in 1939 as W.H. Weaver Construction Company by Herman Weaver. Now, more than 60 years later, the Greensboro company has grown into an award-winning, innovative company with over 150 employees with operations throughout a five-state area in the Southeast. The company constructs luxury hotels, apartment complexes, comprehensive senior-life care facilities, condominiums and office buildings.

Throughout the company's history, the original vision of providing quality construction for good value has been steadfastly maintained. The company joined the national effort during World War II by building residential communities in Jacksonville,

The O. Henry Hotel and Green Valley Grill, Greensboro, North Carolina.

Plymouth, Burlington, Morehead City and Beaufort. After World War II ended, the housing situation had become so tight in North Carolina that leading citizens began a drive to provide living spaces for veterans and their families. Realizing the need for housing, Herman Weaver bought land north of Greensboro and began building the Kirkwood Subdivision. The 65 homes built in this innovative neighborhood were bought up quickly as first homes for veterans.

Using knowledge he gained during the war, Herman Weaver expanded his business in 1948 to the construction of numerous apartment buildings throughout North Carolina. By the end of 1949, the company had completed a total of 738 units. In 1950, W.H. Weaver Construction and T.A. Loving of Goldsboro made North Carolina history as they were awarded the largest private housing development contract ever awarded

in the state—the 1,000 unit, $10 million Mallonee Village at Fort Bragg. Finishing the job in eight months, Weaver and Loving were awarded another $10 million contract for a second 1,000 unit apartment complex in the same village.

The experience of using large crews for big projects like the housing at Fort Bragg led to Weaver's later expansion into extensive residential and subsequently, commercial projects. Other significant projects completed during the 1950s included the Piedmont Airlines home offices and hangers in Winston Salem, a dormitory for East Carolina University, a library for North Carolina AT&T State University, and an office building for IBM in Greensboro.

In 1961, Michael Weaver joined his father and assumed the responsibilities as president. Under Michael Weaver's leadership, the company expanded in both the residential and commercial arenas, and established a solid reputation as a regional innovator in the construction business. A few of the major projects over the next three decades would include the Westinghouse Electric Corporation facilities in Culpepper, Virginia; the Operation Breakthrough project for the U.S. Department of Housing and Urban Development in Macon, Georgia; Fairchild Hiller plants in Winston Salem; the Fieldcrest Cannon headquarters in Greensboro; and the eight story Federal

Building and Courthouse in Raleigh, North Carolina.

Weaver Construction also built the Greensboro/Guilford County Governmental center, which was featured in *Architectural Digest* for its outstanding design and construction techniques. Under various federal programs throughout the Southeast, Weaver Construction Company syndicated and constructed thousands of housing units for low to moderate-income homeowners.

In 1996, the orderly transfer of the ownership of the company to Michael Cooke began. Michael Cooke joined the company in 1988 and became president in 1995. Operating now as Weaver Cooke Construction, Michael Cooke remains the president and chief operating officer of the company.

Under Michael Cooke's leadership the company has grown to over 150 employees and has constructed major projects such as WellSpring Retirement Community facilities in Greensboro; Twin Lakes Retirement Community facilities in Burlington; Wendover Medical Center in Greensboro; Greenwood Development Corporation condominiums in Hilton Head; Oakwood Homes Corporation headquarters and the O. Henry Hotel in Greensboro.

One of the most challenging construction projects Weaver Cooke Construction completed during the last decade is the Natuzzi America's headquarters in High Point. The building, which houses the company headquarters and showroom, is designed in the shape of a ship. The four-story glass and steel structure has a water-filled moat below the building's "bow" for added nautical appeal. Weaver Cooke Construction teams, in daily communication with the internationally renowned architect Mario Bellini in Milan, built the unusual building in 12 months. They received the 1998 Pinnacle Award from Carolinas Association of General Contractors for "Best Building Construction Project" for their work on the project.

Weaver Cooke continues building major projects in this region which include multi-family apartments, condominiums, senior living facilities, commercial offices, adaptive re-use of historic buildings and showrooms for the furniture industry. Weaver Cooke also is a leader in constructing affordable housing throughout North and South Carolina.

Teams from Weaver Cooke offer complete pre-construction services, including design consultation, budget estimates, value engineering, subcontract and supplier selection, and scheduling. Construction services offered are overall construction management, cost and quality control, scheduling and purchasing control. For more than 60 years, thousands of satisfied customers have attested to the company's ability to deliver projects on time, in budget and beyond the customer's expectations.

"The people on the site have been professional, easy to work with, possessed of high personal integrity, and have performed admirably... it has been the best company I have dealt with in more than 25 years in this business", said Dr. Clyde J. Christmas, executive director, Twin Lakes Center, Burlington, North Carolina. BGF President Graham Pope, whose Greensboro headquarters were built by Weaver Cooke, echoes these sentiments. "Working with Weaver as our contractor was truly a good experience. We always knew where we stood; there were no surprises."

Since its founding in 1939, the company has steadfastly maintained a reputation of delivering projects with a total commitment to the customer's building needs, employee safety and superior workmanship.

Natuzzi America's headquarters and showroom, High Point, North Carolina.

WFMY NEWS2

It was 1949. From cramped quarters in a tiny building on Davie Street, shared with a radio station, WFMY-TV made its mark on history.

Adding a television station to its operation was a bold move for WFMY's parent, the Greensboro News Company. On August 18th, 1949, only 1,200 homes in the Piedmont had television sets to watch WFMY News2's first broadcast. It was live, local and lasted just four minutes and 25 seconds. But it made history as the first live television broadcast in the Carolinas.

Soon after that short, yet momentous broadcast, WFMY News2 began broadcasting the major networks. WFMY News2 has been a CBS affiliate from the beginning, but in the early days, the station also carried programs from ABC, NBC, and the now-defunct DuMont Network.

WFMY News2 has built a solid reputation for excellence in local news. Lee Kinard was one year into his 43-year career at WFMY News2 when he created the Good Morning Show in 1957. It went on to be the longest running and highest rated morning news program in the nation.

In February 1960, the station covered the beginning of the civil rights movement from a lunch counter in downtown Greensboro's Woolworth

WFMY News2 honors the Piedmont's unsung heroes with the "2 Those Who Care Service to the Piedmont Awards."

store. The Good Morning Show expanded to one hour to better cover community affairs issues affecting its viewers.

When federally mandated busing began in 1971, the Good Morning Show responded with daily school segments, and expanded again, to two hours. Racial tensions flared again in November 1979 with a fatal meeting between Klan-Nazi supporters and Communist Workers Party supporters. It marked WFMY News2's first use of live television for breaking news.

But viewers asked for a balance of hard news and good news. In 1972 Sandra Hughes became the first African-American woman in the Piedmont to host a talk show, "Sandra and Friends." In 1978 she made history as the first African-American woman in the Southeast to host PM Magazine. Today, Sandra co-anchors WFMY News2's evening newscasts.

Since those early years, WFMY News2 has grown. It moved to its current location in east Greensboro in 1955. In 1980 the station built a 2000-foot tower in Randolph county and formed the nation's first regional news network, "The Carolina News Network," with founding partners WRAL in Raleigh and WSOC in Charlotte.

Community service has been WFMY News2's cornerstone. When Gannett Co., Inc. purchased the station in 1988, WFMY News2 launched 2 Those Who Care Service to the Piedmont Awards. The program has honored 140 unsung heroes and has raised over $600,000 for non-profit organizations.

Since the early days of television in the 1950s, people in the Piedmont have counted on WFMY News2 as their most trusted source for news.

Since 1992 Food 2 Families has collected over 1.2 million pounds of food for Piedmont families. And the station has supported education through its Tools for School campaign, helping over 151,000 school-aged children since 1996.

So much of what WFMY News2 created is now a part of the fabric of this community: George Perry's "Old Rebel," Cordelia Kelly's "What's Cooking Today," Lee Kinard and The Good Morning Show. It's on this solid foundation that WFMY News2 is building its future. In September 1999 the station launched its website just as Hurricane Floyd bore down on eastern North Carolina. There was an immediate thirst for information from the site. Today, wfmynews2.com receives millions of pageviews per month.

What's next for the Piedmont's first television station? Digital. WFMY News2 will launch its high definition television signal in 2002. This new technology and latest bold move will give WFMY News2 even more opportunity to continue its tradition as the Piedmont's most trusted source for television news.

WLXI – TV 61

WLXI Channel 61, located at 2109 Patterson Street, Greensboro, went from Rock to Religious.

This full-power UHF television station was originally licensed to the Consolidated Broadcasting Company in 1984, airing primarily rock music videos. However, in the summer of 1985, the Trinity Broadcasting Network (TBN) of Tustin, California began purchasing airtime on the station. On March 11, 1986, TBN purchased the station and dedicated it to full-time Christian broadcasting. Larry and Karen Patton relocated from Miami to become the station's managers.

TBN's programming included many prominent Christian broadcasters such as, John Hagee, Charles Stanley, D. James Kennedy, and James Robison. Local programs included "Praise the Lord," a talk, music and interview program, and a community affairs program called "Public Report." Volunteers were recruited from the Triad area to receive calls from viewers wanting and needing someone to pray with them individually.

The influence and impact of the station began to expand as pastors and churches saw the value of getting a

Above:
TCT president and founders, Garth and Tina Coonce.

Below:
WLXI has become a center of religious and racial reconciliation in the Triad.

message of hope and help out to viewers through a television station dedicated to preaching, singing, and praying. The Cathedral of His Glory became the first broadcaster with a locally produced program and is still airing their Sunday morning worship service on WLXI.

With a cap on the number of television stations a network could own at that time and wanting to purchase stations in the top 10 markets in the nation, TBN decided to sell WLXI. They approached Dr. Garth W. Coonce, president of Tri-State Christian TV, Inc. (TCT) another network of Christian stations, with the proposal of purchasing channel 61. Negotiations began in 1991 and on January 1, 1992, TCT became the new owners of WLXI, Radiant Life Ministries, Inc.

TCT and Dr. Coonce brought a new and aggressive period of growth to channel 61 with the addition of new programming including the popular "Ask the Pastor" program with a panel of five local pastors and a moderator fielding questions from viewers. In 1997, through the "Must Carry Cable Act," the number of cable subscribers receiving WLXI went from nearly 50,000 to over 275,000. Another bold step was taken in increasing the number of time slots available to local Christian ministries. Over the last few years, the number of Triad broadcasters has grown from one to fifteen.

In May 1999, Radiant Life Ministries, Inc. was the number one Nielsen rated Christian station in the US, and has consistently ranked in the top five since July of 1998. As a religious broadcaster, both TCT and Radiant Life welcome programmers and guests from all denominations and non-denominations. In the Triad, WLXI has become the catalyst for Christian unity and racial reconciliation.

THE ZENKES, INC.

In the 1930s and 1940s, there was located in Greensboro, North Carolina, a very fine furniture establishment. It could be called an "emporium." Recovering from the depression of that time found this small city growing into quite a sophisticated spot. Several institutions of higher learning and many furniture and textile factories nearby put their stamp on the development of the area. Among the leading elements was a retail furniture service by the name of Morrison Neese. The owner, Mr. Morrison, was quite an entrepreneur and while in New York in 1936, lured south one Otto Zenke as a decorator. When Mr. Zenke came to Greensboro, the depression was still evident. It took a couple of years of patience before his talent caught on, and then it was onward and upward all the way. The war years witnessed more growth, especially in the furniture business. People were ready for the advance that was taking place. Otto's brother, Henry, joined him after serving in Europe during World War II, in order to provide structural backgrounds for his brother's work.

Above: International Decorators Showhouse, Washington D.C.

Below: Living room view through bar to library.

Once a year Morrison Neese put on quite a show on two floors of their six-story building, (designed by architect Harry Barton). These areas were redecorated with rooms exquisitely furnished by the designers. Each room was perfect and complete in every detail. One could walk in and sit down as if at home. The public loved it. Invitations were sent out to all parts of the state to clients who looked forward to this special occasion. Thousands of people arrived for two days showing of the finest offered by various manufacturers. Each lady, as she arrived, was given a fresh gardenia. One year, 3,000 blossoms were pinned on the ladies who were dressed up with hats, gloves and sometimes furs. Fresh flowers in abundance were beautifully arranged and the whole affair was grand and glorious.

Morrison Neese is gone and that loyal help has gone too, but the concept of completely finishing a home all at one time still lingers on, being extended by Otto Zenke Inc. and now perpetuated by The Zenkes Inc.

Being an established business in downtown Greensboro for over 50 years is quite an accomplishment and envelops one with a reputation to uphold. Having to watch the downtown disappear and waste away from so close a proximity has been a sad experience. Remaining in business at the same location under these circumstances has been a miracle. While others have moved on, abandoned their sites in downtown Greensboro, the Zenke family, now the Zenkes, Inc., has held on tenaciously to their desire to remain in the same general location with its historic situation during all these changes. They have recently seen a resurgence of interest in the downtown area and they welcome those people who have been courageous enough to make the move.

The family reputation was established by two brothers and is now maintained by Mrs. Henry Christian Zenke and her two children. Having to digest much in the way of art history and practicing art in the furniture business, Henry Christian Zenke III and Virginia Hawthorne Zenke have been exposed to every facet of this profession; and it was usually morning, noon, and night, as well as during working hours. It has always been their pleasure to take a given situation, either do-over or new, and make it livable and always more beautiful. While practicing this theory, the company only does what its clients will let them do. So, of course, they push for the most complete job, not necessarily the most expensive project. It has been said, to their credit, that they know when and where to stop and leave out items that would make the work look overdone. They do not design with an excessive amount of furnishings, fabrics and accessories. They prefer, in-

Above: Sunroom.

Below: Dining room.

stead, the clean look and not what is sometimes thought of as "noisy" decoration.

The Zenkes maintain one of the finest libraries of carpet, fabric and wallpaper samples in the Southeast. Also, they have accessories, antique furniture and reproductions, all of which allows them to work quickly and completely to create undateable rooms. They believe fashion is temporary but style is forever. And the Zenkes believe in style. Most of their clients are so convinced of Virginia's magic that they allow her to have full reign of artistic control.

Working now for the third and fourth generations of families is the company's greatest achievement. Having been employed at the same vocation for over 55 years and living and working on the same block for 50 years is something the Zenkes consider a great honor. Often asked if they call themselves interior designers or interior decorators, they can only reply: we are designers who decorate. Designers dream and plan. Decorators execute and get the job done.

A TIMELINE OF GREENSBORO'S HISTORY

20,000 – 10,000 B.C. More than 20 nomadic Indian groups roamed the Piedmont.

1200 A.D. Indians lived in small family groups in villages and subsisted on farming, hunting, and trading.

1701 English explorer John Lawson traveled 550 miles through the Carolinas.

1710 Keyauwee and Saura tribes no longer in Piedmont; few families remained.

1744 Germans settled in eastern Guilford County.

1745 Friedens Lutheran Church built.

1750 English Quakers (Friends) settled in western and southern Guilford County.

1753 Scotch-Irish settled central Guilford County.

1754 New Garden Monthly Meeting of Friends established.

1756 Buffalo Presbyterian Church established.

1757 Jamestown settled by Quakers.

1765 David Caldwell became pastor of two Presbyterian churches; he later established a classical school for males.

1768 Dolley Madison was born in Guilford County on May 20.

1771 Guilford County established with temporary court location.

1774 Land purchased for county seat (Guilford Courthouse).

1776 Skirmish at Bruce's Crossroads (Summerfield).

1779 Randolph County created from Guilford County.

1781 Battle of Guilford Courthouse on March 15 won by British.

1782–1784 Alexander Martin served as first American governor of North Carolina.

1785 Rockingham County created from Guilford County; Guilford Courthouse renamed Martinsville for governor.

1787 Andrew Jackson admitted to Guilford County bar.

1789 North Carolina became the 12th state in the new nation.

Greensboro was named for General Nathanael Greene, and in 1911 Congress appropriated $30,000 for a monument at the battleground. Sculptor Francis Packer created a bronze equestrian statue that was unveiled on July 3, 1915. It stands 27 feet high. (GHM)

1790 First U.S. census reported 7,291 residents in county.

1807 Legislative act to create Greensborough passed.

1808 Forty-two acres of land deeded to the county commissioners for new county seat on March 25; General Assembly passed an act naming Greensborough (December 15).

1810 Legislative charter written for town of Greensborough.

1816 Greensborough Male Academy chartered.

1824 Presbyterians organized a town congregation.

1826 Levi Coffin born in western Guilford County.

1828 Henry Humphreys began NC's first steam-operated textile mill.

1829 First town census and property assessment.

1830 Peter Doub established Methodist congregation that built town's first church in 1831.

1833 Greensboro College started by Methodists; obtained state charter in 1838.

Boy Scout Troop 1, Greensboro's and perhaps the South's first troop, was organized in 1909. Hundreds of troops have developed from this initial group. (GHM)

The Carnegie Negro Library opened in 1926, two decades after its white counterpart. It still stands on the Bennett College campus but the white one was razed in 1951. (GHM)

1837 Greensboro incorporated with limits of one square mile; New Garden Boarding School started by Quakers; became Guilford College in 1888.

1841 Greensboro held first public school session.

1841–1845 Resident John Motley Morehead served as governor.

1843 Health committee formed after yellow fever epidemic; Manufacture of cigars, snuff, and plug tobacco began.

1849 First volunteer fire company organized.

1851 Work began on NC Railroad in Greensboro (July 11).

1852 Oak Ridge Institute opened.

1853 Calvin Wiley became first superintendent of NC schools.

1856 Tracks of NC Railroad joined near Jamestown; first train arrived on January 29.

1859 Baptist church officially organized.

1861 Greensboro and Guilford residents voted against a referendum for a secession convention (February 28); North Carolina joined the Confederate States of America (May 11).

1862 William Sidney Porter (O. Henry) born on September 11.

1863 Rail line linking Greensboro to Danville, Virginia completed.

1865 President Jefferson Davis met with General Joseph E. Johnston in Greensboro (April 11); Johnston traveled from Greensboro to surrender to General Sherman at Bennett Place (April 26).

1866-1869 Pioneer black churches organized: Providence and St. Matthews (1866); St. James (1867) and Bethel African Methodist Episcopal (1869).

1869 Episcopal church organized.

1870 Greensboro chartered as a city (March 28).

1873 Tobacco Board of Trade established to regulate business.

1875 Public schools for white and black students opened; land acquired for Bennett College; began in 1873.

1877 Chamber of Commerce established; incorporated in 1888; Roman Catholic church constructed.

1882 Green Hill Cemetery opened.

1883 First NC chapter of Woman's Christian Temperance Union established in Greensboro.

1887 City passed first bond issue for $100,000; Guilford Battle Ground Company incorporated.

1888 Cape Fear & Yadkin Valley Railway Company completed.

1890 *Daily Record* began publication.

1891 Sites selected for NC A&T State University and UNCG; Quakers organized a Greensboro meeting; Limits expanded to cover 4 square miles.

1892 Cones built Southern Finishing & Warehouse Company.

1893 Simon Schiffman purchased jewelry store.

1894 Lunsford Richardson introduced Vick's VapoRub.

1896 Brooks Lumber Company opened.

1898 C.C. Fordham's Drug Store built across railroad tracks.

1899 Southern Railroad Depot on

Kathleen Price Byran (second from left) organized the forerunner of the Junior League of Greensboro in 1926. The organization has contributed thousands of dollars to local projects. (GHM)

In March 1943 troops began arriving at the new Greensboro Army Base (Basic Training Camp #10). The rail connections through Greensboro were an important factor for the Army. Courtesy, GHM/ Carol W. Martin Collection

South Elm Street completed.

1900 Greensboro Agricultural Fair began.

1902 Public library opened in city hall; Greensboro Electric Company inaugurated electric streetcar line and opened Lindley Park.

1904 C.C. Hudson Overall Co. (Blue Bell/Wrangler) founded.

1906 Carnegie Library completed.

1908 Merchant Association organized during centennial year.

1909 Greensboro Daily News began publication.

1912 Jefferson Standard Life Insurance Company moved to city.

1917 Wesley Long Hospital opened.

1920 New county courthouse on West Market dedicated.

1923 City limits expanded to 17.84 square miles.

1924 Pilot Life Insurance Co. established; Greensboro Historical Museum founded.

1925 Hebrew Congregation dedicated temple.

1927 King Cotton Hotel and Carolina Theatre opened; War Memorial Stadium completed; Lindley Field selected as regional airport site.

1935 Burlington Mills moved to city.

1937 Otto Zenke began interior design firm.

1943 Basic Training Camp 10 (later ORD) opened; Mary Webb Nicholson killed in plane crash.

1944 George Preddy shot down while flying in Belgium.

1947 Guilford Mills established.

1949 WFMY-TV transmitted live, a first for North Carolina; first female elected to city council.

1951 Dr. William Hampton became first black council member.

1953 Moses H. Cone Memorial Hospital admitted first patient.

1955 Lorillard built Greensboro plant.

1957 City limits extended to more than 49 square miles.

1959 Greensboro Coliseum Complex dedicated.

1960 Woolworth lunch counter sit-ins began on February 1.

William Sullivan is known as the "father of the Coliseum" which finally opened in 1959. The former mayor worked diligently to build support for the facility. (GHM)

Zoe Barbee was the first woman and the first black to win election to the county board of commissioners. Elected in November 1974, she was killed in an accident the next month. (GHM)

1962 Eastern Music Festival founded.

1963 Civil rights protests led by Jesse Jackson.

1966 Wendover Avenue constructed.

1967 Greensboro voted All-American City; *Carolina Peacemaker* began publication.

1968 Henry Frye became first black to serve in the North Carolina House of Representatives in the 20th century.

1968-69 Civil rights protests resulted in curfews enforced by the National Guard and one death.

1971 Greensboro integrated its public schools; Bryan Park dedicated.

1973 Greensboro–Guilford County Governmental Center dedicated.

1974 First black and first female elected to county commission.

1979 Violent conflict at Morningside Homes resulted in five deaths.

1980 Trial of defendants for Morningside murders ended with not guilty verdict; College Hill became first historic district.

1982 City Council adopted district system; Downtown area listed on National Register.

1983 Completion of new airport; renamed PTI in 1987; Henry Frye

Left: In 1963, Dr. Martin Luther King, Jr. (left) visited Greensboro to support the civil rights protests that were led by Jesse Jackson, president of the student body at A & T. When King was assassinated in Memphis on April 4, 1968, a day he had planned to be in Greensboro, Jackson was again by his side. In 1984 and 1988 Jackson was an unsuccessful candidate for the Democratic presidential nomination. He is one of A & T's outstanding graduates. Courtesy, Otis Hairston, Jr.

Top: The roundabout at Hamburger Square still existed in 1966. Visible in the background is Blumenthal's, established in 1926 and still a popular shopping spot. Courtesy, GHM/Carol W. Martin Collection

Bottom: Urban redevelopment in east Greensboro had positive and negative effects. The construction of the new post office on East Market Street required the razing of many black landmarks. Courtesy, GHM/Carol W. Martin Collection

appointed to NC Supreme Court.

1984 Metro (Osborne) Wastewater Treatment Plant opened.

1985 Federal court found defendants liable for deaths at Morningside Homes (1979).

1988 Governmental Plaza named for Medal of Honor recipient Phill McDonald; Tannenbaum Park opened.

1990 Completion of three downtown skyscrapers and renovation of Greensboro Historical Museum and Cultural Center.

1991 Greensboro voted All-American City.

1993 Carolyn Allen became first female mayor; Woolworth's closed; merger of city and county school systems through act of NC legislature; East Market St. Development Corporation formed.

1994 Sit-ins, Inc. formed to create international civil-rights museum.

1996 Downtown Greensboro, Inc. established.

1998 VF, a Fortune 500 firm, moved to Greensboro; Central Library opened on Church Street.

1999 Children's Museum opened.

2000 International House created to assist new immigrants.

BIBLIOGRAPHY

Local history research requires the use of a variety of materials, such as published books and articles, newspapers, city directories and maps, promotional brochures, and family records. Valuable sources for this book include three Greensboro newspapers: the *Greensborough Patriot* (1826-1941, scattered issues); the *Greensboro Record* (1890-1984); the *Greensboro Daily News* (1909-1984) and the *News & Record* (1984-present). All are available at the Greensboro Public Library. Other valuable aids were city directories, dating back as early as 1870, which are preserved at the Library and the Greensboro Historical Museum.

The Information Services Division at the Greensboro Public Library maintains two special collections: the Vertical Files, located in the NC Collection, with materials arranged by topics and names; and the Oral History Collection, videotapes of interviews with interesting Greensboro citizens. The Archives Division, Greensboro Historical Museum, is a repository for family records and sketches, letters, maps, scrapbooks, and unpublished manuscripts. Much of the social history in this book was drawn from these collections.

All students of Greensboro history should be grateful for the body of works created by Ethel Stephens Arnett (1891-1980). Her *Greensboro, North Carolina: The County Seat of Guilford* (Chapel Hill: 1955) is a valuable treatment of the city's history from its beginning to 1955. Later books, all related to Greensboro, are listed in order of their publication: *O. Henry from Polecat Creek* (Greensboro: 1962); *William Swaim, Fighting Editor: The Story of O. Henry's Grandfather* (Greensboro: 1963); *Confederate Guns Were Stacked at Greensboro, North*

Carolina (Greensboro: 1965); *Mrs. James Madison: The Incomparable Dolley* (Greensboro: 1972); *For Whom Our Public Schools Were Named, Greensboro, North Carolina* (Greensboro: 1973); *The Saura and the Keyauwee, in the Land that Became Guilford, Randolph, and Rockingham* (Greensboro: 1975); and *David Caldwell* (Greensboro: 1976).

The following sources are available at the Greensboro Public Library unless otherwise noted.

Albright, James. *Greensboro 1808-1904.* Greensboro: J.J. Stone & Co., 1904.

Album of Greensboro, North Carolina. Greensboro: Chamber of Commerce, 1891. No. 64.19.2. Archives Division, Greensboro Historical Museum.

Art Work of Greensboro, North Carolina. Published in Nine Parts. Chicago: The Gravure Illustration Company, 1904. No. 80.99.1. Archives Division, Greensboro Historical Museum.

Bowles, Elizabeth Ann. *A Good Beginning: The First Four Decades of the University of North Carolina at Greensboro.* Chapel Hill: The University of North Carolina Press, 1967.

Brooks, Aubrey Lee. *A Southern Lawyer: Fifty Years at the Bar.* Chapel Hill: The University of North Carolina Press, 1950.

Brown, Marvin. *Greensboro: An Architectural Record.* Greensboro: Preservation Greensboro, Inc., 1995.

Caldwell, Bettie D. (compiler). *Founders and Builders of Greensboro, 1808-1908.* Greensboro: J.J. Stone & Company, 1925.

Caruthers, Eli W. *A Sketch of the Life and Character of the Rev. David Caldwell, D. D.* Greensborough, North Carolina: Swaim and Sherwood, 1842.

Catlett, Stephen. *Martin's and Miller's Greensboro.* Charleston. SC: Arcadia Publishing, Inc., 1999.

Chafe, William H. *Civilities and Civil Rights: Greensboro, North Carolina and the Black Struggle for Freedom.* New York: Oxford University Press, Inc., 1980.

Cleveland, Edmund J. Diary, May-June, 1865. Southern Historical Collection, Wilson Library, University of North Carolina at Chapel Hill.

Corbitt, David L. *The Formation of the North Carolina Counties, 1663-1943.* Raleigh: State Department of Archives and History, 1950.

Crevecoeur, Hector St. John. *Letters from An American Farmer.* New York: E. P. Dutton and Co., 1912.

Edmonds, Mary Lewis R. *Governor Morehead's Blandwood.* Greensboro: Greensboro Printing Co., 1976.

Fripp, Gayle Hicks. *Greensboro.* Charleston. SC: Arcadia Publishing, Inc., 1997.

_____. *Greensboro Volume II: Neighborhoods.* Charleston. SC: Arcadia Publishing, Inc., 1998

Gibbs, Warmoth T. *History of the North Carolina Agricultural and Technical College: Greensboro, North Carolina.* Dubuque: 1966.

Gilbert, Dorothy Lloyd. *Guilford: A Quaker College.* Greensboro: Jos. J. Stone, 1937.

Greensboro Daily News. May 29, 1971.

Greensboro Record. November 16, 1940.

Hayes, V. T. Scrapbook. No. 79.120.3. Archives Division, Greensboro Historical Museum.

Hinshaw, Seth B. and Mary E. (editors). *Carolina Quakers.* Greensboro: North Carolina Yearly Meeting, 1972.

Holder, Rose H. *McIver of North Carolina.* Chapel Hill: The University of North Carolina Press, 1957.

Isaacs, I.J. (editor). *Progressive Greensboro, the Gate City of North Carolina.* Greensboro: Jos. J. Stone & Co., 1903.

Jones, Abe E., Jr. *Greensboro 27.* Bassett,

Va.: The Bassett Printing Corporation, 1976.

Jordan, Paula S. *Women of Guilford County, North Carolina.* Women of Guilford, 1979.

Kipp, Samuel M., III. "Old Notables and Newcomers: The Economic and Political Elite of Greensboro, North Carolina, 1880-1926," *Journal of Southern History* (August, 1977), 373-394.

Konkle, Burton Alva. *John Motley Morehead and the Development of North Carolina, 1796-1866.* Philadelphia: William J. Campbell, 1922.

Lefler, Hugh T. and Powell, William S. *Colonial North Carolina: A History.* New York: Charles Scribner's Sons, 1973.

Lefler, Hugh T. (editor). *John Lawson's 'A New Voyage to Carolina."* Chapel Hill: The University of North Carolina Press, 1967.

Lefler, Hugh T. and Newsome, Albert R. *North Carolina: The History of a Southern State.* Chapel Hill: The University of North Carolina Press, 1973.

Legislative Papers. 1807. L. P. 223, North Carolina Division of Archives and History, Raleigh, North Carolina.

Noah, Joe, and Sox, Samuel L., Jr. *George Preddy: Top Mustang Ace.* Osceola, WI: Motorbooks International, 1991

O'Keefe, Patrick. *Greensboro: A Pictorial History.* Norfolk, Va.: The Donning Company, 1977.

Olsen, Otto H. *Carpetbagger's Crusade: The Life of Albion Winegar Tourgee.* Baltimore: The Johns Hopkins Press, 1965.

Rankin, Rev. S.M. *History of Buffalo Presbyterian Church and Her People.* Greensboro: Joseph J. Stone & Co., n.d.

Richardson, Smith. *Early History of Richardson-Merrell.* Richardson-Merrell, Inc., 1975.

Robinson, Blackwell P. and Stoesen, Alexander R. *The History of Guilford County, North Carolina, U.S.A. To 1980, A.D.* s.n., n.d.

Rowe, W. W. *The History of the Baptists of Greensboro, North Carolina, 1850-1926.* Greensboro: Jos. J. Stone and Company, 1926.

Schenck, David. Diary. Southern Historical Collection, Wilson Library, University of North Carolina at Chapel Hill.

_____. *North Carolina, 1780-1781. Being a History of the Invasion of the Carolinas By The British Army Under Lord Cornwallis in 1780-1781.* Raleigh: Edwards and Broughton, 1889. Rare Book Collection, No. 72.142.1. Archives Division, Greensboro Historical Museum.

Sieber, Hal. *Holy Ground.* Greensboro, NC: Tudor Publishers, Inc., 1995.

Simpson, John W. *History of the First Presbyterian Church of Greensboro, North Carolina, 1824-1945.* Greensboro, 1947.

Smith, C. Alphonso. *O. Henry Biography.* Garden City, N. Y.: Doubleday, Page & Company, 1924.

Smith, Mary Watson. *The Women of Greensboro, N. C., 1861-1865.* Greensboro: 1919. J. Henry Smith Family Collection. Archives Division, Greensboro Historical Museum.

Smith, Susie M. H. *The Love That Never Failed.* Charlottesville, Va.: The Michie Company, 1928.

Stockard Sallie W. *The History of Guilford County, North Carolina.* Knoxville: Gant-Ogden Co., 1902.

Stoesen, Alexander R. *Guilford College: On the Strength of 150 Years.* Greensboro: Guilford College Trustees, 1987.

_____. *Guilford County: A Brief History.* Raleigh, NC: Division of Archives and History, 1993.

Thayer, Theodore G. *Nathanael Greene: Strategist of the American Revolution.*

New York: Twayne Publishers, 1960.

Tourgee Albion Winegar. *A Fool's Errand By one of the fools....* New York: Fords, Howard, & Hulbert, 1879.

Trelease, Allen W. *Changing Assignments: A Pictorial History of UNCG.* Greensboro: UNCG, 1991.

_____. *The North Carolina Railroad, 1849–1871.* Chapel Hill: The University of North Carolina Press, 1991.

Turrentine, Samuel Bryant. *A Romance of Education.* Greensboro: Piedmont Press, 1946.

Wadelington, Charles W. and Knapp, Richard F. *Charlotte Hawkins Brown and Palmer Memorial Institute.* Chapel Hill & London: The University of North Carolina Press, 1999.

Warner, Stafford Allen. *Yardley Warner: The Freedman's Friend, His Life and Times.* Didcot, Great Britain: The Wessex Press, 1957.

Weaver, C.E. (compiler). *City of Greensboro, N.C.: Pen and Picture Sketches.* Richmond, Va.: Central Publishing Co., Inc., 1917.

"West Market Street Methodist Episcopal Church, South: A History of Its Growth and Influence for One Hundred Years from Its Foundation in 1830, until October 12th, 1930." Greensboro, 1934.

Wheaton, Elizabeth. *Codename Greenkill: The 1979 Greensboro Killings.* Athens and London: The University of Georgia Press, 1987.

White Water, Colored Water. Greensboro, NC: Project Homestead, 1993.

Wolff, Miles. *Lunch at the Five and Ten: The Greensboro Sit-Ins, A Contemporary History.* New York: Stein and Day, 1970.

World Leadership in Denims: Through Thirty Years of Progress. Greensboro: The Proximity Mfg. Co., 1925.

ACKNOWLEDGEMENTS

A community's history is much like a puzzle; some of the parts are easy to place, while others are scattered, even lost. Years of research have produced more material than will fit into this book's pages, and omitting anecdotes, characters, descriptions and summaries has been a most difficult duty. Writing the text has been a challenge and a privilege; one hopes that it will give each reader an assembled picture puzzle of Greensboro.

A number of people and organizations made this project possible. William J. Moore, Director of the Greensboro Historical Museum, recommended the author and gave encouragement and support. Sandy Neerman, Head of the Library/Museum Department of the City of Greensboro, endorsed this new edition and allowed time away from other duties. Mayor Keith Holliday and City Manager Ed Kitchen have promoted its development, while Mayor Pro Tem Yvonne Johnson and Councilwoman Claudette Burroughs-White have served as advisors.

Members of the Greensboro Historical Museum, Inc. have been helpful in many ways, as have volunteers who have donated their services to make research and writing time possible. Staff members also assisted with a variety of tasks. My special thanks go to Stephen Catlett and Christine Dumoulin (Archives) and Kathy Devereux who provided specialized services, and to Linda Evans and Betty K. Phipps who carried out some of my usual tasks. I also want to acknowledge Helen Snow and the Reference Division of the Greensboro Public Library for their help in answering so many questions.

The City Clerk of Greensboro provided copies of Greensboro's charters and access to other records, while other city departments furnished background information, photographs and maps.

A number of individuals provided historical information and research information. James G.W. MacLamroc and Alexander Stoesen were helpful in various areas, while Charles Weill Jr. answered many economic development questions. A.H. Peeler, Grace Lewis, Nelson Johnson, Hal Sieber and Yvonne Johnson assisted in gathering material on Greensboro's African American citizens, events and neighborhoods. Drs. Joffre Coe (UNC) and J. Ned Woodall (Wake Forest) furnished technical information on Native American, as did Ruth Revels (Guilford Native American Association). Marc Bush (Greensboro Coliseum Complex), Ray Gibbs (DGI), Mark Sills (Faith-Action), and Mac Sims (East Market Street Development Corporation) provided material on their agencies.

I am also grateful for information provided by the North Carolina Division of Archives and History; the Southern Historical Collection (UNC Wilson Library); William R. Perkins Library (Duke); the Friends Historical Collection (Guilford); and the Walter C. Jackson Library (UNCG). Clippings from the *News & Record* and other printed sources have helped with many historical facts.

Special appreciation goes to Terry, who supported and encouraged me throughout this project.

Gayle Hicks Fripp

PHOTOGRAPHIC ACKNOWLEDGEMENTS

Managing a project of this scope would be an impossible task without aid from many people. The following individuals and institutions agreed to a special one-time use with other stipulations: Otis Hairston, Jr.; Mark Wagoner, Productions; Aerial Photography Services; and the *News and Record*. Images from the *News & Record* are reprinted with its permission and the "reprint does not constitute or imply any endorsement or sponsorship of any product, service, company or organization."

Many industries, institutions and organizations made photographs available for this publication. Included are: Bennett College; Carolina Theatre; Center for NC Art; City of Greensboro (Greensboro Coliseum Complex; Greensboro Parks & Recreation Department; Greensboro Public Library; Housing and Community Development; and Organizational Development & Communications); East Market Street Development Corporation; Evergreens, Inc.; FaithAction; Friends Historical Collection (Guilford College); Greensboro Children's Museum; Greensboro Jaycees; Greensboro Millennium Committee and Charles Lowe; Greensboro Symphony Orchestra; Guilford Courthouse National Military Park and Don Long; NC A & T State University; NC Division of Archives and History; Proctor & Gamble (Richardson-Vicks); UNCG (Jackson Library Archives and Publications Office); and Wake Forest University, Archeological Department.

Individuals who loaned their photographs include: Miss Ailene Beeson; Hal Sieber; Photographer Jack Moebes; Mrs. Louise Reynolds; Mrs. Anita Rivers; Dr. T. E. Sikes Jr.; and Photographer Jim Stratford.

We also acknowledge the many organizations and citizens who offered other images for us to copy and preserve in our Archives.

Gayle Hicks Fripp

INDEX

244

These two young ladies, with hats and an umbrella to protect them from the sun, were photographed on South Elm Street as they waited for a turn-of-the-century parade. The brick street and the Bank of Guilford are clues to a vanished era. (GHM)